Paddling
Pennsylvania

D1599107

0 11557 03626 8

Paddling
Pennsylvania

Canoeing and Kayaking
the Keystone State's
Rivers and Lakes

Jeff Mitchell

STACKPOLE
BOOKS

Published by
STACKPOLE BOOKS
5067 Ritter Road
Mechanicsburg, PA 17055
www.stackpolebooks.com

Printed in the United States of America

10 9 8 7 6 5 4 3 2 1

FIRST EDITION

Cover design by Wendy Reynolds

Cover: Leigh Ann Jennings paddles the Susquehanna River at Tunkhannock with a view of Miller Mountain in the distance.

All photos by the author.

Paddling is an inherently risky activity with ever-changing conditions and numerous natural and man-made hazards. Please choose rivers and creeks that are appropriate for your ability. It is also important to exercise caution on lakes and ponds. All persons paddling the rivers, creeks, lakes, ponds, swamps, and other waterways in this guide do so at their own risk; this guide is not a substitute for your own common sense, caution, and taking necessary safety precautions. The author and publisher disclaim any and all liability for conditions along the rivers, creeks, lakes, ponds, swamps, and other waterways in this guide, occurrences along them, and the accuracy of the data, conditions, and information contained herein.

Library of Congress Cataloging-in-Publication Data

Mitchell, Jeff, 1974–
    Paddling Pennsylvania : canoeing and kayaking the keystone state's rivers and lakes / Jeff Mitchell. — 1st ed.
        p.   cm.
    Includes index.
    ISBN-13: 978-0-8117-3626-8 (pbk.)
    ISBN-10: 0-8117-3626-1 (pbk.)
    1. Canoes and canoeing—Pennsylvania—Guidebooks. 2. Kayaking—Pennsylvania—Guidebooks. 3. Pennsylvania—Guidebooks. I. Title.
GV776.P4M58   2010
797.1220978—dc22
                                                                                2009035640

To Kaitlyn and Christian

Contents

Preface

Sliding onto the water and breaking its surface with a paddle is like entering a different world—one that melts away the stress of our modern lives, a world that is governed by nature's endless cycles and rhythms that will continue long after we are gone. All too often, our lives are cordoned off by the asphalt and macadam of the highways, streets, and roads that we build around ourselves. Yet our rivers and creeks are blissfully unaware of such limitations as they meander and bend, following courses that defy logic, always taking the most scenic routes. Being on the water offers a perspective of how we have been blessed with a beautiful world, a world with which humanity is inextricably intertwined despite our efforts to control and exploit it. Paddling offers us the solace and space to appreciate the incredible landscapes, history, and ecology of the places we call home.

I still think back to a paddling trip I did on the Clarion River with my friend Steve Davis a number of years ago. The air hung hot and heavy as the humidity faded the deep green forests and masked the distant mountains. We proceeded down the river into a gorge with massive boulders, deep pools, and swirling rapids, and we camped among the ferns and fished for smallmouth. Towering white pine trees rose like the columns of some sylvan temple while eagles, hawks, egrets, and herons followed their daily routines, unaware of our special sojourn. The soft murmur of the current reflected the sunlight in the morning and put us to sleep at night. At the time, I felt as if we were passing through a special place. And, in fact, we were.

See you on the river.

Acknowledgments

Special thanks to all my friends and family, including Joe and Tessa Mitchell, my parents, Leigh Ann Jennings, Steve Davis, Bryan Mulvihill, Bob Holliday, Jeff Sensenig, Dan Wrona, Ashley Lenig, Jay and Kristen Lewis, BCCKC, Paul and Paula Litwin, Rick and Nadine Dixon, Ed Kintner, Chuck Pirone, and Carissa Longo.

This book would not be possible without the assistance, support, and patience of Kyle Weaver and Brett Keener at Stackpole Books.

Finally, I express my appreciation to all those volunteers who support watershed organizations, clean our rivers, creeks, lakes, ponds, and reservoirs, and maintain and promote our water trails.

Introduction

Pennsylvania may derive its name from its forests, and it may be famous for its rolling, green mountains, but it is really a land of rivers and creeks, with more waterway miles than any state but Alaska. Rivers defined this state, providing routes for transportation and shipping lanes to convey coal and timber. They were highways through a wilderness, helping to build cities and industrialize a nation.

Unfortunately, man wasn't so kind to the rivers and streams upon which he depended so heavily. Clear-cut forests resulted in massive erosion and devastating forest fires that clogged waterways with silt and sediment. Acid mine drainage rendered countless miles of rivers and streams lifeless. And finally, thousands of dams combined with dredging and channeling altered the natural flow of the rivers, preventing the natural migration and destroying the habitats of many aquatic species.

But then something began to change. People realized that rivers and creeks offered incredible recreational and environmental benefits. Water trails were established on several rivers and creeks to introduce people to these beautiful waterways. Greenway and comprehensive plans were established to protect and enjoy the rivers. Towns and cities that once shunned rivers are now establishing attractive riverfronts, trails, parks, and access areas. Kayaking is one of the fastest growing outdoor recreational activities in Pennsylvania. Instead of exploiting the rivers and streams, we realize their worth by appreciating them for their outdoor recreation, ecological, and scenic values.

Pennsylvania's rivers and streams are known for their beauty. Some meander through pastoral countryside, while others cut through impressive canyons, water gaps, and gorges. These waterways offer a glimpse to the past, with the many old canals, bridge abutments, covered bridges, viaducts, and even forgotten towns that lie along their routes. Paddling also protects our waterways by introducing people to the beauty of the rivers, creeks, and lakes upon which our communities depend. By exposing people to our beautiful waterways, their value is appreciated and a realization is created of what could be lost if we do not preserve them.

Simply put, Pennsylvania offers some of the finest paddling in the country. Few states can match our incredible selection of large rivers, creeks, lakes, ponds, and reservoirs. Whether you want to paddle the massive Susquehanna or the intimate Tionesta, the vast Lake Erie or the hidden wilderness of Shumans Lake, you will find it all in the Keystone State.

Purpose and Scope of this Guide

This guide primarily focuses on sizeable flatwater rivers and streams, although riffles and rapids exist on many of the rivers and streams covered. This is not a guide to whitewater rivers and creeks. Industrialized rivers, or those open to heavy commercial traffic, are generally not included. Many lakes and ponds are also covered, but only those that are open to the public and featuring scenic value and limited shoreline development. An overview description of each river, creek, lake, or pond is provided. If you are planning an extended trip on a river or creek, it is advisable you obtain a more detailed guide if one is available. It is important to understand that the character and difficulty of rivers and streams can vary greatly depending on flows. A flood can dramatically change a river or creek with new braids, islands, strainers, and rapids.

This guide is organized by watersheds—the reason being that rivers and streams cross political and regional boundaries that makes organizing a guide by those criteria difficult. The Susquehanna River alone crosses or adjoins fifteen different counties and three different regions of the state.

Safety

Even the most benign creek can become deadly. It is absolutely crucial that you take the necessary steps, and learn important skills, to help ensure your safety while on the water. Please be aware of the following hazards while on the water.

Strainers: Strainers are trees that have fallen into a river or creek, and they are the most dangerous features found on the water. Avoid strainers at all costs and never attempt to paddle through one. If you are out of your boat and the current is taking you towards a strainer and you cannot avoid it, do not try to swim underneath it. Instead, climb over it. Strainers are dangerous because there are branches under the water that can trap and drown a paddler. Furthermore, the powerful current will force a person down into the water when trapped in a strainer. Strainers are often found along islands or bends where the river is cutting into the bank.

Lowhead dams: These are the second most dangerous features on the water. As a general rule, always portage a dam; do not paddle over any dam unless it is breached and there is a safe route. Dams are dangerous because they create recirculating hydraulics, also known as holes, that can trap and drown a paddler. These hydraulics are caused by the water flowing over the dam. Dams are usually identified by a horizon line on a river or creek.

Wing dams: Wing dams exist on a few rivers and creeks, particularly the Delaware River. Wing dams extend from each shore partway into the river or creek, leaving an opening, usually in the middle, through which the river or creek flows. The opening often has very fast and powerful currents with large

MAP LEGEND

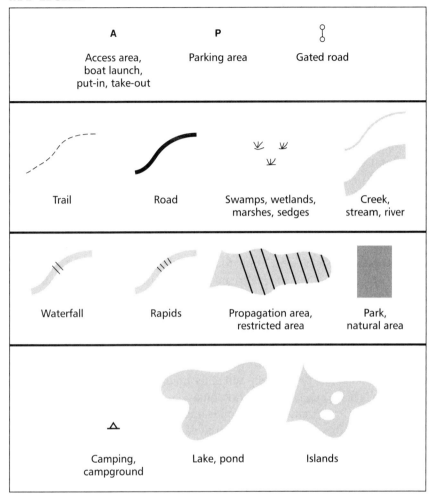

waves and rapids. Always paddle straight through the opening, or portage; never paddle over the wings, as there may be powerful hydraulics that can capsize a boat and cause drowning.

Rapids: All of the rivers and creeks in this guide are primarily flatwater with easy riffles and rapids. High flows can create significantly more difficult waves and holes that can swamp and flip a canoe or kayak. Do not boat during high flows. If you swim in a rapid, float feet first, try to hold onto your paddle and, if you can, the upstream end of the boat.

Foot entrapment: As a general rule, do not attempt to stand up in deep, fast-moving water since your feet can become trapped in the riverbed, particularly if the riverbed is comprised of boulders, large cobblestones, trees, branches, or roots. If your feet become trapped, the current can force you underwater. Wait to stand up when you reach calm water or a shallow riffle. If you can, swim to calmer water; otherwise, float downstream feet first. Never jump feet first into moving current since your feet can become entrapped.

Hypothermia and exposure: These conditions can endanger a paddler any time of the year, including summer. Make sure to bring rainwear, waterproof clothing, and garments made with synthetic materials that can wick away moisture and conserve body heat. It is generally not a good idea to wear cotton since it dries slowly and does not insulate when wet, which can lead to hypothermia. Wearing a life preserver will provide additional protection from hypothermia.

Drowning: Drowning can result from a variety of factors, such as hypothermia, exposure, foot entrapment, exhaustion, or most frequently, failure to wear a life preserver. You should always wear a suitable preserver while on the water. Strong currents and long distances to shore can be difficult for any swimmer to overcome without a preserver. Most deaths are the result of people not wearing a life preserver.

Dehydration: It may seem ironic to face dehydration on the river, but you are more susceptible than you realize due to exposure to the sun and wind and the exertion required when paddling. Always bring enough water and/or a water filter.

Poison ivy and other poisonous plants and insects: Thanks to plenty of water and thick soils, poison ivy is a common presence along rivers and creeks, as are other poisonous plants. Learn to identify these plants. The locations in this guide also attract bloodthirsty and other troublesome insects. Protect yourself with repellant, bug netting, and clothing.

Equipment: Proper equipment is critical to help ensure your safety. Whenever you are on the water it is important to have these items:

Life preserver
Whistle
Cell phone
Wading shoes
Clothing made from wool or synthetic materials, such
    as polypropylene or fleece
Throw rope
Sufficient water and food
Water filter for longer trips
Rain jacket, hat, sunglasses
Sunblock
First-aid kit
Camera and binoculars
GPS—may be helpful finding islands on which to camp,
    or to navigate the larger swamps in this book, such
    as Conneaut Marsh or Hartstown Swamp.

Other safety precautions:

- If you capsize, hold onto the upstream end of the boat and swim to the shore or an eddy. If you are in a difficult current and cannot manage your boat, let it go and swim to shore.
- If you collide with an obstacle, such as a rock, while in a boat, lean into the obstacle to help prevent capsizing.
- Always scout any section of the river that may appear challenging, dangerous, or does not present a clear route.
- Never boat alone; always bring a friend and let someone know where you are going and when you expect to return.

When to Paddle

For the rivers and streams in this guide, sufficient flow is obviously dependent on rainfall. A wet year can result in many rivers and streams being runnable most of the time, and a dry year just the opposite.

As a general rule, the major rivers (Delaware, Schuylkill, Susquehanna, Juniata, West Branch Susquehanna, Allegheny, Youghiogheny) are runnable year-round, although you can expect to drag your boat across riffles and gravel bars. The other creeks and streams are usually runnable up until May or June, and again in late October or November. Heavy rainfalls may permit paddling for a few days to a week over the summer.

Rivers and streams in the southeastern corner of the state may be ice-free all winter long.

Access

As a general rule, established access areas with signs, ramps, and parking are available on the larger rivers and more popular creeks. Many of the lesser-known creeks in this guide do not have established access areas, so you will

---

Acronyms

The destinations in this guide, particularly the lakes and ponds, are owned and managed by various governmental agencies and departments identified by their acronyms for convenience. They are:

DCNR: Pennsylvania Department of Conservation and Natural Resources
NPS: National Park Service
PFBC: Pennsylvania Fish and Boat Commission
PGC: Pennsylvania Game Commission
USACE: United States Army Corps of Engineers
USFS/ANF: United States Forest Service/Allegheny National Forest
USGS: United States Geological Survey

have to park along the road or in a pull-off, usually near a bridge. The banks to reach the stream or creek are often steep and brushy.

Almost every lake and pond in this guide has an access area of some kind that can be reached by a vehicle; however, there are a few that require you to hike in with your boat, offering a more challenging and isolated paddling experience.

Permits and Fees

Depending on which governmental agency or department or private entity owns the lake, pond, or launch areas, permits or fees may be required. This money is crucial in maintaining the access areas that are so important to paddlers.

DCNR and PFBC: Non-powered boats must have one of the following: launching or mooring permits from Pennsylvania state parks, or boat registration or launching permit from the PFBC.

USACE: Small fees are generally required to access USACE lakes. Fees are generally paid by the honor system at the parking and launch areas.

PGC: No permits or fees are required; however, DCNR or PFBC permits may be required at some lakes.

Privately owned lakes and ponds open to the public: May require their own permits or fees. Some may require DCNR or PFBC permits.

County and local government-owned lakes and ponds: May require their own permits and fees. Some may require DCNR or PFBC permits.

State and National Scenic Rivers

Pennsylvania is home to several rivers and creeks that have been designated as state or national scenic rivers. This list is limited to those rivers and creeks covered in this guide.

State Scenic Rivers
Brandywine Creek
Lehigh River
Little Schuylkill River
Octoraro Creek
Pine Creek
Schuylkill River
Tulpehocken Creek
Yellow Breeches Creek

National Scenic Rivers
Allegheny River
Clarion River
Delaware River

Pennsylvania Water Trails

Pennsylvania has an excellent system of officially recognized water trails established by local groups and the Pennsylvania Fish and Boat Commission. Many of these rivers and creeks have maps and guides that are free to the public.

Most of the rivers and creeks in this guide are not part of the water trail system. The PFBC and DCNR are actively looking to expand the water trail system, so if you have a local river or creek you'd like to include, go to www.fish.state.pa .us/watertrails/trailindex.htm for more information. The following rivers and creeks are part of the system:

Delaware River
Lehigh River
Schuylkill River
North Branch Susquehanna River
West Branch Susquehanna River
Pine Creek
Susquehanna River
Raystown Branch Juniata River
Juniata River
Conodoguinet Creek
Swatara Creek
Conestoga River
Yellow Breeches Creek
Allegheny River
Clarion River
Kiskiminitas and Conemaugh Rivers
Monongahela River
Youghiogheny River
Three Rivers Water Trail

Camping

Many rivers flow through public land where camping is permitted. However, most of the rivers in this guide flow through private land where camping may be prohibited or restricted. Always obey posted lands and respect the rights of the landowner. Obtain permission from the landowner when camping on private land. It is also important to use existing campsites where available; avoid creating new campsites.

Rivers and streams that offer primitive camping open to the public:
Delaware River
Susquehanna River
West Branch Susquehanna River
Pine Creek
Juniata River
Little Juniata River
Frankstown Branch Juniata River
Allegheny River
Clarion River
Tionesta Creek
Youghiogheny River

Lakes and ponds that offer primitive camping open to the public:
Raystown Lake
Allegheny Reservoir
Tionesta Lake

Best Lakes, Ponds, and Reservoirs for Birdwatching, Wildlife, and Plantlife

These lakes and ponds are known for their opportunities to observe birds, wildlife, and plantlife.

Shohola Lake
Pecks Pond
Bruce Lake
Egypt Meadow Lake
Lower Lake
Gouldsboro Lake
Bradys Lake
Long Pond
State Game Lands 250 Pond
Lake John
Splashdam Pond
Lake Jean
Faylor Lake
Octoraro Reservoir
Shumans Lake
Lake Chillisquaque
George B. Stevenson Reservoir
Shaggers Inn Shallow Water Impoundment
Black Moshannon Lake
Raystown Lake
Beaver Meadows Lake
Lake Pleasant
Conneaut Marsh
Lake Wilhelm
Cranberry Glade Lake
Pymatuning Reservoir
Hartstown Swamp
Shenango River Lake
Lake Arthur
Glade Dam Lake
Presque Isle Bay
Lake Erie

Hike-in Lakes, Ponds, and Reservoirs

For those looking for a unique and challenging paddling experience where you are likely to have the water to yourself, there are several lakes and ponds that can be accessed only by hiking in with your boat and gear.

Bruce Lake	Splashdam Pond
Egypt Meadow Lake	Beech Lake
Lake John	McWilliams Reservoir
Shumans Lake	

Useful Web Sites

Paddlers should become familiar with the PFBC's Web site, www.fish.state .pa.us. This site contains a wealth of information for paddlers, including permit and fishing license information, as well as other regulations. The Web site contains county guides where you can select a county and view a clickable map with access areas, trout waters, special regulation areas, and rivers, lakes, and ponds open to the public. The county guides are located at www.fish.state .pa.us/county.htm. This site also allows you to order free water trail guides, regional maps, and other publications.

The USGS maintains many gauges across the state that monitor water flow and river and creek levels. Paddlers use these gauges to help determine if a river or creek is runnable. To access this information, go to http://water.usgs .gov/waterwatch/ and click on Pennsylvania. The levels described in this book are generally minimum levels.

I did not include the internet addresses that describe the locations in this guide because those addresses change so frequently. A simple internet search of the rivers, creeks, lakes, ponds, swamps, and other waterways in this guide will reveal a wealth of information, including current conditions. It is important to educate yourself as much as possible about the places you intend to paddle.

Get Involved

Our rivers, streams, and lakes face a variety of threats and challenges from pollution, overdevelopment, and lack of access. Water is our most precious resource, and sadly, it is often exploited and polluted. There are numerous paddling and watershed organizations that need your help. Consider helping with lake and river cleanups; establish a water trail on a local creek; petition local governments to build access areas; and write your elected officials to protect our rivers and watersheds. Rivers, streams, and lakes cannot defend themselves and can become victims of political agendas, greed, and narrow minds. Paddling enables us to enjoy what should be held in the public trust and offers an opportunity to appreciate the great beauty of our state—and also gives us an appreciation of what can also be lost.

What can you do?

- Join a watershed association. Numerous streams and rivers in the state have their own watershed associations. These groups do invaluable work in protecting our watersheds. The Pennsylvania Organization for Watersheds and Rivers (POWR) is the statewide organization for watershed associations. Their Web site is www.pawatersheds.org.
- Help with a river or lake cleanup.
- Pick up litter as you paddle. It is a great example to others.
- Join a paddling club. Many clubs exist across the state, and some are free to join; a list of these clubs is below. These clubs increase awareness, provide recreational opportunities, and help with river cleanups.

Most Beautiful Rivers and Creeks

Whether they flow through deep canyons or pastoral countryside, these rivers and creeks are widely regarded as the most scenic in Pennsylvania.

Delaware River	Juniata River
Balls Eddy to Portland	Tuscarora Creek
Susquehanna River	Aughwhick Creek
Towanda to Falls	Raystown Branch Juniata River
Sunbury to Royalton	Everett to Juniata River
Wyalusing Creek	Frankstown Branch Juniata River
Tunkhannock Creek	Little Juniata River
Nescopeck Creek	Allegheny River
Catawissa Creek	Port Allegany to Eldred
West Branch Susquehanna River	Kinzua Dam to Warren
Shawville to Renovo	Franklin to Emlenton
Loyalsock Creek	Brokenstraw Creek
Pine Creek	Tionesta Creek
Kettle Creek	Oil Creek
First Fork Sinnemahoning Creek	French Creek
Driftwood Branch Sinnemahoning	Clarion River
Creek	Red Bank Creek
Bennett Branch Sinnemahoning	Mahoning Creek
Creek	Youghiogheny River
Sinnemahoning Creek	Shenango River
Moshannon Creek	Elk Creek
Clearfield Creek	

Most Beautiful Lakes, Ponds, and Reservoirs

These are the most beautiful lakes and ponds in the Pennsylvania. Consider this a list of "must-do" destinations. Each contains different qualities, but they all are generally undeveloped. Some are completely undeveloped and feature wilderness qualities; others feature unique habitats and diverse and plentiful wildlife.

Belmont Lake
Upper Woods Pond
Lower Woods Pond
White Oak Pond
Shohola Lake
Pecks Pond
Bruce Lake
Egypt Meadow Lake
Lower Lake
Tobyhanna Lake
Bradys Lake
Long Pond
Beltzville Lake
Lake Nockamixon
Tioga Lake
Lackawanna Lake
State Game Lands 250 Pond
The Meadows and Beech Lake
Lake John
Splashdam Pond
Lake Jean
McWilliams and Klines Reservoirs
Letterkenny Reservoir
Shumans Lake
Bearwallow Pond

Hunters Lake
Kettle Creek Reservoir
George B. Stevenson Reservoir
Black Moshannon Lake
Raystown Lake
Shawnee Lake
Long Pine Run Reservoir
Meadow Grounds Lake
Lake Koon and Lake Gordon
Allegheny Reservoir
Beaver Meadows Lake
Howard Eaton Reservoir
Union City Reservoir
Mahoning Creek Lake
Quemahoning Reservoir
High Point Lake
Cranberry Glade Lake
Laurel Hill Lake
Pymatuning Reservoir
Lake Arthur
Raccoon Lake
Cross Creek Lake
Presque Isle Bay
Lake Erie

Paddling Clubs and Organizations

Please consider joining and supporting the following paddling clubs and related organizations:

American Canoe Association, www.americancanoe.org
American Rivers, www.americanrivers.org
Benscreek Canoe and Kayak Club (Johnstown),
    www.benscreekcanoeclub.com

Canoe Club of Greater Harrisburg, www.ccghpa.com
Keystone Canoe Club, www.keystonecanoeclub.com
Lancaster Canoe Club, www.lancastercanoeclub.com
Lehigh Valley Canoe Club, www.enter.net/ ~ lvcc/
Pennsylvania Organization for Watersheds and Rivers (POWR),
    www.pawatersheds.org
Philadelphia Canoe Club, www.philacanoe.org
Three Rivers Paddling Club (Pittsburgh),
    www.threeriverspaddlingclub.com

River (and Lake) Karma

While paddling, you may hear the expression "river karma." What does this mean? By doing something good for the river, the river will be good to you. Trust me—it is always best to have the river on your side. Paddlers usually like to ensure good karma by picking up litter they may find along a river or lake. It is easy to throw litter in your kayak or canoe and dispose of it properly when you take out. Since litter flows downstream, our rivers and creeks suffer from it. Every little bit helps.

Delaware River Watershed

The famous Delaware forms the eastern boundary of Pennsylvania, which shares the river with New York and New Jersey. It is by far the most popular river for canoeing and kayaking in the state, attracting tens of thousands of people every year. Several canoe liveries operate on the river above the Delaware Water Gap. The Delaware offers beautiful scenery, exciting rapids, superb water quality, excellent fishing, and many fine primitive campsites between Matamoras and the Delaware Water Gap. It is also unique in that the main stem of the river does not have a dam, so the Delaware is home to shad and eels, species rarely seen on other rivers.

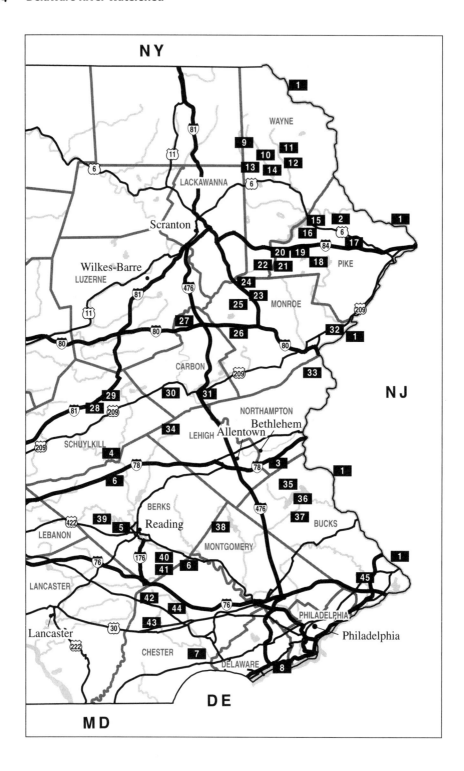

 # Rivers and Creeks

1. Delaware River

Balls Eddy to Narrowsburg

Length: 45.4 miles	

Length: 45.4 miles

Water level: 2.5 to 4 feet on the NPS gauge at Narrowsburg. Exercise caution at higher flows.

Difficulty: Easy to moderate

Hazards: Skinners Falls and other rapids

Scenery: Very good to excellent

Highlights: Cliffs, bald eagles, Skinners Falls

Fishing: Trout, smallmouth bass, shad, eel, striped bass, walleye, pickerel, muskellunge, sunfish, bluegills, carp, catfish, suckers

Camping: Limited to private campgrounds along the river

This section begins on the West Branch Delaware River as it meanders between steep wooded hillsides. There are a few small islands below Balls Eddy. Just below Hancock, New York, the East Branch joins to form the Delaware River. Below the confluence, there is a series of islands with channels between them. The mountains rise approximately 800 feet above the river with cliffs and rock outcrops. Fields lie along the river, and forests of hardwoods, hemlock, and white pine cover the mountains. Much of this section is not heavily paddled but is very popular with anglers. You will also encounter numerous weirs, used to trap eels. The weirs are V-shaped rock wings. Do not paddle over the wings—instead go to the left or right, or through the center chute if a trap isn't present.

Only riffles and easy Class I rapids are encountered to the Buckingham PFBC access. Further downstream is Frisbie Island and the village of Equinunk on the right; there are limited services and no established access at the village. Between Equinunk and Long Eddy, the state highways leave both sides of the river and the Delaware flows through a beautiful canyon with a few small islands, easy riffles, and Class I rapids.

New York Route 97 returns to the left shore of the river below Long Eddy. More easy riffles are encountered; in places, the river cuts into the bedrock with ledges. The combination of easy riffles, Class I rapids, small islands, and steep, wooded mountainsides typifies the Delaware to the Damascus PFBC access on the right. The river is calm to the next bridge at Milanville, with occasional islands. Immediately downstream is the start of Skinners Falls, a strong Class II rapid that is one of the most challenging on the entire river. The rapids

1. Delaware River, Balls Eddy to Narrowsburg

are formed by shale and sandstone ledges with potholes carved by the river that are several feet deep. In high flows, the rapids have big waves and holes. It is not a very difficult rapid, but you will want to keep your boat straight. The safest channel is along the right shore; the rapids can be scouted and portaged on the left. Below Skinners Falls the river is more popular with paddlers, thanks to several outfitters and liveries.

The river is relatively quiet to Narrowsburg with only easy rapids and riffles. The scenery at Narrowsburg is impressive as the river squeezes between high cliffs and ledges and then opens into a large pool, known as Big Eddy. Big Eddy, at 113 feet deep, is also the deepest spot on the river. The Narrowsburg PFBC access is just downstream on the right.

Narrowsburg to Matamoras

Length: 34 miles

Water level: 2.5 to 4 feet on the NPS gauge at Narrowsburg. Exercise caution at higher flows.

Difficulty: Moderate

Hazards: Several whitewater rapids; four rapids are Class II; more than twenty are Class I.

Scenery: Excellent

Highlights: Cliffs, rapids, wet-weather waterfalls, bald eagles, good fishing, Roebling Bridge, Elephant Feet Rocks

Fishing: Trout, smallmouth bass, shad, eel, striped bass, walleye, pickerel, muskellunge, sunfish, bluegills, carp, catfish, suckers

Camping: Limited to private campgrounds along the river; Delaware State Forest is the only place for free, primitive camping.

This is arguably the Delaware River at its most scenic. Cliffs tower above the river as it flows through a canyon of forested hills and mountains. In wet weather, waterfalls cascade from these cliffs. The river also features many rapids, the most of any river in this guide; as a result, those who paddle this section should be experienced. The rapids are not complicated, but they do require maneuvering to avoid rocks, and in higher water, holes. Due to the good water quality, fishing is very popular along this section of the Delaware, so be sure to share the river with anglers. The only drawback to this section is its popularity. On summer weekends, the river will be overrun with canoes and rafts. Several raft and canoe liveries operate along this stretch of water. The liveries also operate several private campgrounds, enabling overnight trips. Most of these campgrounds are on the New York side of the river.

Downstream from Narrowsburg, observe Darbytown Falls, which drops more than 100 feet along Peggy Run on the Pennsylvania shore. Easy Class I rapids

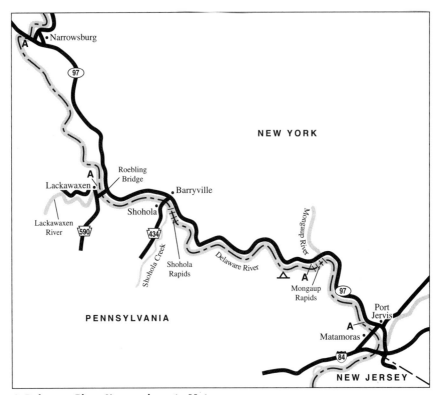

1. Delaware River, Narrowsburg to Matamoras

follow to a railroad bridge; immediately below is Bridge No. 9 Rift, an easy Class II rapid. The Tenmile River joins from the New York side, and farther downstream, Masthope Creek joins from the Pennsylvania side. Easy rapids continue periodically along the river; watch for boulders. The next notable rapid is Westcolang Rift, a long Class II rapid with two-foot waves. There is a Class I rapid, followed by Class II Narrow Falls Rift, a tricky rapid where cross-currents often tip canoes. The main channel is towards the right. New York Route 97 rejoins along the left and will stay in close proximity to Port Jervis. There is also a private campground on the left. Down to Lackawaxen, the Delaware is mostly forested and undeveloped, with few homes and mountains that rise 800 feet above the river.

The Lackawaxen River (see page 26), a major tributary, joins from the right with the PFBC Zane Grey Access at the juncture of the two rivers on the right; Zane Grey was a famous author of Westerns in the late 1800s and early 1900s who lived in Lackawaxen from 1906 to 1918.

Immediately downstream is one of the river's highlights: the impressive Roebling Bridge, the oldest suspension bridge in the country. Named after its engineer, John Roebling, the bridge was completed in 1849 to carry the Delaware & Hudson Canal over the Delaware River; it is now open to automobiles. Roebling went on to design the world-famous Brooklyn Bridge in New York City.

From Lackawaxen to Shohola there are more Class I rapids and riffles and one Class II rapid, Big Cedar Rift. Several private campgrounds are located on the left; most of them are operated by various canoe liveries. Immediately downstream from the Shohola-Barryville Bridge is Shohola Rift, also known as Shohola Rapids. At a half-mile in length, they are the longest and among the most challenging rapids on the Delaware. The clearest channel is to the right. Easy riffles and Class I rapids continue periodically for eleven miles as the river flows between steep wooded mountainsides. A few more private campgrounds are available on the left. About 2.5 miles below the Pond Eddy Bridge, on the right, is the only primitive camping along this upper section of the Delaware. This camping area is located in Pennsylvania's Delaware State Forest, and you must get a permit first before camping.

The Mongaup River joins from the left, which also marks the beginning of Class II Mongaup Rift, or Mongaup Rapids. There is an access on the left above the confluence with the Mongaup River, which is very popular with whitewater paddlers who enjoy running the rapids that lead directly into the Delaware during release weekends. The Mongaup Rift or Rapids begin as the river bounces over ledges, but the main flow is narrowed with big three-foot waves along a cliff on the right. Expect to take on water. Below the rapids, high cliffs and rock outcrops rise over the river, particularly on the left where New York Route 97 hugs the cliffs high above, making for an exceptionally scenic drive. Pass under a railroad bridge, which marks the downstream boundary of the Upper Delaware National Scenic and Recreational River. On the left is an access area, and on the right, outcrops and cliffs known as Elephant Feet Rocks. Down to Port Jervis, the river is mostly wooded and undeveloped with 700-foot mountains and relatively few islands. Paddle two miles farther to reach the PFBC Matamoras access on the right.

Matamoras to Portland

Length: 48 miles

Water level: 2.5 to 4 feet on the NPS gauge at Narrowsburg. Exercise caution at higher flows.

Difficulty: Easy

Hazards: Strainers along islands

Scenery: Very good

Highlights: Undeveloped river with many islands open to primitive camping, Delaware Water Gap National Recreation Area, bald eagles

Fishing: Trout, smallmouth bass, shad, eel, striped bass, walleye, pickerel, muskellunge, sunfish, bluegills, carp, catfish, suckers

Camping: Numerous primitive campsites available within the Delaware Water Gap National Recreation Area, mostly on islands, but also along the shore.

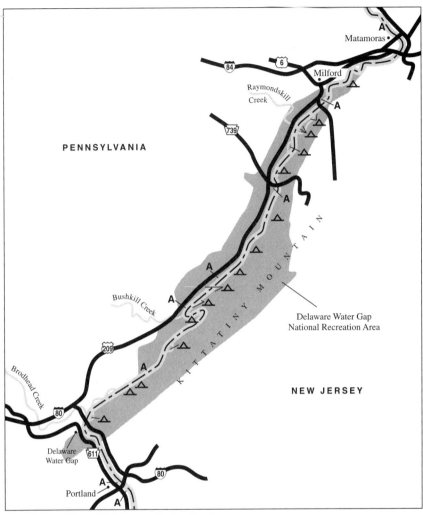

1. Delaware River, Matamoras to Portland

This section provides a superb multi-day float trip. Because much of this section of the river is protected by the Delaware Water Gap National Recreation Area, it is undeveloped with a surprising sense of isolation. The river flows down a valley between the Kittatinny Mountains of New Jersey on the left and the Pocono Mountains of Pennsylvania on the right. Mountains rise to about 500 feet above the river; the terrain rises gradually on the New Jersey side, but cliffs and wooded bluffs are common on the Pennsylvania side. Fields often lie along the river and islands are more common than in previous sections. With the exception of riffles over gravel bars, the river is calm and is suitable for beginners at normal flows. Riffles and easy rapids are usually located where the river encounters islands. This section also features many primitive campsites managed by the National Park Service; most of these sites are actually in New Jersey. Only camp at designated sites. Like the previous, this section of river is popular with paddlers, so expect company.

From the Matamoras access, paddle under the Mid-Delaware Bridge, and soon thereafter, the I-84 bridge. On the left, the Neversink River joins at Carpenters Point, also known as Tri-State Rock, where the states of Pennsylvania, New York, and New Jersey meet. From here on out, New York is left behind and New Jersey will be on river left. On the right is a private campground. Every mile or two you will encounter islands that rise 10–15 feet above the river with riparian forests of tulip poplar, silver maple, and sycamore with an understory of ferns. On river right from Punkys Island is another private campground. The downstream end of Punkys Island marks the beginning of the Delaware Water Gap National Recreation Area, where primitive campsites are available on a variety of islands and on either shore of the river.

The next access is at Milford Beach, on river right, just upstream of the U.S. 206 bridge. Downstream is Minisink Island, one of the largest islands on the Delaware and was once home to an Indian community. Take the channel to the right where there are several campsites on the island. Raymondskill Creek joins to the right; less than a mile upstream on that creek is spectacular Raymondskill Falls, one of the highest in Pennsylvania. There are impressive shale cliffs on the Pennsylvania side that harbor prickly pear cactus. Their yellow blooms can be seen in May from the river. Campsites are also available on Namanock Island, a mile downstream.

Three-and-a-half miles downstream is Dingmans Bridge and Dingmans Ferry Access, on river right below the bridge; a half-mile below the access on river left is full-service Dingmans Campground with showers. For the fifteen miles to Depew Access on the New Jersey side, the river placidly flows through its valley framed by the ridge of Kittatinny Mountain to the east. There are primitive campsites every mile or so on either side of the river and on Shapnack, Buck, and Depew islands. Wind can become a nuisance, particularly where the river makes an S-turn at Walpack Bend. One drawback is that traffic can often be heard from busy U.S. 209. There is an access area on river left below Depew Island.

A mile and a half downstream is Poxono Island, which does not offer camping, and two miles farther on river right is the Smithfield Beach Access. Just downstream is Tocks Island; this small, narrow island may seem insignificant today, but it was selected to be the site of a dam in the 1960s. That proposal helped lead to the creation of the Delaware Water Gap National Recreation Area. The Tocks Island Dam would have created a reservoir 37 miles long. As a flood control project, its fluctuating water levels would have created exposed mud flats. The dam would have flooded countless sites with historical, scenic, and ecological significance. The effort to defeat the dam was one of the first environmental movements, and victories, of its kind in the nation. Thanks to that movement, the Delaware will continue to flow freely and provide future generations with superb paddling, camping, and fishing.

Below Tocks, islands become more common. Campsites exist on Labar Island and on the Pennsylvania shore. Pass two large islands, Depue and Shawnee Island, the latter the site of a golf course and resort. The main channel flows to the left of these islands. Broadhead Creek joins from the right with gravel bars; just downstream is Schellenberger Island with two campsites. These are the last primitive campsites open to the public in the Delaware Water Gap National Recreation Area. The imposing, rugged terrain of the water gap begins to rise around you as you paddle under the busy I-80 bridge, which also serves as the Appalachian Trail's crossing. The river bends left into the gap; on the left is Kittatinny Access area and a visitor's center with restrooms, water, and parking.

The Delaware Water Gap is a place of imposing natural beauty. The mountains are crowned with towering cliffs as they rise 1,300 feet above the river. You may even spy rock climbers on the cliffs. The scenery is truly impressive and spectacular. Arrow Island lies at the outlet from the water gap and small Slateford Creek joins from the right. This marks the southern boundary of the national recreation area. For the remainder of the river, most of the islands and shore is privately owned and primitive camping is very limited. The towering Kittatinny Mountain gives way to pastoral scenery and wooded hills. Paddle under a railroad bridge and reach a pedestrian bridge 1.5 miles farther at the town of Portland. An access area with a steep ramp is located under the pedestrian bridge on river right.

Portland to Riegelsville

Length: 34 miles

Water level: USGS Belvidere gauge should be at least 3.4 feet. USGS Riegelsville gauge should be 2.8 feet.

Difficulty: Easy

Hazards: Foul Rift

Scenery: Good

Highlights: Miniature water gap below Hog Rift, north of Easton

Fishing: Smallmouth bass, largemouth bass, muskellunge, trout

Camping: Only occasional public campgrounds; no primitive camping open to the public.

For the remainder of its course after leaving the water gap, the Delaware is a changed river. Expect more development, homes, cottages, and some industry along the river. However, fields and wooded hills are still common. Primitive camping is almost nonexistent since most of the land surrounding the river is privately owned; camping is largely limited to private campgrounds along the river. You can even expect to see powerboats in the long, deep pools.

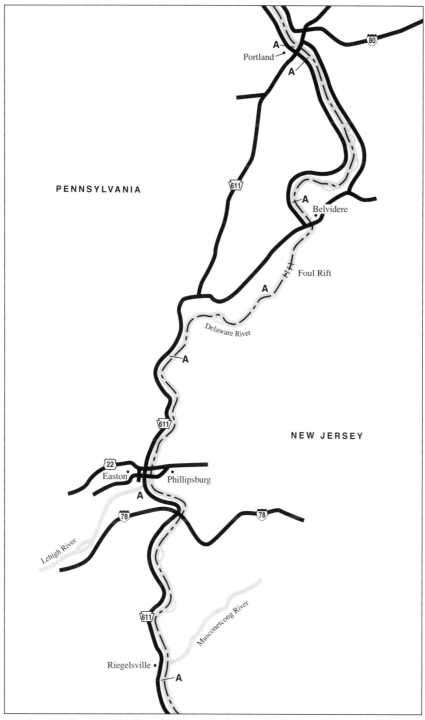

1. Delaware River, Portland to Riegelsville

Heading downstream to Riverton, pass a private campground to the right on Attins Island. You then encounter several islands with Class I riffles and reach a public access on river right, just upstream from Riverton. Below Belvidere, New Jersey, is Foul Rift, a strong Class II rapid; it is a long ledge rapid that should not be attempted by novice paddlers. Portage is possible on the left, but it is not an established carry. The erosive power of the river has exposed the bedrock along the shores below the rapid. There is an industrial or electrical generation plant below the rapid on the right.

From Foul Rift to Easton, the Delaware meanders through pastoral scenery, riffles and Class I rapids, and a few small islands. The scenic highlight of this section is a beautiful miniature water gap just below Hog Rift, where the river squeezes between wooded bluffs 400 feet high. Just downstream is Easton, featuring the Front Street access area located just upstream of the confluence with the Lehigh River, on the right. The Lehigh flows over a spillway before joining the Delaware; this spillway impounded water for the Delaware Canal. This beautiful canal has been restored and features a bike path, locks, and historical displays. It can often be seen from the river.

There is another 400-foot-deep water gap between Coffeetown and Riegelsville. For the remaining ten miles to the Rielgelsville access, the river passes several islands and occasional Class I riffles. The scenery is pastoral with wooded hills and fields. The Riegelsville access is on the right, less than a mile below the bridge.

Riegelsville to Yardley

Length: 35 miles

Water level: USGS Riegelsville gauge should be a minimum of 2.8 feet.

Difficulty: Easy to moderate

Hazards: Wells Falls, Scudders Falls, wing dams

Scenery: Good to very good

Highlights: Nockamixon Cliffs, Delaware Canal State Park, Washington Crossing State Park

Fishing: Smallmouth bass, shad, eel, striped bass, walleye, pickerel, muskellunge, sunfish, bluegills, carp, catfish, suckers

Camping: Limited to commercial campgrounds, Tinicum County Park, and Bulls Island State Park in New Jersey; river is surrounded mostly by private land.

For the remainder of this section the Delaware flows through pastoral countryside of fields and wooded hills. This final section of the river has surprisingly limited development, and much of the river is wooded, pastoral, and scenic.

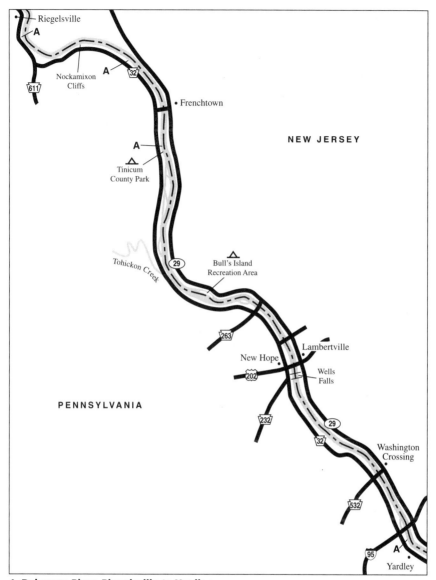

1. Delaware River, Riegelsville to Yardley

This section includes historical features, including the site of George Washington's famed crossing of the Delaware and the canal.

The scenic highlight of this section begins not far below the put-in, where cliffs known as the Nockamixon Cliffs or the Palisades of the Delaware rise 300 feet on river right. These cliffs face north and harbor rare plants found in more northerly and arctic habitats. The cliffs are also home to ninety species of birds. The river flows downstream among strings of islands, along with easy riffles and Class I rapids. Access is found at Upper Black Eddy, Erwinna, and Tinicum County Park; camping is located at Dogwood Haven Campground and Tinicum County Park. There is a long chain of islands below the park. The scenery along the river improves as the setting becomes more forested and undeveloped. Point Pleasant is on the right where the Tohickon Creek joins; forested hills rise to 300 feet above the river.

Encounter the Raritan, or Lumberville, Dam at Bulls Island, upstream of the Lumberville-Raven Rocks pedestrian bridge. The rapid formed by the wing dam is Class I–II with large wave trains. This is the first of three such wing dams on this section. Always take the center chute and never go over the dams, where there can be lethal hydraulics. On river left is Bulls Island with camping and access; this is the last public camping on the river.

Continue seven miles downstream to the scenic towns of New Hope, Pennsylvania, and Lambertville, New Jersey. Pass under two bridges and reach the Lambertville access on the left. These towns have many shops, restaurants, and galleries. Just downstream is one of the most difficult rapids on the entire river, Wells Falls, which are partially formed by a wing dam. Four-foot wave trains are often formed by the Class II–III rapids. The clearest line is towards the left side of the chute. The falls can be portaged over either wing dam into the eddy below; do not be too proud to portage this rapid, as people have died here. Only experienced paddlers should attempt to run Wells Falls.

The river then calms down and passes by Washington Crossing; a few miles further the river leads to another wing dam at Scudders Falls. This Class I rapid is not difficult as long as you remain in the center chute. Pass a few islands and go under the I-95 bridge. The takeout at Yardley PFBC access is on river right.

2. Lackawaxen River

Section: Threshmans private access to Delaware River

Length: 9 miles

Water level: Usually dependent on releases from Lake Wallenpaupack; 1,200 cfs is a good flow.

Hazards: Class I–II rapids

Difficulty: Moderate

Scenery: Good to very good

Highlights: Canal remnants and mountain scenery

Fishing: Trout

Camping: None

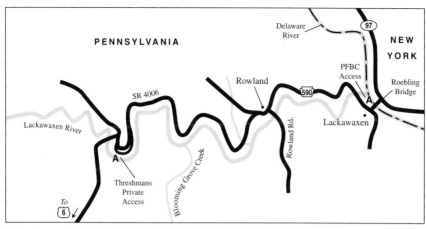

2. Lackawaxen River

The Lackawaxen River drains a large area of Pike and Wayne counties. Thanks to water releases for electrical generation from PP&L's Lake Wallenpaupack, this scenic river is often run during the summer when most rivers of similar size are too low to float much of anything. The releases are usually during weekdays but are also scheduled on a few weekends. Expect to see bald eagles, kingfishers, and ospreys on this river. The Lackawaxen is also popular with trout anglers.

Be aware this river has mild whitewater rapids. A recreational kayak can handle these rapids, but a spray skirt is recommended. Do not attempt this river in a recreational kayak during high flows, particularly below the Rowlands Road bridge. It is advisable that you have some experience before paddling this river.

The typical put-in is Threshmans, a private put-in where you must pay to access the river. SR 4006 and PA 590 also follow the river closely, and there are various places where you can pull off and access the river. The take-out is the Zane Grey PFBC access where the Lackawaxen joins the Delaware.

Down to the Rowlands Road bridge, the river is easy with simple riffles and a few wave trains with long pools. Forested bluffs and mountains rise to about 400 feet above the river and in several places impressive old stone walls line the river—the walls to the left were for the old canal, and those to the right for the railroad. The surrounding forests have towering white pine trees. Development is scant with only a few cottages and homes, which are usually on the left.

Below the Rowlands Road bridge, the rapids become more frequent, although they are still fairly easy. The hardest rapid is a long Class II one mile below the bridge; this rapid is marked by large boulders on the right. Stay toward the left. Mountains rise to 600 feet above the river. A few easy rapids, wave trains, and short pools are below down to the PFBC access at the Delaware River.

3. Lehigh River

Bowmanstown to Kimmets Lock

Length: 21 miles

Water level: USGS Bethlehem gauge should be 1.5 feet.

Difficulty: Easy to moderate

Hazards: Easy whitewater rapids, two lowdams

Scenery: Poor to good

Highlights: Blue Mountain, easy rapids, canal remnants, Lehigh Gap

Fishing: Smallmouth bass, trout, muskellunge

Camping: None available

The Lehigh is one of the most popular rivers in eastern Pennsylvania. The section between White Haven and Jim Thorpe is famous for its beautiful canyon scenery and Class II–III rapids; as a result, it is not appropriate for flatwater kayaks and canoes. This guide covers the Lehigh's tamer section between Bowmanstown and Easton.

This float trip is far from pristine and does not offer the scenery found in the whitewater section between White Haven and Jim Thorpe, but it is still an enjoyable paddle. Historically, the Lehigh's value was in transportation, whether it be as a canal more than a century ago or as a pathway for the railroads and highways that follow the river today. The river flows through the urbanized and fast-growing Lehigh Valley.

Below Bowmanstown, Blue Mountain rises like a giant wall to the south; busy PA 248 is on the left. Pass a few islands and watch for a lowdam that should be portaged with a pumphouse on the left less than a mile from the put-in. The river flows through a valley with defunct industry and factories. The surrounding hills and mountains, including Blue Mountain, are largely devoid of vegetation due to the now-defunct zinc smelting in Palmerton. While the scenery is less than appealing, there is a delightful series of easy rapids and riffles to the beginning of the Lehigh Gap, where Aquashicola Creek joins from the left. Pass through the rugged, 1,000-foot-deep gap, which is cloaked with extensive talus slopes and cliffs. The gap's rugged scenery is compromised by the highway, railroad, and lack of vegetation thanks to the zinc smelting.

Pass under the SR 4024 bridge over which the Appalachian Trail crosses. More rapids lie downstream to Walnutport; while these rapids are easy, they can become heavy in high water. Notice the small, symmetrical islands that were once bridge abutments. Other islands occur only occasionally along the river. Below Walnutport, you may also notice remnants of a canal on the left. From Walnutport to Northampton, the Lehigh flows through a more rural, scenic setting with riparian forests and bluffs. Watch for rapids and swift currents through a breached dam above the PA 154 bridge at Treichlers. Below Treich-

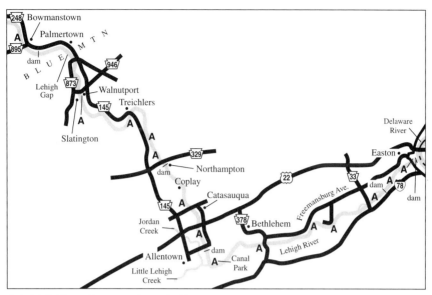

3. Lehigh River, Bowmanstown to Easton

lers, there are 300-foot bluffs and easy rapids. Portage the dam below the PA 329 bridge on the right. There is a potential access at Canal Park in Northampton on the left. Easy rapids and riffles are below, including a breached dam at North Catasauqua and Whitehall above the Lehigh/Eugene Street bridge, where there can be big waves. Development increases along the river as you near Allentown. Take out at the Kimmets Lock access on the left.

Kimmets Lock or Canal Park to Easton

Length: 18 miles

Water level: USGS Bethlehem gauge should be 1.2 feet.

Difficulty: Easy

Hazards: Dams, a few easy rapids and riffles

Scenery: Poor to good

Highlights: Canal remnants, scenic section between Freemansburg and Glendon

Fishing: Smallmouth bass, trout, muskellunge

Camping: None available

This section begins at Kimmets Lock, but you will want to start at Canal Park since there is a dam a mile below Kimmets Lock that you must portage. There are easy rapids below the dam. At Canal Park, Jordan Creek joins from the right. Below the park, the scenery improves with a forested ridge on the right and a riparian forest on the left with an old canal; encounter islands two miles below the park. The right bank stays wooded down to Bethlehem.

Industry and development return to the river at Bethlehem, although trees often border the river. Notice the massive, defunct Bethlehem Steel plants on the right. From Freemansburg to Glendon, the river flows through an attractive and rural setting with 400-foot forested hills. Below the PA 33 bridge, pass a small island, and then a larger one, as you near Glendon; take the left channel, since there is a dam immediately after the larger island that should be portaged on the left. Paddle through Easton and take out on the left above another dam just before the confluence of the Lehigh into the Delaware. This dam feeds the Delaware Canal to the right.

This section of the Lehigh is easier to paddle than the previous since there are more and longer pools and fewer rapids. This section also provides some good fishing opportunities for trout and smallmouth bass since the river is infused with several limestone streams.

4. Little Schuylkill River

Section: PA 443 to Port Clinton

Length: 18.4 miles

Water level: USGS gauge at Berne should be above 6.1 feet.

Difficulty: Easy to moderate

Hazards: Possible strainers, easy rapids

Scenery: Good to very good

Highlights: Mountain scenery

Fishing: Trout

Camping: No public camping; the river flows through private land.

The Little Schuylkill is a popular trip for paddlers and is generally recognized as offering the finest river paddling in the Schuylkill River watershed. Most paddlers begin at New Ringgold or Hecla, but if the water is high enough, begin at PA 443 or a township road (Atlas/River Rd.) bridge a mile downstream to enjoy the most scenic part of the river as it meanders for five miles through an isolated gorge. If you begin from the PA 442 bridge in South Tamaqua, expect to encounter a sedimentation pond and low dam that must be portaged.

The river has occasional islands and plenty of riffles with easy rapids that can be classified as Class I-plus or Class II in high water through a gorge 400 feet deep. There is almost always a current, riffles, or easy rapids, and few long, flat stretches. Steep forested banks of hardwoods, hemlocks, and rhododendron surround the river. PA 443 returns to the river at Hecla down to New Ringgold, which the Little Schuylkill mostly avoids. Below, the river becomes scenic and largely undeveloped. The lower half has more fields with nice views of Hawk Mountain and Blue Mountain, which rise roughly 1,000 feet above the river on the left, and rolling fields and hills on the right. Surprisingly for this coal mining region, the Little Schuylkill has good water quality and is a trout stream, so be sure to share the river with anglers.

Below the PA 61 bridge, the river makes a sharp left and braids around an island; watch for strainers. Paddle through an 800-foot-deep gorge, accompanied by busy PA 61 on the left. In Port Clinton, there are remnants of a small dam that can be run. Take out at the Broad Street bridge, or where the Little Schuylkill joins the Schuylkill River. A great place to eat afterwards is the Port Clinton Hotel, where you might encounter backpackers on the Appalachian Trail, which also passes through town.

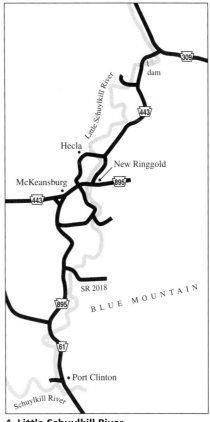

4. Little Schuylkill River

5. Tulpehocken Creek

Section:	Blue Marsh Lake to Schuylkill River
Length:	6 miles
Water level:	USGS gauge at Blue Marsh Dam should be 2.6 feet.
Difficulty:	Easy
Hazards:	Lowdams, possible strainers
Scenery:	Good
Highlights:	Red Bridge, Grings Mill, canal remnants
Fishing:	Trout, carp
Camping:	None

This short segment of the Tulpehocken is popular with Reading-area paddlers and trout anglers. The creek offers attractive pastoral scenery, often bordered by a thick riparian forest and several county parks. The creek has easy riffles and

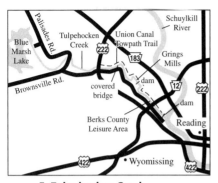

5. Tulpehocken Creek

pools. Buildings and homes occasionally dot the landscape. Put in below the Blue Marsh Dam and pass wooded bluffs on the right as the creek curves to the left. A half mile below the U.S. 222 bridge is Red Bridge, a beautiful covered bridge that was formerly known as Wertz's Bridge. It was built in 1867 and is 204 feet long, the longest single span for a covered bridge in the state.

A mile farther on the left is Grings Mills, which boasts impressive stonework. Here also is a lowdam that must be portaged. The Union Canal Towpath Trail, a biking and walking trail, follows the creek for 4.5 miles on the left. The creek is attractive to the end, though the surroundings do become more developed and urbanized. Most people take out at the Berks County Leisure Area on the right just upstream of the PA 12 bridge. Geese, ducks, great blue herons, ospreys, and hawks are often seen along the creek. If you decide to continue on to the Schuylkill River, there is another lowdam on the Tulpehocken just before the confluence that must be portaged.

6. Schuylkill River

Port Clinton to Reading

Length: 26.5 miles

Water level: USGS gauge at Berne should be 5.1 feet.

Difficulty: Easy

Hazards: Dams

Scenery: Good

Highlights: Pastoral scenery, wildlife

Fishing: Smallmouth bass, channel catfish, shad, striped bass

Camping: No public primitive camping is available along the river. Almost all land along the river is privately owned; camp where you have permission.

At Port Clinton the Schuylkill slices through Blue Mountain via a rugged water gap to enter the rolling and pastoral hills of southeastern Pennsylvania. After putting in, enjoy the last of some impressive mountain scenery as Blue Mountain towers more than 1,000 feet on the left. Don't expect to stay in your boat for long, since there is a big dam you must portage on the right. Below the dam is an island; the main channel is to the right. Development and traffic noise

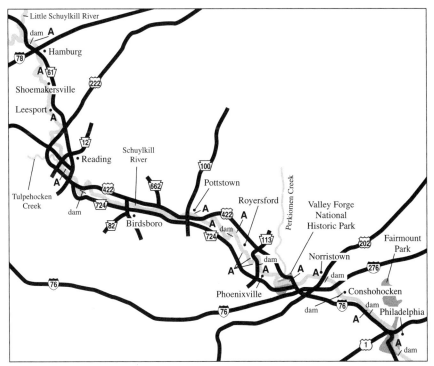

6. Schuylkill River, Port Clinton to Fairmount Park, Philadelphia

become more common as the river passes under I-78 and by Hamburg, and flows under PA 61.

Below Hamburg, the river becomes scenic and pastoral. The river is bordered by a forest as fields stretch beyond. There are even relatively few homes until you near Shoemakersville. Because PA 61 is close by, traffic can be heard on the river and some more development is encountered at Leesport. As you proceed downstream, homes become more common on the left shore as PA 61 comes close to the river. Maiden Creek joins from the left, and homes become common on the left, while the right shore is undeveloped.

The river passes under the U.S. 222 bridge and flows through remnants of two dams removed in 2007. Housing developments become common on the left and the Reading airport is on the right, but the Schuylkill is still attractive. After the PA 12 bridge, the river enters Reading and passes mills and other industry on the left. However, the scenery is fairly good since the river is bordered by a string of trees. The Tulpehocken Creek, a famous trout fishery, joins from the right. U.S. 222/422 follows the river closely on the right as the city of Reading rises on the left. Despite this busy, urban setting, the river still offers some pleasant paddling since it is often cordoned off by trees. Take out on the left at Riverfront Park.

The Schuylkill has relatively few islands and is usually confined to a single channel; strainers are rarely a major problem. The river is notoriously shallow and languid in summer, so many people paddle in the spring, fall, or even balmy winter days. The Schuylkill represents a major flyway for birds; ospreys, green herons, kingfishers, great blue herons, mergansers, wood ducks, warblers, and countless songbirds are often seen.

Reading to Fairmount Park, Philadelphia

Length: 62 miles

Water level: USGS gauge at Berne should be 5.1 feet.

Difficulty: Easy

Hazards: Six dams

Scenery: Fair to good

Highlights: Pastoral scenery, wildlife

Fishing: Smallmouth bass, catfish, rock bass

Camping: Primitive camping open to the public is virtually nonexistent. Most land along the river is privately owned.

This section begins and ends in urban settings. Put in at Reading's Riverfront Park and run the remnants of the Reading Dam through the center, or portage left. The river twists away from Reading as forested hills rise 400 feet above the river to the north. Four miles below the put-in, reach the Titus Station Wing Dam where, during normal or low flows, you can run left or portage right. However, in high water, a portage is necessary. An industrial plant is on the left.

The Schuylkill flows through the heavily populated southeastern corner of the state, yet surprisingly it maintains a rural and pastoral character all the way to Valley Forge. Although trains and highways follow the river's corridor, they are usually out of sight. Thick riparian forests buffer the river, and there are only occasional cottages and homes. Bridges cross the river on average every three or four miles. Small islands dot the river approximately every five miles. Aside from the dams, the river is easy with riffles and long pools. Be aware of a strong current under the PA 82 bridge and between islands at Birdsboro, which can pull boats into the bridge abutments; keep to the left.

There is an interesting maze of islands with a thick riparian forest below the South Hanover Street Bridge in Pottstown. Also below the bridge is a park on the right with potential access. The river becomes wooded and passes the nuclear power plant in Limerick on the left. Nine miles below Pottstown is the Vincent Dam; portage to the left. The Black Rock Dam is a little more than a mile below Upper Schuylkill Valley Park and feeds a canal to the left; portage to the right.

Below Valley Forge, there are several islands and the setting becomes urbanized, although the river is still often lined with trees. Three dams remain—Norristown Dam, where you portage right (this dam is located immediately after an island with a power plant on it); Plymouth Dam, where you portage right; and Flat Rock Dam, where you again portage right. Be aware of rapids below Flat Rock Dam that can reach Class I–III difficulty depending on water level. Below Flat Rock Dam the setting is heavily urbanized and industrialized, with busy I-76 on the right.

The Schuylkill now reaches Fairmount Park in Philadelphia, where you take out on river left at Kelly Drive. Look for the East Park Canoe House with a red tile roof. You can continue downstream to see the world-famous Boathouse Row and the Philadelphia Museum of Art on the left, but be aware Fairmount Dam is just downstream. There is no easy take-out, so paddle upstream, which is a long pool thanks to Fairmount Dam.

7. Brandywine Creek

Section: Lenape to Brandywine Creek State Park, Delaware

Length: 11.2 miles

Water level: USGS gauge at Chadds Ford should be 1.5 feet.

Difficulty: Easy

Hazards: Three lowdams

Scenery: Good

Highlights: Pastoral scenery

Fishing: Smallmouth bass, rock bass, carp

Camping: Primitive camping is not available along the creek; most land is privately owned.

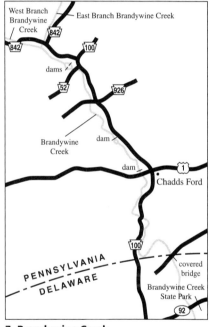

7. Brandywine Creek

Brandywine Creek meanders through the rolling countryside of Chester County and its horse farms, museums, and botanical gardens. It is surprising that a creek located so close to urban areas has still retained much of its pastoral charm. Relatively few homes crowd the banks and shore. The one minor drawback is that power lines tend to follow the creek. The Brandywine is also a very popular creek with paddlers; it is home to canoe liveries, so you can expect company on summer weekends.

The creek offers a pleasant paddle through thick riparian forests that span the creek and bucolic farms that abut the shore. The creek bed is often sandy, and the flow can be a bit languid in summer. There are three lowdams. The first is at an island a mile below the put-in and can be carried to the left. Just below on the left is Brandywine Outfitters. The second dam is three miles farther and can also be portaged on the left; it also diverts water around an island.

The last dam is just above the U.S. 1 bridge and has a slot that may be paddled through; approach with caution.

Below U.S. 1, the Brandywine flows through more forests and is more scenic and isolated. After crossing into Delaware, paddle under a covered bridge. The best place to take out is on the left after Thompson Bridge Road (Route 92) in Delaware's Brandywine Creek State Park.

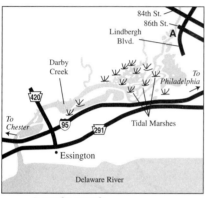

8. Darby Creek

8. Darby Creek

Section: John Heinz National Wildlife Refuge

Length: 5 miles

Water level: High tide

Difficulty: Easy

Hazards: Being stranded in low tide

Scenery: Poor to good

Highlights: Diverse wildlife

Fishing: Smallmouth bass, channel catfish, shad, striped bass

Camping: None

Who would think that the heart of the Philadelphia metro area would offer such unique paddling? Yet, there it is—within view of the city's skyscrapers and underneath the airliners that fly into the international airport. It is a little odd paddling through the serenity of the refuge while being surrounded by the bustle of millions of people. What makes this section of Darby Creek and the national wildlife refuge that protects it so unique is that it represents the last remaining significant tidal wetlands and marshes in Pennsylvania. As a result, you can only paddle two hours before or after high tide. It is very important to be mindful of the tidal schedule.

Being in an urban area, Darby Creek is not a wilderness, nor is it untouched. The tanks of an oil refinery are on the right at the beginning of the trip. The skyscrapers of Philadelphia's downtown rise in the distance. Industry and residential areas lie beyond the refuge; busy I-95 is along the southern border of the refuge. As you proceed downstream, the setting becomes more natural. Sedges and marshlands spread across the landscape, hemmed in by woodlands. Take time to explore the winding channels and marshy islets.

The highlight of this trip is the incredible diversity of plants and wildlife. The refuge is home to more than three hundred species of birds. Expect buggy conditions on hot, humid days. Although you can take out along the Delaware River, most paddlers make a circuit and put in and take out at the refuge's visitor center.

🚣 Lakes, Ponds, and Reservoirs

9. Belmont Lake

Size: 172 acres

Ownership: PFBC

Horsepower restrictions: Electric motors

Scenery: Excellent

Fishing: Muskellunge, walleye

Location: At the intersection of PA 371 in Belmont Corner, take PA 670 north for 2.2 miles and turn right to the lake.

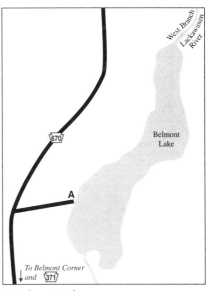

9. Belmont Lake

A beautiful and serene place to paddle, Belmont is notable as a large PFBC lake that is undeveloped and isolated. Wooded hillsides and ridges rise 300–400 feet above the lake. There are hemlocks at the northern end of the lake and a grove of spruce trees at its southern end. Mount Ararat, one of the highest points in eastern Pennsylvania, rises 700 feet above the lake to the northeast. The lake itself is set at a high elevation of approximately 1,800 feet. Belmont's graceful shoreline does not feature many bays or inlets, but take time to explore the inlet of the West Branch Lackawaxen River at the north end. One launch on the west shore provides access. The surrounding countryside is some of the most scenic in the state and offers views of the Catskills to the northeast.

10. Miller Pond

Size: 61 acres

Ownership: PFBC

Horsepower restrictions: Electric motors

Scenery: Very good

Fishing: Largemouth bass, chain pickerel, bluegill, brown bullhead, pumpkinseed, yellow perch

Location: From Honesdale, follow PA 670 north for almost 10 miles. Turn right onto PA 247 and follow it 1.6 miles. Turn left on Miller Pond Road (SR 4029) and drive 1 mile. Turn right to reach the lake.

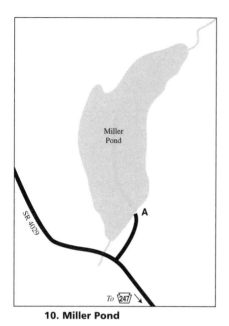

This small, peaceful pond is surrounded by wooded hillsides that rise 200 feet. Hemlocks and hardwoods comprise the forest. There are two small inlets and wetlands at the north end of the pond, where the inlet is located. One launch provides access.

10. Miller Pond

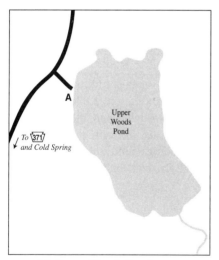

11. Upper Woods Pond

11. Upper Woods Pond

Size: 80 acres

Ownership: PFBC

Horsepower restrictions: Electric motors

Scenery: Very good to excellent

Fishing: Brook and rainbow trout

Location: From PA 317 at Cold Spring, follow SR 4007 2.4 miles; bear right towards the lake and then turn right to the launch.

Upper Woods Pond may look like other ponds or small lakes in Pennsylvania, but it is a unique place. First, it is a natural lake; the vast majority of lakes in the state are man-made. Second, it was formed by glaciers thousands of years ago. It reaches a surprising depth of 72 feet, features excellent water quality, and is home to both brook and rainbow trout. There are a few small coves at the north end. The pond is surrounded by low wooded hillsides and State Game Lands 159, and the forest is mostly comprised of hardwoods. One launch provides access on the northwest shore.

12. Lower Woods Pond

Size: 91 acres

Ownership: PFBC

Horsepower restrictions: Electric motors

Scenery: Very good to excellent

Fishing: Largemouth bass, bluegill, chain pickerel, walleye

Location: From Cold Spring, follow PA 371 towards Damascus for 1.5 miles. Turn left onto Lower Woods Road and go .3 mile. Turn left onto the road to the pond.

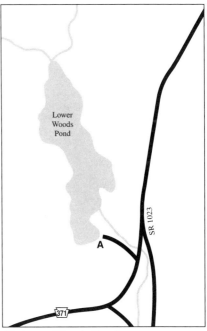

12. Lower Woods Pond

Located downstream from Upper Woods Pond, beautiful Lower Woods Pond is nestled in a secluded, wooded valley with low, rolling hills. This pond features a graceful shoreline with quiet coves and bays that offer great flatwater paddling. The inlet is located at the north end of the pond. One launch provides access.

13. White Oak Pond

Size: 175 acres

Ownership: PFBC

Horsepower restrictions: Electric motors

Scenery: Very good

Fishing: Bluegill, brown bullhead, yellow bullhead, black crappie, chain pickerel, pumpkinseed, yellow perch

Location: From Waymart, follow PA 296 north for 4 miles. Turn right onto SR 4004 (White Oak Drive); follow 1 mile to the lake on the left.

White Oak Pond offers some of the best lake paddling in Wayne County thanks to its fairly large size and coves, islets, and inlets that invite exploration. The narrow bay at the pond's inlet is a great place to paddle. White Oak is surrounded by wooded hillsides and fields; the ridge of the Moosic Mountains rises to the west. There are a few cottages along the south shore.

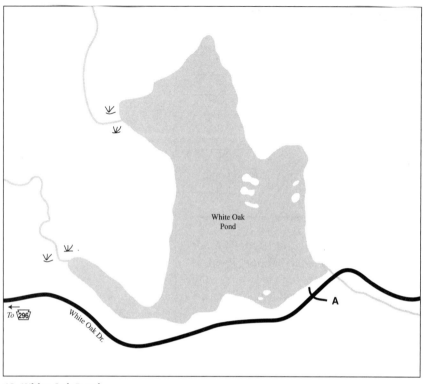

White Oak
Pond

To 296

White Oak Dr.

A

13. White Oak Pond

14. Prompton Lake

Size: 290 acres

Ownership: USACE (the land around the lake is owned by DCNR and managed as Prompton State Park, which is undeveloped)

Horsepower restrictions: 10 hp

Scenery: Good to very good

Fishing: Largemouth bass, bluegill, walleye

Location: From Honesdale, follow U.S. 6 west for 4.3 miles and then turn right onto PA 170. Follow for 2 miles to an access area on the right.

This long, narrow lake stretches for about 2.5 miles in a forested valley. At its midsection, the lake becomes so narrow it is almost divided in half. The setting is scenic and undeveloped; the surrounding ridges are forested with hemlocks and pine along the northeastern shore. A particularly interesting section is the northern end where the West Branch Lack-awaxen River feeds the lake, creating a delta formed by sediments deposited by the river. This is a good place to observe wildlife and try your luck fishing.

Prompton is also popular with mountain bikers since many trails surround the lake; don't be surprised if you see them as you paddle.

The lake is formed by a large flood-control dam operated by the USACE, while the surrounding land is managed as the undeveloped Prompton State Park. As a flood control project, the lake level is variable. A boat launch is located on the western shore.

15. Decker Pond

Size: 40 acres

Ownership: PGC

Horsepower restrictions: Unpowered boats only

Scenery: Good to very good

Fishing: Crappie, bluegill, chain pickerel

Location: The pond is 1.5 miles east of Wilsonville on the left side of U.S. 6 at the east end of Lake Wallenpaupack.

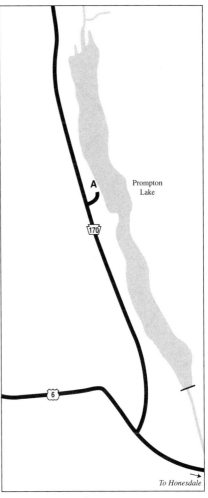

14. Prompton Lake

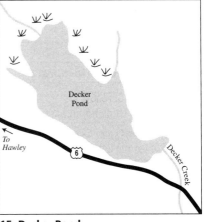

15. Decker Pond

This small pond is located along U.S. 6 and is protected by State Game Lands 183, just east of busy Lake Wallenpaupack. Decker offers good opportunities for wildlife and bird watching with extensive wetlands and a few coves along its northern and western shores. The pond is shallow and has heavy vegetative cover in summer; there are also tree stumps and some dead tree trunks in the pond. With the exception of U.S. 6 along part of the southern shore, the pond is undeveloped and scenic.

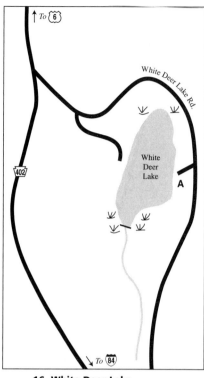

16. White Deer Lake

Size: 40 acres

Ownership: DCNR

Horsepower restrictions: Unpowered boats only

Scenery: Good to very good

Fishing: Crappie, bluegill, yellow perch, pumpkinseed, bullhead, chain pickerel

Location: From Exit 30 on I-84, take PA 402 north for 1.8 miles to a pull-off and dirt road on the right. Follow the road for 1 mile to the launch, where you turn left.

This hidden jewel is nestled in the northern part of Delaware State Forest. One boat launch provides access on the eastern shore. Typical of the Pocono Plateau, a low, rolling topography surrounds the lake. Hardwoods predominate, but there are hemlock and pine at the northern and southern ends of the lake; there are surprisingly few lily pads. Paddlers will want to explore the southern end, which is also the outlet, with its wetlands and sedges that harbor plants and wildlife. There are also some wetlands on the northern end. There are a few cottages along the shore, but the lake is mostly undeveloped. While White Deer Lake attracts some anglers, don't be surprised if you have the place all to yourself.

17. Shohola Lake

Size: 1,137 acres

Ownership: PGC

Horsepower restrictions: Electric motors

Scenery: Very good to excellent

Fishing: Largemouth bass, smallmouth bass, pickerel, catfish, bluegill

Location: From Exit 46 on I-84, take U.S. 6 west 8.8 miles to a PGC sign and access road on the left. Follow the sign to a boat launch on the left.

Beautiful Shohola Lake is a must-do for any paddler who enjoys lakes. It offers everything—isolation, superb scenery, islands, coves, inlets, and plentiful

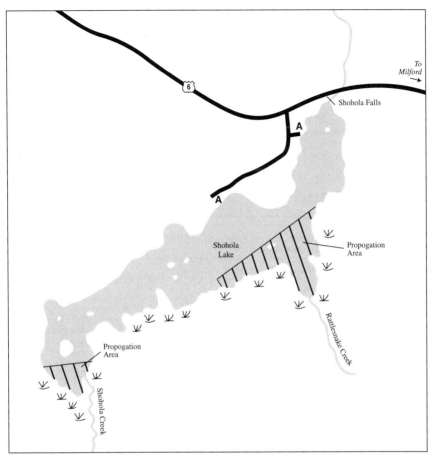

17. Shohola Lake

wildlife. The lake is surrounded by State Game Lands 180 and sits atop the Pocono Plateau; forested hills rise to about 300 feet above the lake. Extensive wetlands and sedges surround the lake, particularly on the southern shore, where there are also many small coves, bays, and islands. The northern shore meanders with larger bays and coves. Shohola Lake is very shallow, being only 8.2 feet at its deepest and having an average depth of 4.9 feet.

Besides wetlands, Shohola also features quite a bit of standing timber. This combination makes Shohola the perfect place for wildlife. The lake is home to, or otherwise attracts, turtles, herons, egrets, muskrats, beavers, bald eagles, ospreys, and numerous ducks and other waterfowl. You may want to avoid the lake in humid weather since conditions can become buggy.

Be aware that boats are not permitted in the two propagation areas on the southern shore, which includes the inlets of Rattlesnake and Shohola creeks. These protected areas allow waterfowl to reproduce and raise their young without being disturbed.

The lake attracts anglers who ply the lake in aluminum boats, but this is really an environment best suited for kayaks or canoes. You can easily spend a few days exploring this lake and its many coves, wetlands, inlets, and islands. And since Shohola is more than three miles long, it offers a lot of places to explore.

While you're there, do not miss the spectacular Shohola Falls immediately below the dam. This 70–80 foot falls tumbles over a series of ledges and enters an incredible slot gorge. In high water, whitewater paddlers run the falls and the big rapids in the gorge below.

18. Pecks Pond

Size: Approx. 450 acres

Ownership: DCNR, Delaware State Forest

Horsepower restrictions: Electric motors

Scenery: Very good to excellent

Fishing: Largemouth bass, catfish, sunfish, bluegill, carp

Location: From I-84, take Exit 30 and follow PA 402 south for 6.5 miles. Turn left onto Brewster Road and then make a second left onto Pecks Pond Road. Bear right to the launch.

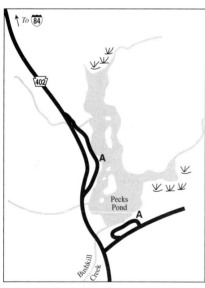

18. Pecks Pond

Pecks Pond is one of the finest destinations for lake paddling in the state. With the exception of cottages on the western and southern shores at its southwestern corner, this large lake is mostly undeveloped and is surrounded by the Delaware State Forest. Forested hills rise to almost 200 feet and several islands dot the central section of the pond. Extensive wetlands can be found at the northern and eastern ends of the lake, where there are stream inlets that invite exploration. Several small streams feed Pecks Pond, which serves as the source of popular Bushkill Creek. The forest is mostly hardwoods with towering white pine trees. In the summer, lily pads adorn the shore and shallow areas of the lake with beautiful blooms. The pond is well known for its diverse plantlife, which includes sundews that often grow on tree stumps in the lake.

The scenery is exceptional and the lake is known for its excellent fishing. Two launches provide access and there is a picnic area on the southern shore.

19. Bruce Lake

Size: Approx. 50 acres

Ownership: DCNR, Delaware State Forest

Horsepower restrictions: Unpowered boats only

Scenery: Excellent

Fishing: Trout, smallmouth bass, panfish

Location: From I-84, take Exit 26 and proceed south on PA 390 towards Promised Land. After .3 mile, turn left into a gravel parking area. Follow the trails and gated forest road 3 miles to the lake. The easiest place to put in is along the northern shore.

Bruce Lake, the centerpiece of a 4,300-acre state natural area of the same name, may be the crown jewel of Delaware State Forest. This is a unique lake. First, it is natural, formed by glaciers thousands of years ago. Second, it is completely

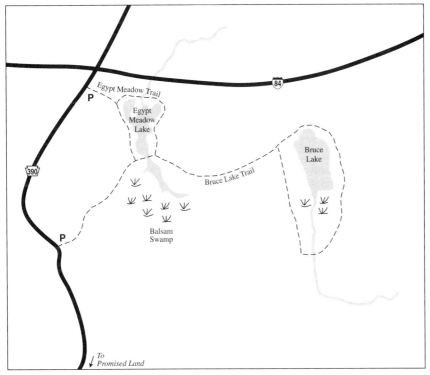

19. Bruce Lake
20. Egypt Meadow Lake

spring-fed, so it is pristine with clear water, unlike the dark tannin waters of most lakes in the Poconos. Third, it is completely undisturbed and undeveloped. And fourth, this is one of the most difficult lakes to reach in this guide since it requires a three-mile hike, one way, to reach it. Bruce Lake rarely sees a boat, and if you hope to paddle here, an inflatable boat that you can carry in a pack is your best bet.

The surrounding topography is low and rolling. Cliffs and ledge rise along the northern and northeastern shores of the lake. Many plants more commonly found farther north live here, including black spruce, balsam fir, tamarack, and shrub leatherleaf. Although you get the feeling you are miles from anywhere, I-84 is only a half mile to the north and you can occasionally hear traffic from the northern shore of the lake. Bruce Lake is popular with hikers, so don't be surprised to see them, particularly along the northern shore.

The highlight of this lake is the large, floating sphagnum moss bog at its southwestern end, a feature found on few other lakes in this guide. This bog is home to many rare and unique plants, including orchids, pitcher plants, and cranberries. Since this bog is difficult to reach by foot, it is ideal to explore by boat.

The lake's outlet is also at the southern end; Bruce Lake is the source of Shohola Creek, which joins the Delaware River about fifteen miles away.

20. Egypt Meadow Lake

Size: Approx. 70 acres	
Ownership: DCNR, Delaware State Forest	
Horsepower restrictions: Unpowered boats only	
Scenery: Excellent	
Fishing: Largemouth bass, pickerel, muskellunge, yellow perch, sunfish, crappie	
Location: From I-84, take Exit 26 and proceed south on PA 390 towards Promised Land. After .3 mile, turn left into a gravel parking area. Follow the gated forest road .4 mile to the lake. The easiest place to put in is the spillway along the Egypt Meadow Trail.	

Haven't heard of Egypt Meadow Lake? Well, now that you have, this hidden jewel is well worth the effort it takes to paddle it. A friend once said to me this was his favorite lake to paddle in the region, and it is easy to see why.

This exotic-sounding lake is set within the Bruce Lake Natural Area and it is completely undeveloped. A small bridge, over which a gated forest road passes, essentially divides the lake. Small boulders adorn the shore, and rolling wooded hills with bluffs of ledges rise above it. Mountain laurel, hemlock, white pine, and hardwoods comprise the forest. This lake is a pleasure because it offers many coves and inlets that make it seem larger than it is. Don't be surprised if you see hikers, since trails encircle the northern half of the lake. The southern half is shallower with stumps, wetlands, and sedges. The lake is partially fed by the Balsam Swamp to the south, one of the largest in the area. The swamp is home to diverse plant and wildlife.

The price to paddle Egypt Meadow Lake is that you must hike in about .4 mile from PA 390 along a gated, grassy old forest road. This extra effort will offer you a chance to paddle a serene lake that sees few other boats.

21. Promised Land Lake

Size: 422 acres

Ownership: DCNR, Promised Land State Park

Horsepower restrictions: Electric motors

Scenery: Very good

Fishing: Largemouth bass, smallmouth bass, pickerel, muskellunge, yellow perch, sunfish, catfish

Location: Promised Land State Park is located off Exit 26 of I-84. Take PA 309 south 3 miles to the park. There are access areas off North Shore Road and Pickerel Point Road.

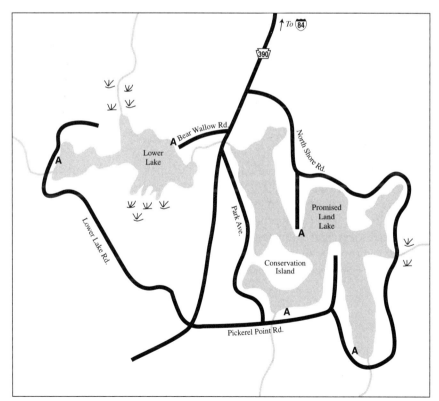

21. Promised Land Lake
22. Lower Lake

Promised Land Lake is an excellent place to paddle with many coves, bays, and inlets surrounded by a forest of hemlock, pine, and rhododendron. The lake is surrounded by low rolling hills of the Pocono Plateau and the shoreline is mostly undeveloped. Even though powerboats are prohibited, the lake does receive a lot of use from anglers and paddlers; the state park is very popular in the summer, so you shouldn't expect to have the lake to yourself. There are cottages set back from the shore along the western section of the lake. Ideal places to explore are Conservation Island, Ridgefield Point, and Pickerel Point. The eastern side of the lake is more isolated while the northwest corner near the picnic area receives the most boat traffic. Big Inlet and islets on the eastern shore are worth exploring. Three boat launches access the lake.

22. Lower Lake

Size: 173 acres

Ownership: DCNR, Promised Land State Park

Horsepower restrictions: Electric motors

Scenery: Excellent

Fishing: Largemouth bass, smallmouth bass, pickerel, muskellunge, yellow perch, sunfish, catfish. The lake is also an approved trout water and is stocked with brook, brown, and rainbow trout.

Location: Promised Land State Park is located off Exit 26 of I-84. Take PA 309 south 3 miles to the park. There are access areas off Bear Wallow Road and Lower Lake Road.

Lower Lake offers superb scenery similar to its upstream sister lake, Promised Land Lake. Hemlocks, pine, and rhododendron grace a shoreline with many coves and bays. Good places to paddle are the inlets, sedges, and wetlands along the northern and southern shores, and the inlet from Promised Land Lake. Lower Lake narrows and then opens up behind its dam. Lily pads cover parts of the lake and carnivorous sundews grow on old tree stumps. Lower Lake receives less boat traffic than Promised Land Lake and offers more isolation and opportunities to view wildlife; many paddlers consider it the more scenic of the two. Two boat launches access the lake.

23. Tobyhanna Lake

Size: 170 acres

Ownership: DCNR, Tobyhanna State Park

Horsepower restrictions: Electric motors

Scenery: Very good to excellent

Fishing: Smallmouth bass, largemouth bass, pickerel, sunfish, catfish, yellow perch, walleye, crappie, muskellunge

Location: From I-380, take Exit 8 and follow PA 423 north 3 miles to the park.

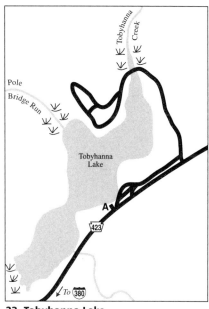

23. Tobyhanna Lake

This beautiful lake sits atop the Pocono Plateau at an elevation of approximately 2,000 feet. Except for the dam, Tobyhanna Lake is almost completely undeveloped with many coves, bays, and wetlands. Low forested hills surround the lake. Due to the horsepower restrictions, the lake is rarely crowded, although it is popular with anglers. Paddlers will want to explore the two coves at the northern end of the lake, particularly the inlet of Tobyhanna Creek as it meanders through wetlands. Wetlands also lie at the southwestern end of the lake. One boat launch provides access to the lake.

24. Gouldsboro Lake

Size: 250 acres

Ownership: DCNR, Gouldsboro State Park

Horsepower restrictions: Electric motors

Scenery: Good to very good

Fishing: Largemouth bass, bluegill, bullhead, sunfish

Location: From I-380, take Exit 13 and follow PA 507 east 2 miles to Gouldsboro. Turn right at the park sign and follow the road 1.5 miles to the park. Lot 4 provides the best access.

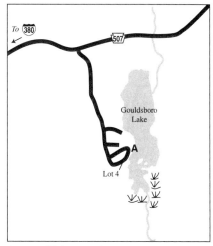

24. Gouldsboro Lake

Gouldsboro Lake is situated atop the Pocono Plateau and is surrounded by rolling hills of hardwoods, hemlock, and laurel. The lake is more than a mile long and a half-mile wide. The dam and a few cottages are located at the northern end; paddlers will be more interested in the lake's southern half, which features coves, inlets, islands, wetlands, and sedges. This is a great place to observe wildlife, birds, and a variety of plants. The lake is fairly shallow and the water is known for its dark color, a natural result of the swamps and bogs that drain into it. One boat launch located at the midpoint of the lake on the western shore provides access.

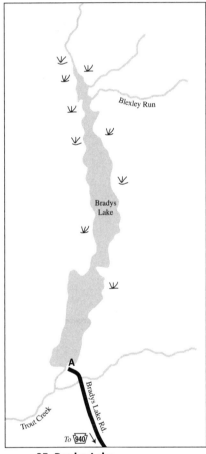

25. Bradys Lake

25. Bradys Lake

Size: 229 acres

Ownership: PGC

Horsepower restrictions: Electric motors

Scenery: Excellent

Fishing: Largemouth bass, crappie, bluegill

Location: From Exit 284 of I-80, take PA 115 north for 1.3 miles. Turn right onto PA 940 and go 5 miles. Turn left onto Bradys Lake Road and follow for 3.4 miles to the parking area.

Bradys Lake is a beautiful gem that is beloved by paddlers. Like several Pocono lakes and ponds, Bradys was built in 1915 for the production of ice. Due to its superb scenery and isolated setting, it became popular with anglers and paddlers over the years. However, the lake's dam began to deteriorate and had to be removed. As a result, the lake was drained and paddlers feared this precious body of water was lost forever. Thankfully, a new dam was built in 2007 and the lake began to refill in 2008.

The lake is long and narrow; it is more than two miles long and about 1/3-mile wide. It features an irregular shoreline with many small islets, coves, and bays. Sedges, wetlands, and blueberries line the shore, especially at the northern end, while the forest is composed of hemlock, pine, hardwoods, mountain laurel, and spruce. State Game Lands 127 completely surrounds the lake, which is undeveloped and sits on top of the Pocono plateau. The terrain around Bradys Lake is gradual. A few small streams enter the lake along its northern half. The scenery is excellent and paddlers have compared Bradys Lake with lakes in Maine, the Adirondacks, or Canada. If you enjoy paddling isolated, beautiful lakes, Bradys Lake should be at the top of your list. One boat launch at the dam on the southern end of the lake provides access.

26. Long Pond

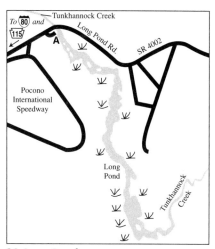

26. Long Pond

Size: Approx. 100 acres

Ownership: Nature Conservancy

Horsepower restrictions: Unpowered boats only

Scenery: Excellent

Fishing: Largemouth bass, panfish

Location: From Exit 284 on I-80, take PA 115 south for 3.1 miles; turn left onto Long Pond Road and follow for 1.5 miles to a pull-off on the right at the outlet of Long Pond. There is a riffle and beaver dam at the outlet, so you will have to hike a short distance upstream to reach the pond. This access is undeveloped and parking may be limited or restricted.

It is hard to imagine that right next to Pocono International Speedway lies one of Pennsylvania's most interesting paddling destinations. Long Pond is unique; it is fed by Tunkhannock Creek and resembles a winding inland estuary as compared to a pond. Depending on flows, there can be a slight current, particularly through the narrower sections of the pond. Long Pond is part of a 2,000-acre wetland and is surrounded by extensive meadows, sedges, and swamps. Beyond the meadows are forests of hemlock, spruce, tamarack, and hardwoods with an understory of sheep and mountain laurel and rhodora. Several islands dot the narrow channels along the northern half of the pond.

Long Pond is renowned for its biological diversity and is home to thirty-two species of plants and animals rare to Pennsylvania, including several species of moths. This special place is reminiscent of habitats found much further north.

The pond is more than two miles long and is very narrow. Its waters are dark thanks to the natural tannin from the swamps that flow into the pond.

27. Francis E. Walter Reservoir

Size: 80 acres (normal pool)

Ownership: USACE

Horsepower restrictions: 10 hp

Scenery: Good to very good

Fishing: Muskellunge, walleye, northern pike, trout

Location: From White Haven, follow SR 2041 north for 6 miles to a sign for the dam. Turn right and follow the road for 1.1 miles to a gravel road and access area on the left. You can also continue a mile, cross over the dam, and turn left to another access on the other side of the lake.

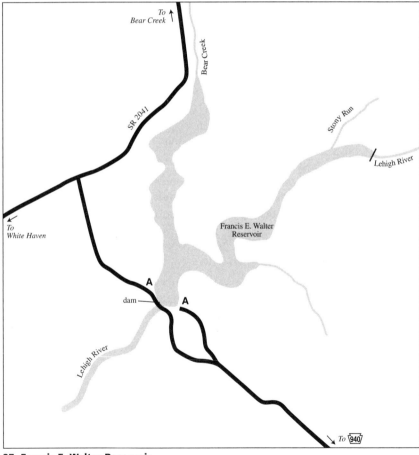

27. Francis E. Walter Reservoir

Francis E. Walter is a unique place to paddle. This is a flood-control project, so the normal pool of the lake is kept much lower than the capacity of the dam. As a result, exposed shorelines of meadows that are devoid of trees surround the lake. Scags, or the trunks of dead, standing trees, rise on the gentler slopes along the shore and protrude out of the water, particularly along the Bear Creek inlet. The scenery is made interesting, if not surreal, by the steep slopes of boulders, ledges, cliffs, and talus that are bleached white. Be sure to explore the inlets of both Bear Creek and the Lehigh River; the inlet to the latter features canyonlike scenery and wooded bluffs. Steep hills rise 200–500 feet above the lake.

The size and characteristics of this lake can change dramatically depending on the level of the pool. The pool of the lake is generally kept much larger than 80 acres. If you paddle here on a sunny day, you'll notice the water takes the hue of a remarkable deep, dark, indigo blue. Aside from the massive dam, the shoreline is completely undeveloped and isolated. Two boat launches provide access near the dam.

28. Locust Lake

Size: 52 acres

Ownership: DCNR, Locust Lake State Park

Horsepower restrictions: Electric motors

Scenery: Good to very good

Fishing: Pickerel, largemouth bass, smallmouth bass, bluegill, sunfish, brown trout, brook trout

Location: From I-81, take Exit 131A; turn left onto Moren Road and follow for 1 mile. Make a sharp left onto Burma Road and follow for 1 mile. Bear left onto Brockton Mountain Drive for 1.5 miles and bear right onto Moss Glen Road. Turn right onto Locust Lake Road into the park.

This small, oval-shaped lake is nestled along the forested Locust Ridge. Locust Lake is formed by a long dam. With the exception of the inlet of Locust Creek, the lake does not feature many coves or inlets. Locust Lake has typical state park amenities, including a beach and fishing pier. Two boat launches provide access.

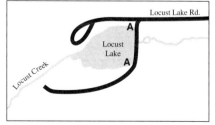

28. Locust Lake

29. Tuscarora Lake

Size: 96 acres

Ownership: DCNR, Tuscarora State Park

Horsepower restrictions: Electric motors

Scenery: Good to very good

Fishing: Largemouth bass, smallmouth bass, muskellunge, pickerel, catfish, yellow perch, sunfish

Location: From Tamaqua, follow PA 309 north for 1 mile. Turn left onto SR 1018 and follow 2 miles to the park.

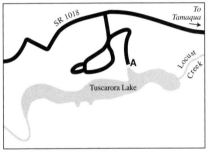

29. Tuscarora Lake

The forested Locust Ridge rises 500 feet to the south of the lake, while wooded hills rising 200 feet are to the north. The lake is surrounded by a mixed forest of hardwoods, pine, and hemlock. Located in Tuscarora State Park, Tuscarora Lake features the typical recreational amenities of a beach, picnic areas, and concessions. Paddlers will want to explore the southern shore where there is more isolation and several small coves; the western end features the winding inlet of Locust Creek. One boat launch on the north shore provides access.

30. Mauch Chunk Lake

Size: 330 acres

Ownership: PFBC

Horsepower restrictions: Electric motors

Scenery: Good to very good

Fishing: Largemouth bass, bluegill, bullhead, crappie, perch, pumpkinseed, walleye

Location: The lake is 3 miles southwest of Jim Thorpe along SR 3012.

This long, narrow lake stretches 3 miles in a valley between Pisgah Mountain and Mauch Chunk Ridge; the latter rises prominently 500 feet along the southern shore. The lake does not feature many coves or bays, but the inlet at the western end does have sedges and wetlands. The southern shore offers more isolation. Mauch Chunk Lake is managed as a county park with camping, picnic areas, and a beach. Two launches provide access—one near the dam, and the other towards the western end of the lake.

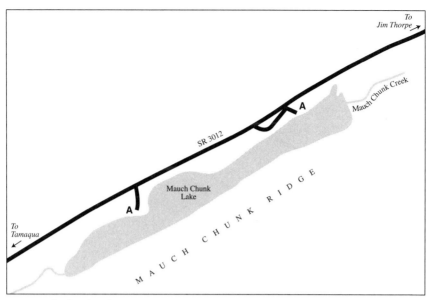

30. Mauch Chunk Lake

31. Beltzville Lake

Size: 949 acres

Ownership: DCNR, Beltzville State Park

Horsepower restrictions: Unlimited horsepower

Scenery: Very Good

Fishing: Trout, striped bass, largemouth bass, smallmouth bass, walleye, perch, muskellunge

Location: Beltzville State Park is located off Interchange 74 of I-476 (Pennsylvania Turnpike Northeast Extension). Follow Pohopoco Drive to the Pine Run access, or U.S. 209 to the Preachers Camp access.

Beltzville Lake offers fine water quality and scenery: a 400-foot forested ridge rises to the south of the lake, while rolling fields and forests are to the north. Due to its size and unlimited horsepower restrictions, the lake is very popular with motorboats, particularly close to the dam at the western end of the lake. For less interference from motorboats, explore the coves and small bays along the northern shore of the lake; Pine Run cove is scenic with good opportunities to observe wildlife.

However, it is Wild Creek and Pohopoco coves at the eastern end of the lake that make Beltzville a real pleasure to paddle. These coves are located in no-wake zones and attract few motorboats. The scenery of these coves is excellent with bluffs and towering forests; there is also a surprising sense of isolation.

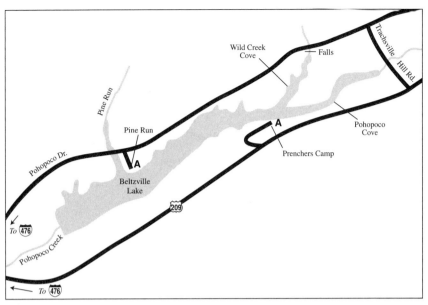

31. Beltzville Lake

Wild Creek Cove is particularly beautiful; paddle to the end of this winding cove and hike a short trail to a cascading waterfall. To reach these coves, it is best to use the Preachers Camp access.

32. Hidden Lake

32. Hidden Lake

Size: Approx. 40 acres

Ownership: NPS

Horsepower restrictions: Electric motors

Scenery: Very good

Fishing: Bluegill, largemouth bass, bullhead, perch, trout

Location: The lake is located 4.5 miles northeast of Marshalls Creek off U.S. 209.

When one thinks of paddling in the Delaware Water Gap National Recreation Area, the popular Delaware River comes to mind. However, the recreation area has a few ponds and small lakes, most notably Hidden Lake. This undeveloped, narrow lake stretches 3/4 mile and is surrounded by woodlands and scenic mountain ridges to the south that rise 400 feet above the lake. Hidden Lake offers a few small coves and wetlands at its southwestern end.

33. Minsi Lake

Size: 117 acres

Ownership: PFBC

Horsepower restrictions: Electric motors

Scenery: Good to very good

Fishing: Largemouth bass, perch, walleye, rainbow trout

Location: From Bangor, follow N. Main Street north for 1 mile and turn right onto Creek Road for 2 miles. Turn right onto Lake Minsi Drive for 1.3 miles. There are boat launches off Blue Mountain Drive and East Shore Drive.

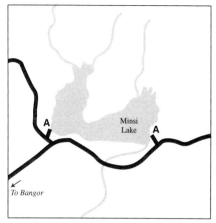

33. Minsi Lake

Minsi Lake is a peaceful paddling destination that is particularly convenient for paddlers in the Poconos or Lehigh Valley. The lake is surrounded by the rolling woodlands of a 300-acre county park. Several small streams feed this U-shaped lake at two coves at the northern end. The northwest cove is a scenic place to explore. Hardwoods comprise most of the forest that surrounds the lake. The long ridge of Kittatinny Mountain rises 2 miles to the north. Two launches provide access to the lake.

34. Leaser Lake

Size: 117 acres

Ownership: PFBC

Horsepower restrictions: Electric motors

Scenery: Good

Fishing: Bluegill, largemouth bass, bullhead, perch, trout

Location: From New Tripoli at PA 309, follow PA 143 towards Jacksonville for 5 miles to the lake. Access areas are off Pleasure Court, Ontelaunee Road, and Leaser Road.

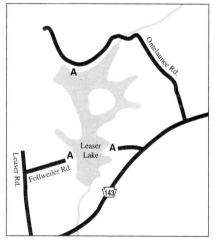

34. Leaser Lake

Located close to the Lehigh Valley and featuring many coves, bays, inlets, and a large island, Leaser Lake is a superb place to paddle. This relatively small lake offers many places to explore with its winding shoreline. Woodlands and fields surround the lake, as do a few homes; the ridge of Blue Mountain rises to the north. A small stream feeds the lake at its northern end.

Leaser Lake is owned by the PFBC, but is managed as a Lehigh County park. Three launches provide access. At the time of this writing, the lake was drawn down to 40 acres until the dam can be repaired.

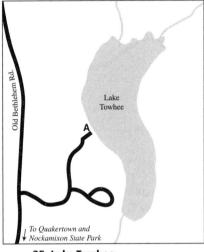

35. Lake Towhee

Size: 50 acres

Ownership: Lake Towhee Park, Bucks County

Horsepower restrictions: Electric motors only

Scenery: Good

Fishing: Largemouth bass, catfish, bluegill, sunfish

Location: From Quakertown, follow PA 313 towards Lake Nockamixon to West Thatcher Road and follow for 1.8 miles. Continue straight onto Creamery Road for .4 mile and turn right onto Cider Press Lane for 1 mile. Turn left onto Old Bethlehem Road for .8 mile and turn right into the park.

35. Lake Towhee

This small lake is surrounded by a county park covering 500 acres. A thick deciduous forest lies along the shore and the lake is mostly covered by lily pads in summer. Set in the bucolic countryside of northern Bucks County, Lake Towhee is a serene place for local paddlers to visit. One launch provides access.

36. Lake Nockamixon

Size: 1,450 acres

Ownership: DCNR, Nockamixon State Park

Horsepower restrictions: 20 hp

Scenery: Good to very good

Fishing: Walleye, muskellunge, pickerel, smallmouth bass, largemouth bass, striped bass hybrids, channel catfish, carp, bluegill, sunfish

Location: From I-476 (Pennsylvania Turnpike Northeast Extension), get off at Interchange 44 (Quakertown) and follow PA 663 to Quakertown. Follow PA 313 for 4 miles and turn left onto PA 563. Follow this road into the state park.

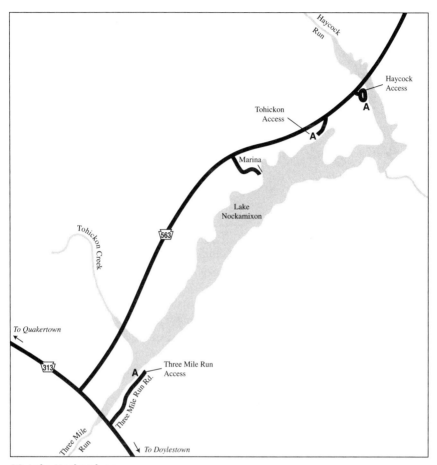

36. Lake Nockamixon

This large lake is surrounded by forested hills and a few fields in the pastoral countryside of Bucks County. The forested summit of Haycock Mountain rises 600 vertical feet above the lake to the north. Due to its size the lake is very popular with anglers and sailboaters. Expect the lake to be crowded on summer weekends; the middle section of the lake receives the most boat traffic and also has a large marina. Four boat launches access the lake, but the Three Mile Run and Haycock launches are better suited for paddlers since they provide more direct access to some of the more scenic, and less crowded, areas of the lake. Ideal places to explore are the inlets of Tohickon Creek, Three Mile Run, and the large inlet of Haycock Run. The meandering shoreline features many coves, inlets, and bays. The area behind the dam is also interesting as the lake narrows into an undeveloped gorge-like setting where wooded bluffs rise above the shore.

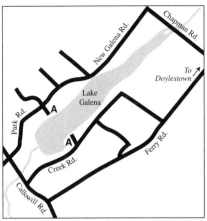

37. Lake Galena

37. Lake Galena

Size: 365 acres

Ownership: Bucks County

Horsepower restrictions: Electric motors

Scenery: Good to very good

Fishing: Largemouth bass, walleye, catfish, bluegill, carp

Location: From Doylestown, follow PA 313 west for 3 miles and turn left onto New Galena Road. Follow the road for 2–3 miles to reach access areas on the left.

Set amidst the rolling fields and woodlands of Bucks County, Lake Galena is a worthwhile paddling destination. The lake is surrounded by the 1,500-acre Peace Valley County Park. Due to the low topography around the lake, winds can be a problem and windsurfing and sailing are both popular. Galena Lake is nearly 3 miles long but does not feature many sizable coves or bays. The most interesting place to explore is the winding inlet at the eastern end where there is also an islet. It's a great place to enjoy birdwatching: more than 250 species visit the park. Several boat launches provide access.

38. Green Lane Reservoir

Size: 800 acres

Ownership: Green Lane Park, Montgomery County

Horsepower restrictions: Electric motors

Scenery: Good

Fishing: Largemouth bass, walleye, catfish, bluegill, carp

Location: From Red Hill, follow PA 29 north to West 11th Street. Turn left and follow for .3 mile. Continue onto Walt Road for .5 mile to the access areas.

This large lake is set in the bucolic countryside of northern Montgomery County. Like much of southeastern Pennsylvania, this area is feeling the pressure of residential development. Thankfully Green Lane Reservoir is protected by a county park and although some houses can been seen from the lake, the setting is serene and relatively undeveloped.

A dam on Perkiomen Creek forms this reservoir, which is narrow at its southern end behind the dam, but grows wider with many bays and coves at its

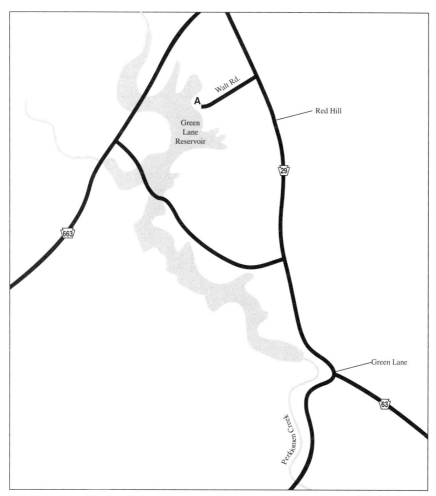

38. Green Lane Reservoir

northern end. For the paddler, the highlight is the many coves Green Lane has to offer along with wetlands and sedges that attract much wildlife; in fact, more than 250 species of birds frequent the lake. The islets at the inlet of Perkiomen Creek at the lake's northern end are good places to explore, as is the section behind the dam where forested hills and bluffs rise 300 feet above the shore; this is the most isolated part of the lake and arguably its most scenic.

The terrain is low and rolling with forests, fields, and meadows. Three bridges cross over the lake.

39. Blue Marsh Lake

Size: 1,150 acres

Ownership: USACE

Horsepower restrictions: Unlimited

Scenery: Good to very good

Fishing: Largemouth bass, smallmouth bass, walleye, catfish, perch, crappie, carp, bluegill, sunfish, muskellunge, brook trout, brown trout, rainbow trout

Location: The lake is located 6 miles northwest of Reading via PA 183. Access areas are located off Palisades Drive, Brownsville Road, and PA 183.

Blue Marsh is a large, meandering lake with three long, narrow, twisting inlets; countless coves and bays; and a large island in the lake's main body. The lake is popular with motorboats and traffic is heavy in the summer. Thankfully, all those coves and inlets—and their no-wake zones—provide more seclusion for paddlers. Spring Creek forms the western inlet; Tulpehocken Creek forms the northwestern inlet; and smaller Licking Creek forms the northern inlet. The inlets of Spring and Tulpehocken creeks also have islets.

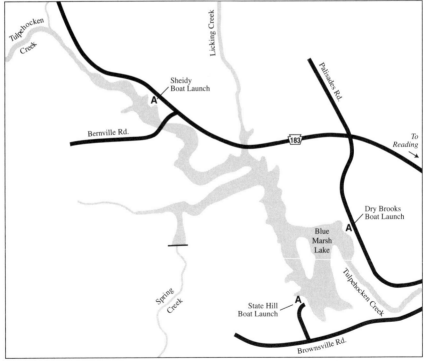

39. Blue Marsh Lake

Pastoral hills, fields, and rolling woodlands surround the lake and rise 200–300 feet, creating surprisingly steep terrain. As the lake is a flood-control project, its water level is variable and the shoreline can be exposed rock and mud. Blue Marsh is well known for its birdlife, with ospreys, hawks, and a variety of waterfowl.

Two USACE access areas are located at the southern part of the lake; a fee is required. The PFBC Sheidy Road Access is at the northern end where Tulpehocken Creek enters the lake; a permit is required for this access.

Besides paddling, Blue Marsh has picnic facilities, playgrounds, hiking trails, and it is particularly well known for its mountain biking trails.

40. Scotts Run Lake

Size: 22 acres

Ownership: DCNR, French Creek State Park

Horsepower restrictions: Electric motors

Scenery: Good

Fishing: Trout

Location: The state park is bisected by PA 345 between Birdsboro and Warwick. Use Scott Run Road to reach the lake.

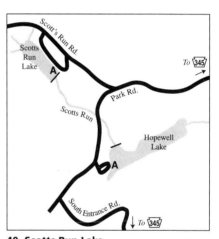

40. Scotts Run Lake
41. Hopewell Lake

This small, hidden gem set among the forested hills of French Creek State Park is a pleasure to paddle. Hardwoods comprise most of the forest, but there are some hemlocks along the northeast shore. The northern end of the lake is fed by small streams and springs, which contribute to the lake's fine water quality. As a coldwater fishery, Scotts Run Lake is home to trout. This small, oval-shaped lake doesn't offer coves or inlets, but it does offer serenity, a quality you will find less of on French Creek State Park's other lake, Hopewell Lake. One boat launch provides access.

41. Hopewell Lake

Size: 68 acres

Ownership: DCNR, French Creek State Park

Horsepower restrictions: Electric motors

Scenery: Good

Fishing: Pickerel, walleye, largemouth bass, muskellunge, smallmouth bass, panfish

Location: The state park is bisected by PA 345 between Birdsboro and Warwick. Use Park Road to reach the lake.

Hopewell Lake is set among the forested hills of French Creek State Park, a sylvan oasis close to the Philadelphia urban area. Paddlers will enjoy the small coves along its shore. With picnic areas, parking, concessions, a pool, and boat rental, do not expect as much isolation on Hopewell as you would expect on nearby Scotts Run Lake. Regardless, with its clean water and serene setting, Hopewell Lake is a pleasure to paddle. For anglers, Hopewell is a big bass lake and special regulations apply. One boat launch on the western end of the lake provides access.

42. Struble Lake

42. Struble Lake

Size: 386 acres

Ownership: PFBC

Horsepower restrictions: Electric motors

Scenery: Good

Fishing: Largemouth bass, bluegill, catfish, crappie, perch, walleye

Location: From Morgantown, follow Mill and Morgantown roads south 4 miles to the lake.

Struble Lake is fairly large but is unlikely to attract many paddlers except those that live locally. An old railroad grade crosses the western end and houses can be seen along the eastern shore. Low fields and woodlands also surround parts of Struble Lake, and forested hills rise to the north. Since the lake is fairly open with few inlets and coves, wind can be a problem. One boat launch provides access.

43. Chambers Lake

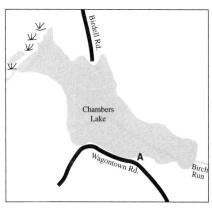

Size: 90 acres

Ownership: Chester County (Hibernia County Park)

Horsepower restrictions: Electric motors

Scenery: Good to very good

Fishing: Panfish, channel catfish, chain pickerel, smallmouth bass, largemouth bass

Location: From Coatesville, follow PA 82 north for 1.8 miles and turn left onto PA 340 for 1.3 miles. Turn right onto Wagontown Road and follow 1.6 miles to the lake.

43. Chambers Lake

Nestled within the 900 bucolic acres of Hibernia County Park, Chambers Lake is a serene place to paddle for those living in crowded southeast Pennsylvania. Low hills of hardwood forests and fields surround the lake. The northwest end of the lake features the inlet of Birch Run as well as wetlands and sedges that offer great opportunities to view wildlife, plants, and birds. The second access is along Wagontown Road.

Chambers Lake offers great fishing and is one of only three lakes in the state designated as a Panfish Enhancement Area. Hibernia County Park also offers many miles of trails, camping, playgrounds, and picnic facilities.

44. Marsh Creek Lake

Size: 535 acres

Ownership: DCNR, Marsh Creek State Park

Horsepower restrictions: Electric motors

Scenery: Good to very good

Fishing: Muskellunge, largemouth bass, channel catfish, crappie, walleye, bluegill

Location: The park is 2 miles west of Eagle.

With low, rolling woodlands and many coves, bays, and inlets, Marsh Creek offers some of the finest lake paddling in southeastern Pennsylvania. Good places to paddle are the two long, narrow inlets on the eastern shore and the long, narrow cove on the north end where Marsh Creek enters the lake. There

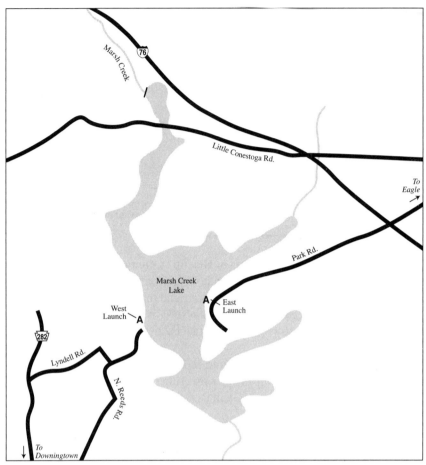

44. Marsh Creek Lake

are fewer coves or bays on the western shore. Although the setting is natural, housing developments are encroaching around the park and some homes can be seen from the lake.

Sailboats are a common sight at Marsh Creek and you can expect more boat traffic due the lake's proximity to populated areas, but the many long, narrow coves will always offer a serene place to paddle. Two boat launches, one each on the western and eastern shores, provide access.

45. Lake Luxembourg

Size: 174 acres

Ownership: Core Creek Park, Bucks County

Horsepower restrictions: Electric motors

Scenery: Good

Fishing: Muskellunge, largemouth bass, catfish, carp, walleye, bluegill

Location: The lake is located 2 miles north of Langhorne. Use Park Road off of Bridgetown Pike to access the park and lake.

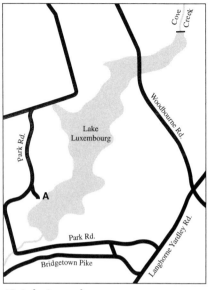

45. Lake Luxembourg

This lake is surrounded by 1,200 acres of Core Creek Park, owned by Bucks County. Thanks to the horsepower restrictions, Lake Luxembourg is a pleasant and peaceful place to paddle among the bustle of Philadelphia's suburbs. The surrounding terrain is low, with forests and fields; as a result, conditions can get windy. Housing developments lie beyond the park but are mostly out of sight from the lake. Paddlers will enjoy the many coves and small bays that line the shore, as well as the inlet of Core Creek at the northern end of the park where there are sedges and wetlands.

One launch near the dam provides access. The park also features trails, picnic facilities, playgrounds, and athletic fields.

Susquehanna River Watershed

The Susquehanna is the largest river not only in Pennsylvania, but the eastern seaboard of the United States. Stretching 444 miles from Cooperstown, New York, to the Chesapeake Bay in Maryland, it is also one of the longest commercially unnavigable rivers in the country. Despite its length, size, and fine scenery, the Susquehanna offers surprising isolation and is not nearly as popular with paddlers as the Delaware River. However, that is beginning to change. The Susquehanna continues to attract more and more paddlers to its serpentine route as it winds between mountains and cuts through ridges.

While the stretch between New York and Sunbury is occasionally referred to as the North Branch Susquehanna River, it is more commonly known as the Susquehanna River. As a result, the river between New York and Maryland border is described singularly as the Susquehanna and the West Branch Susquehanna River is described separately.

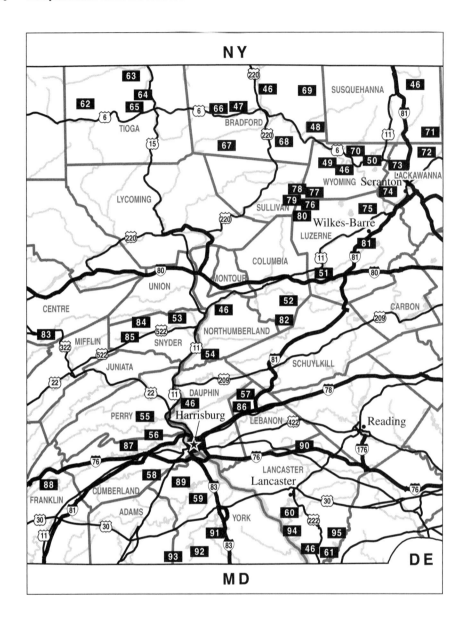

 Rivers and Creeks

46. Susquehanna River

New York Border to Hallstead

Length: 13 miles	
Water level: USGS Windsor, New York, gauge should be 3.0 feet.	
Difficulty: Easy	
Hazards: Lowhead dam below Susquehanna	
Scenery: Very good	
Highlights: Pastoral scenery, Starrucca Viaduct	
Fishing: Smallmouth bass, panfish	
Camping: Primitive camping is possible, but most land is privately owned.	

It is here that the Susquehanna first visits Pennsylvania, only to bend back north into New York. This section is a scenic float and offers some of the most rural and isolated scenery in Pennsylvania, with wooded mountains rising 400 feet above the river and its adjacent small farms. The river is easy, although there is a low power dam below the town of Susquehanna that must be portaged on the left.

The first public access is at the PFBC Oakland access, about a mile south of the New York border. Just upstream of the access is a primitive camping area

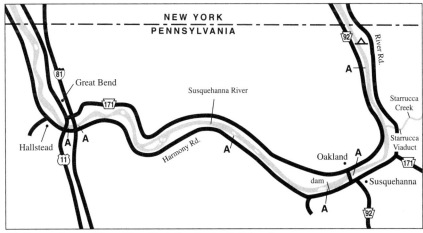

46. Susquehanna River, New York Border to Hallstead

owned by the Rail-Trail Council of Northeast Pennsylvania; it is adjacent to the D&H Rail Trail. A permit is required to camp.

The first highlight is the impressive Starrucca Viaduct in Lanesboro, on the left. Although it isn't massive, this viaduct is unique with its high, graceful stone arches. I think it is the most beautiful viaduct I have ever seen. The town of Susquehanna is on the left, nestled along steep, wooded hillsides. Watch for the low power dam below town. Portage to the left; in high water be very careful and take out at the PA 42/171 bridge, where there is a municipal access.

The section between Susquehanna and Hallstead is the most scenic, featuring beautiful rural isolation with fields and wooded hills that rise to heights of 500 feet above the river. Small islands dot the river. The PFBC Great Bend access is on the left halfway between the two towns. Two miles below this access is a cluster of islands known as the Finger Islands, a great place for bird-watching; these islands may also collect strainers and create tricky currents. Islands become more common down to the take-out. Civilization returns with Hallstead and busy I-80. Take out at either the I-81 bridge access or the PFBC Hallstead access at U.S. 11, both on the left.

Sayre to Laceyville

Length: 45 miles

Water level: USGS gauge at Waverly, New York, should be 0-5 feet; Towanda USGS gauge should be .5 feet.

Difficulty: Easy

Hazards: None

Scenery: Very good

Highlights: Standing Stone, bald eagles, good fishing, cliffs

Fishing: Smallmouth bass, trout, muskellunge

Camping: Primitive camping is occasionally available along the river.

The Susquehanna reenters Pennsylvania at Sayre and flows down a wide valley contained by wooded hillsides and low mountains. The first access is the PFBC Sayre access along SR 1043. Below the PA 1056/Susquehanna Street bridge in Athens is Harrigan Island, where camping is allowed. Paddle past historic Tioga Point to the confluence with the Chemung River; a string of small islands lie downstream. The river flows down a broad farming valley surrounded by mountains. The Susquehanna is lined with trees and farmlands, with relatively few cottages along the shore. Three miles below Ulster is Hornbrook County Park on the left, where there is an access area. Camping is also allowed by permit/fee. Above Towanda, large cliffs with landslide scars loom on the left. The Susquehanna flows between clusters of islands with great opportunities to

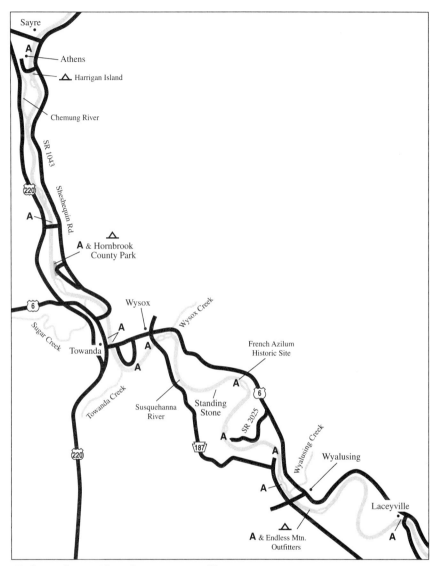

46. Susquehanna River, Sayre to Laceyville

observe wildlife, including bald eagles and ospreys. Towanda Riverfront Park on the left offers a convenient take-out or put-in with parking; there are also access points on the right, in the borough of Towanda. Beneath the U.S. 6 bridge is a riffle that can have large waves in high water.

Pass islands to the right, as well as the confluence with Towanda Creek. The PFBC Wysox access is on the left; steep wooded bluffs and cliffs rise 700 feet on the right. Just before the PA 187 bridge on the left is a municipal access. The river flows between more islands and passes Riverside Acres Campground on the right. A highlight of this section, Standing Stone, is a few miles downstream on the right. This rectangular boulder was deposited by glaciers and rises 24 feet out of the river. A mile farther on the right is the French Azilum Historic Site, with access, parking, and camping by permit/fee. French Azilum was a settlement built for refugees and, some say, Marie Antoinette during the French Revolution.

From this point to the PFBC access at Terrytown, the river flows between cliffs and ledges that rise 300–600 feet on alternating banks, giving the Susquehanna a beautiful canyon-like setting. The cliffs are particularly notable above Wyalusing, across from the Terrytown access. Wyalusing is mostly inaccessible from the river. A mile and a half below the PA 187 bridge are islands. On the channel to the right is Endless Mountains Outfitters, which offers shuttles, tours, and camping. The scenery is similar down to Laceyville, with cliffs, farmlands, and occasional cottages. On the right above Laceyville are impressive rock outcrops and cliffs. As you approach the bridge at Laceyville, take the channel to the left to an access area on the left, immediately above or below the bridge. Laceyville is a quaint, river-friendly town that offers a market and restaurant within easy walking distance of the river. There is parking in town at the SR 3001 bridge.

Laceyville to Falls

Length: 33 miles	
Water level: USGS Meshoppen gauge should be 7.5 feet.	
Difficulty: Easy	
Hazards: None	
Scenery: Very good to excellent	
Highlights: Vosburg Neck, remnants of North Branch Canal, bald eagles, good fishing, impressive mountain scenery	
Fishing: Smallmouth bass, trout, muskellunge	
Camping: Camping is available on several islands.	

With several islands open to camping, impressive mountain scenery, towering cliffs, historical features, wildlife, and river-friendly towns, this section of the Susquehanna is one of the finest overnight paddling trips in the state.

From Laceyville to Mehoopany, the Susquehanna flows through a more isolated valley with steep wooded hillsides and rising mountains. Three islands are encountered between Laceyville and Meshoppen; two of them are open to primitive camping. Just below Meshoppen on the left is a small access area. At Mehoopany, there is a private access on the right below the PA 87 bridge. The river passes a massive Proctor & Gamble plant on the left that is mostly out of sight except for its smokestack. Below the plant, enjoy some easy riffles

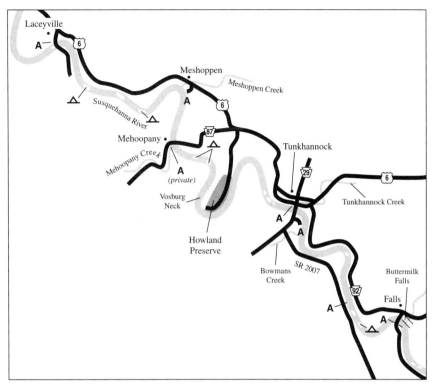

46. Susquehanna River, Laceyville to Falls

and several islands that are ideal for camping. Remains of the canal wall are on the right.

The section between Mehoopany and Tunkhannock is one of the finest along the entire river as you paddle around the Vosburg Neck, an oxbow loop. Incredible sheer mountains rise more than 1,000 feet above the river, and the higher mountains off to the right rise 1,700 feet above the river. On the left is the impressive stonework of the former North Branch Canal. Also to the left is Camp Lackawanna, where camping is permitted for a fee and with prior permission. The Endless Mountains Nature Center is also located at Camp Lackawanna and offers a variety of programs and exhibits. Trails there explore the impressive remains of the North Branch Canal, which, from the river, are hidden in the cloak of the forest. The entire Vosburg Neck is now protected by Camp Lackawanna and the North Branch Land Trust's Howland Preserve. This area is truly a gem along the Susquehanna River. The section of the river from Mehoopany to Tunkhannock is also the course of one of the oldest canoe races in the country, the Tunkhannock Downriver Canoe and Kayak Race, organized by the Tunkhannock Kiwanis Club and held in late July.

Downstream, impressive cliffs rise several hundred feet, alternating on the left and right; there are towering waterfalls here in wet weather. In typical fashion along this river, mountains and cliffs rise on alternating sides. Pass a series of islands with an easy riffle and reach Tunkhannock; access is on the left, at Riverside Park. Tunkhannock is one of the more river-friendly towns with a variety of restaurants, cafes, and stores within walking distance from Riverside Park. Camping is allowed in the park by permit. Pass under the PA 29 bridge where the Tunkhannock Creek, another stream popular with paddlers, joins from the left. A mile downstream is the PFBC Tunkhannock access on the right. Miller Mountain towers ahead as it rises more than 1,500 feet above the river.

Scenic mountains rise above the river as you head downstream. There is a new PFBC access on the right at White's Ferry. Paddle past a series of islands (the second one is open to camping) and reach Falls with huge red cliffs on the left. A PFBC access is on the right, after the bridge. Across the river is the mouth of Buttermilk Creek; paddle under the railroad bridge to see beautiful waterfalls.

Falls to Shickshinny

Length: 36.8 miles

Water level: USGS Wilkes-Barre gauge should be 1 foot.

Difficulty: Easy

Hazards: None

Scenery: Fair to very good

Highlights: Campbells Ledge

Fishing: Smallmouth bass, trout, muskellunge

Camping: None; most land is privately owned.

Below Falls, the river passes impressive red sandstone and shale cliffs that rise 400 feet above the water. When the sun sets, these cliffs are blood red. The river valley opens with similar scenery as before. There are two islands near the boundary of Wyoming and Luzerne counties as the river approaches some impressive mountains and steep, wooded bluffs. The PFBC Apple Tree access is on the right. Enter a canyonlike setting as Campbells Ledge, a local landmark, towers above the river off to the left.

Below the ledge, the river enters the Wyoming Valley with many towns and cities and intense development. The Lackawanna River, stained orange from acid mine drainage, joins from the left. Despite the urban setting, the river is often bordered by a wall of sycamore or oak or levees and dikes to protect the valley from flooding. The development is most intense as the Susquehanna flows between Kingston and Wilkes-Barre, where several bridges span the river. The impressive dome of the Luzerne County Courthouse is visible to the left and Nesbitt Park on the right provides parking and access.

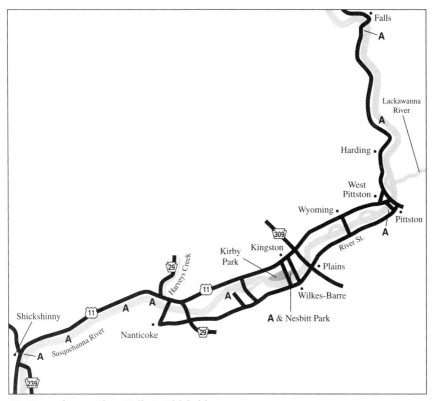

46. Susquehanna River, Falls to Shickshinny

The development begins to recede below Richard Island. Below the PA 29 bridge, the river returns to a more natural setting as it flows between two ridges. U.S. 11 is on the right. Tilbury Knob, a massive sandstone outcrop popular with rock climbers, rises 800 feet on the right. Just below is a series of rapids that can reach Class II in difficulty. From here to Harrisburg, the Susquehanna flows through the ridge and valley region. You will notice the terrain is different than that above Campbells Ledge.

The river flows between high, forested ridges with cliffs and outcrops. Pass about four small islands before reaching the PA 239 bridge at Shickshinny. Take out at the municipal access on the right, a half mile before the bridge.

Shickshinny to Northumberland (Shikellamy State Park)

Length: 46.1 miles

Water level: USGS Danville gauge should be 3.0 feet.

Difficulty: Easy

Hazards: None

Scenery: Good

Highlights: Islands

Fishing: Smallmouth bass, trout, muskellunge

Camping: Camping is available at campgrounds or riverside parks. Primitive camping is limited.

Beneath Shickshinny, the Susquehanna slices through a ridge and passes two islands as it enters a wide, bucolic valley. Paddle almost 2 miles farther to Gould Island. Ahead is the small town of Wapwallopen on the left; the Berwick nuclear power plant rises on the right. This is also the site of the Susquehanna Riverlands Environmental Preserve, featuring trails, unique riparian habitats, and an access area. Steep bluffs rise on the left. As you reach the PA 93 bridge in Berwick, watch for a rapid known as Nescopeck Falls, which is hazardous in low water; stay to the right.

Immediately below the rapids and the bridge, the Nescopeck Creek, a popular whitewater stream, joins from the left. The Test Track Park is just below Berwick on the right and also offers camping by permit. The 15-mile stretch between Berwick and Bloomsburg is the most developed with a series of towns

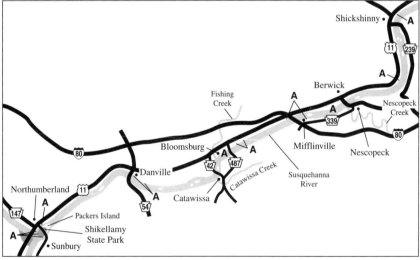

46. Susquehanna River, Shickshinny to Northumberland (Shikellamy State Park)

and the I-80 bridge, although there are wooded bluffs on the left that rise more than 600 feet above the river. This segment also features a string of small, narrow islands. There are access points in both Mifflinville and Bloomsburg. Between Bloomsburg and Danville, the river flows through a scenic rural setting with cliffs, low ridges, and several islands. Remnants of the North Branch Canal wall are along the right. The PFBC Danville access is about a mile and a half above the PA 54 bridge on the right. Another access point is the Montgomery Park Municipal access on the right before the PA 54 bridge.

Below Danville, a ridge rises on the right while pastoral hills and fields are to the left. Three and nine miles below Danville, respectively, are private campgrounds on the right. Seven miles below Danville marks the summer pool of Lake Augusta when the Sunbury Fabridam is inflated; expect heavy powerboat traffic in summer. Take out at Shikellamy State Park on Packers Island, after the PA 147 bridge. Take the left channel when you reach the island. You can also take out at two municipal access areas in Northumberland on the right. Here the Susquehanna River joins with the West Branch Susquehanna River and nearly doubles in size. Across the river are the towering cliffs of Shikellamy State Park. The Sunbury Fabridam is two miles downstream from the juncture of the West Branch and it must be portaged.

Sunbury to Clemson Island/Halifax

Length: 31.7 miles	
Water level: USGS Sunbury gauge should be 5.7 feet; do not paddle if over 11 feet.	
Difficulty: Easy	
Hazards: A few ledges, McKees Half Falls, countless rocks in low water	
Scenery: Good to very good	
Highlights: Countless islands, mountain ridges, water gaps, superb primitive camping on numerous islands	
Fishing: Smallmouth bass, trout, muskellunge, rock bass	
Camping: Public, primitive camping is available on about ten islands. There are only a few commercial campgrounds along the river.	

This section begins at the Sunbury PFBC launch below the Fabridam. Do not even think of running this dam under any circumstances. When inflated, it creates a lethal hydraulic. When deflated in winter, it can damage and capsize your boat. There is also a power plant lowdam at Hummels Wharf that straddles both sides of Byers Island.

Below Sunbury, the mighty Susquehanna comes into its own with the addition of the waters of the West Branch. The river changes significantly from the upstream sections. First, it is very wide, often more than a mile wide. Second,

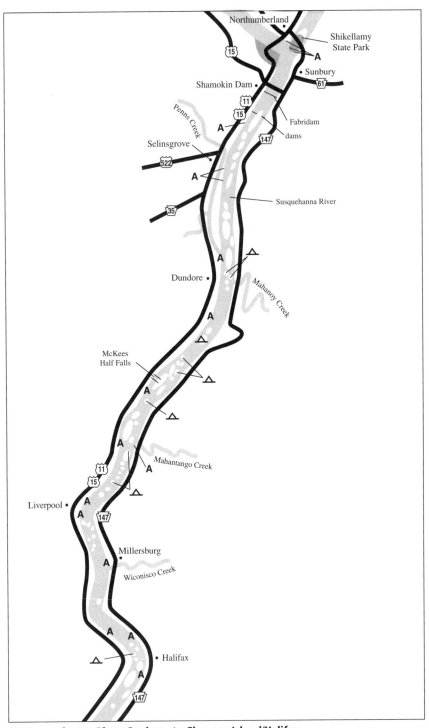

46. Susquehanna River, Sunbury to Clemson Island/Halifax

there are hundreds, if not thousands, of islands and islets. No other river in Pennsylvania, and possibly the nation, has so many islands. In low water, sections of the riverbed become a sea of rocks. Due to the river's width, do not expect it to carry you easily down with its current, particularly in low water. Paddling will be required, especially when there is a headwind. However, with so many islands on this wide river, paddling the Susquehanna is like paddling many rivers in one since there are countless routes you can take. Several islands are open to public, primitive camping is available, and there are superb opportunities to observe wildlife.

Paddlers tend to stick to the western, or river right, shore since that is where most access points are located. For a more isolated paddling experience, explore the eastern, or river left, shore since PA 147 is not nearly as busy as U.S. 11/15.

The scenery is attractive with long ridges separated by forested hills and pastoral valleys. The river has sliced through the many ridges via impressive water gaps with steep bluffs and cliffs. These ridges rise more than 800 feet above the river, and there are many smaller hills and bluffs along the shore.

McKees Half Falls sounds more intimidating than it actually is; it is a minor ledge rapid that cuts diagonally across the river, creating waves. It is easy to navigate in normal flows; the easiest routes are to the left.

With an influx of limestone streams, this section of the Susquehanna is a superb smallmouth fishery. Also expect to see herons, egrets, ospreys, ducks, geese, kingfishers, and an occasional bald eagle.

There is a commercial campground across the river from Millersburg, which is also home to a ferry. This section is unique in that from Sunbury to Clarks Ferry not a single bridge open to vehicles crosses the river. The takeout is at a Pennsylvania Game Commission access on river right, at Clemson Island. Across the river, just upstream from Halifax, is another access area.

Clemson Island/Halifax to Royalton

Length: 31.3 miles

Water level: Do not paddle if USGS Harrisburg gauge is over 6 feet.

Difficulty: Easy to moderate

Hazards: A few rapids, 2-foot weir at Harrisburg

Scenery: Fair to good

Highlights: Countless islands, mountain ridges, water gaps, Statue of Liberty, Dauphin Narrows, Sheets Island

Fishing: Smallmouth bass, trout, muskellunge, rock bass

Camping: Public, primitive camping is available on about ten islands.

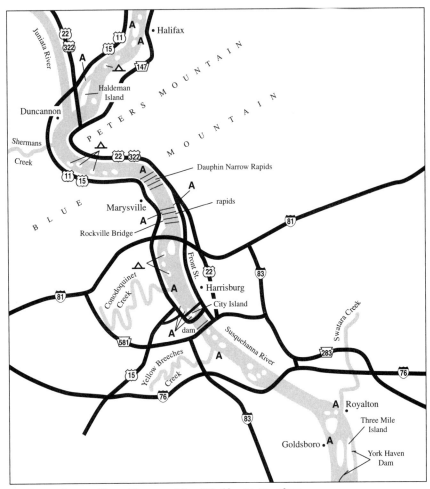

46. Susquehanna River, Clemson Island/Halifax to Royalton

Below Halifax, the Susquehanna flows along Peters Mountain and passes several small islands before reaching Haldeman Island on river left, which is one of the largest islands on the river. Access to Haldeman Island is largely restricted because it is a wildlife propagation area. The Juniata River joins from the left and the Susquehanna grows into a massive river, wider than most lakes, which can intimidate the beginning paddler. Duncannon is on the left with access under the railroad bridge. Traffic is noticeable from the surrounding highways and railroad.

The river turns to the south and slices through Peters Mountain via another water gap with buttresses of cliffs and ledges. Pass a series of small islands, several of which are open to camping. The river cuts through Second Mountain (keep to the left through the rapids) and soon thereafter, slices through Blue Mountain. This is the Dauphin Narrows and these water gaps have been designated as a National Natural Landmark. Rocks begin to emerge from the riverbed and rapids form; keep to river left. Pass to the left of a 25-foot replica of the Statue of Liberty and paddle underneath the famous Rockville Bridge, the longest stone arch bridge in the world. Keep to the left of the rapids below, among the most difficult on the river.

The river opens up and passes more islands; a few are open to camping. The setting becomes urbanized with highway and road bridges and the Harrisburg skyline to the left. The islands also return and a few are open to camping. It is a bit odd to camp primitively in the middle of a bustling urban setting. Fortunately, the river is buffered with a wall of trees. McCormick's Island is one of the largest on the river and offers a nice place to rest at its southern tip. Next to McCormick's Island is smaller Wade Island, featuring Pennsylvania's largest multi-species rookery and home to great egrets and black-crowned night herons. If you love to watch birds, you cannot miss Wade Island. Stay off the island however; access to the island is prohibited. Sheets Island Natural Area features a beautiful hardwood riparian forest. City Island is a convenient place to stop and rest, but camping is not permitted.

Just upstream of the I-83 bridge is a two-foot weir; portage on the left. A string of islands in the middle of the river follow and Harrisburg's airport is on the left. Below the Pennsylvania Turnpike bridge, the right shore is mostly wooded and scenic. Take out at the Royalton or Goldsboro PFBC access areas. Downstream the current slows behind Frederic Lake, formed by a lowdam above Conewago Falls. This lake is channeled by three islands, including the infamous Three Mile Island. Do not run the dam, although you may portage it to the left.

Falmouth to Peach Bottom

Length: 38 miles

Water level: Has water all year due to dams

Difficulty: Easy

Hazards: Conewago Falls, rapids, dams

Scenery: Good to very good

Highlights: Potholes and rock formations at Conewago Falls, Upper and Lower Bear islands, Johnsons Island, scenic tributary streams, Susquehanna River Gorge, bald eagles, ospreys

Fishing: Smallmouth bass, trout, muskellunge, rock bass

Camping: Generally limited to commercial campgrounds along the river.

This last remaining section of the great Susquehanna in Pennsylvania is a mixed bag for paddlers. It offers some exceptional scenery, but much of it is essentially lake paddling since three large hydroelectric dams span the river, taking advan-

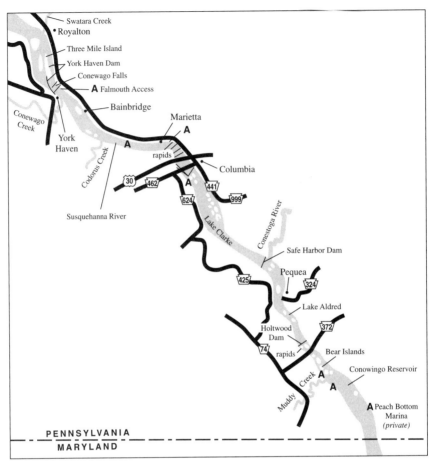

46. Susquehanna River, Falmouth to Peach Bottom

tage of its descent to the Chesapeake Bay. Behind these dams are large lakes where there are cottages, second homes, and plenty of powerboat traffic.

Begin beneath the rapids of Conewago Falls and explore the fascinating potholes and rock formations carved into the bedrock of the river. Pass a few islands and wooded bluffs on the right. Below Marietta, the river narrows and turns right with rapids above the U.S. 30 bridge; to the left is Chickies Rock, a massive rock outcrop popular with climbers. The rapids aren't difficult, but large waves do form on river left in high water. Downstream from Columbia, the current slows as the river enters Lake Clarke, formed by the Safe Harbor Dam. There are a string of islands on river left. This marks the beginning of the Susquehanna River Gorge, where the river carves a 400–600-foot-deep gorge through the River Hills. The gorge is particularly beautiful with cliffs and steep wooded bluffs.

Immediately below Lake Clarke is narrow Lake Aldred, formed by the Holtwood Dam. Here the gorge is at its most impressive as it squeezes the river.

Several islands dot the lake and invite exploration. Several side streams, particularly Otter Creek, Tucquan Creek, and Kellys Run, are known for their beauty. Paddlers enjoy visiting the Sculptured Rocks just below the Safe Harbor Dam. These rocky islets feature small beaches and Indian hieroglyphics that have been largely erased by erosion and vandalism.

Below Lake Aldred is the Conowingo Reservoir, formed by the Conowingo Dam in Maryland. Boating is restricted between the Holtwood Dam and the PA 372 bridge because of the large rapids, waves, and dangerous currents. This restricted section attracts whitewater paddlers who enjoy some of the largest surf waves in the eastern United States. One of the most scenic areas of this section of the river is Upper and Lower Bear islands. Take your time exploring these beautiful islands with their towering buttresses of schist rock outcrops. The glen of Muddy Creek on river right is also worth visiting. Johnsons Island is further downstream on the left and is famous as being the world's first bald eagle preserve. The Peach Bottom nuclear plant is on the right downstream from Johnsons Island.

The surrounding gorge is scenic with its towering wooded bluffs. It is well worth your while to visit the overlooks at Susquehannock State Park. Take out at either of two private access areas, Coal Cabin Beach or Peach Bottom.

47. Sugar Creek

Section: Burlington to North Towanda

Length: 11 miles

Water level: No online gauge available. Creek is generally running in early and mid-spring. The USGS gauge along Towanda Creek at Monroeton should be approximately 400–500 cfs.

Difficulty: Easy

Hazards: Potential strainers

Scenery: Good to very good

Highlights: Shale cliffs, wooded bluffs, easy rapids

Fishing: Smallmouth bass

Camping: None

Sugar Creek is an enjoyable float through the pastoral countryside of Bradford County. Fields and wooded hills and mountains, particularly off to the right, surround the creek. The creek is usually bordered by trees but does braid in the beginning of this section, so watch for strainers. U.S. 6 passes through the valley but generally stays away from the creek.

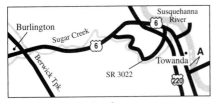

47. Sugar Creek

No large rapids exist on this section, but there are several easy riffles over cobblestones and gravel. Smallmouth bass is the primary fish species, but the creek also holds some trout, rock bass, and muskellunge in the deeper holes.

The stretch below the last U.S. 6 crossing to the take-out is the most scenic with steep hillsides and wooded bluffs that rise up to 600 feet above the creek. About two miles below the last U.S. 6 bridge is a pretty gorge area with shale cliffs on the right rising to about 50 feet and easy ledge rapids that can grow more difficult in higher water. Take-out is problematic at Sugar Creek Road in North Towanda. Instead it is best to continue on to the Susquehanna River; you will see some remnants of the North Branch Canal before reaching the river. Be aware that brush and strainers may cause problems at the mouth of the creek where it joins the river. Continue down the river for three miles and take out at Riverfront Park on the left, across from Towanda. This short section of the river is very scenic with an archipelago of islands and towering shale and sandstone cliffs on the left.

48. Wyalusing Creek

Stevensville to Wyalusing

Length: 11.5 miles

Water level: The painted gauge at SR 1007 should be 1.5 feet. As a rough correlation, the USGS gauge along Towanda Creek at Monroeton should be approximately 400–500 cfs.

Difficulty: Easy

Hazards: Strainers, often along islands and near take-out

Scenery: Very good

Highlights: Rural scenery, isolated setting, good smallmouth fishery

Fishing: Smallmouth bass and trout

Camping: No public camping, many potential sites on private land

The Wyalusing is a large creek that drains an expansive area of Susquehanna and Bradford counties. The creek flows down a farm valley with wooded hillsides and bluffs. Because all the surrounding land is privately owned, no camping is allowed without permission. The Wyalusing is a very good smallmouth stream with several deep pools.

A good place to put in is the SR 1007 bridge at Stevensville. The creek is often surrounded by forests and occasional fields. The creek is easy with no difficulties. Some riffles can be long, and are often interspersed with pools. Camptown is a small, attractive town with potential access at the PA 706 bridge. A mile below Camptown, the creek braids around three islands; watch for strainers and shallow water. Two miles below the second PA 706 bridge is a unique, old, iron, one-lane bridge along County Bridge Road (T 467). This bridge is a possible take-out.

As you near Wyalusing, the creek meanders through an impressive forest of sycamore and oak trees, and strainers can be a problem. The last take-out along the creek is the bridge for U.S. 6, but it will require a steep climb up to the road on the left. You can continue to the Susquehanna River, but be aware that strainers often build up along the railroad bridge abutments. If you continue on to the river, you can take out with permission at Endless Mountain Outfitters, a private access, on the right at Sugar Run.

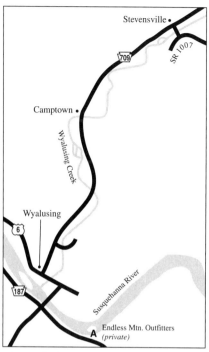

48. Wyalusing Creek

49. Mehoopany Creek

Section: Forkston to Mehoopany	
Length: 6.5 miles	
Water level: No online gauge available. The creek is usually running in early to mid-spring.	
Difficulty: Easy	
Hazards: Strainers, Class I riffles; Class II in high water	
Scenery: Very good	
Highlights: Rugged scenery, isolated, seasonal waterfalls	
Fishing: Smallmouth bass, trout	
Camping: None	

At Forkston, the North Branch Mehoopany joins with Mehoopany Creek to create a sizeable mountain stream. The creek flows down a narrow, twisting valley that at times seems more like a canyon with soaring ridges to the south and steep hills with fields and forests. The Mehoopany often flows up against cliffs and steep bluffs in a setting that is largely undeveloped.

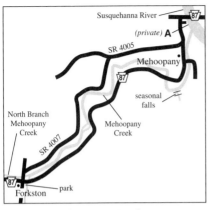

Susquehanna River

(private) **A**

SR 4005

Mehoopany

seasonal
falls

North Branch
Mehoopany
Creek

SR 4007

Mehoopany
Creek

Forkston   park

49. Mehoopany Creek

The creek is not difficult. The rapids are easy and straightforward; they are formed where there are gravel bars and cobblestones. However, some paddling experience and a spray skirt is advisable if paddling a kayak. The Mehoopany does braid in a few places, particularly two miles below Forkston, so be sure to watch for strainers.

As you near the town of Mehoopany, cliffs rise above the creek. Paddle under the PA 87 bridge and watch for towering seasonal waterfalls on the right. These falls reach a height of 200–300 feet, and one has been historically known as Maynard Falls. In winter, there are incredible columns of ice.

The creek largely avoids Mehoopany. Be aware that the SR 3003 bridge in Mehoopany often collects strainers. This bridge is a possible take-out, but it would be difficult due to the steep banks and limited parking. The better option is to paddle under a canopy of large sycamore trees to the Susquehanna River, and then paddle upstream a short distance to a private take-out on the left (if you are paddling upstream) just before the PA 87 bridge.

50. Tunkhannock Creek

Section: Nicholson to Tunkhannock

Length: 15.9 miles

Water level: USGS gauge at Dixon should be 2.0 feet.

Difficulty: Easy

Hazards: Strainers, often along islands; Class I riffles

Scenery: Good to very good

Highlights: Tunkhannock Viaduct, bald eagles, good fishing

Fishing: Smallmouth bass, trout, muskellunge

Camping: Primitive camping allowed at Lazybrook Park with permission; otherwise, most of the land along the creek is privately owned.

The Tunkhannock Creek is an ideal canoe trip that explores the farmlands and wooded hillsides of Wyoming County. Put in at Nicholson, either at the SR 1031 or SR 1017 bridge. You can also begin at the juncture of PA 92 and PA 374 three miles upstream from Nicholson, but there are braids downstream that can collect strainers. Otherwise, begin at SR 1031 to enjoy the incredible views of the Tunkhannock Viaduct, under which the Tunkhannock flows. The viaduct is the largest concrete railroad bridge in the world.

The Tunkhannock largely avoids the town of Nicholson, and Martins Creek joins from the left as the Tunkhannock grows to the size of a small river. Much of the creek is undeveloped and farmlands and large sycamore trees line the creek. Many of the steeper hillsides are adorned with hemlock and rhododendrons. Bald eagles are an increasingly common sight along the creek. The creek often makes sharp ninety-degree bends and the faster water is often along islands where strainers are also more likely.

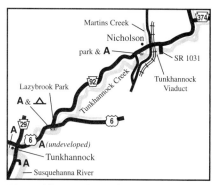

50. Tunkhannock Creek

The South Branch Tunkhannock Creek joins from the right to form a large pool ideal for swimming or fishing. Reach an island and take the channel to the right along bouncy riffles. Pass under the U.S. 6 bridge and reach a public park on the right with access and camping. Bounce over another riffle and float by a private campground to the left. The creek flows under U.S. 6 again as mountains rise to the south; you will paddle around Shadowbrook Golf Resort. Pass under U.S. 6 again, with an undeveloped access and parking on the left, as the creek bends right and flows along the base of Avery Mountain. The town of Tunkhannock is largely hidden by large sycamore trees as you paddle under the bypass and the railroad bridge and reach the Susquehanna River. Paddle up the river for .3 mile to the take-out at Riverside Park, or head downriver to a PFBC access 1 mile on the right.

51. Nescopeck Creek

Section: Hollow Road to Susquehanna River

Length: 12.6 miles

Water level: An approximate correlation is 80 cfs on the USGS Wapwallopen gauge

Difficulty: Easy

Hazards: Class I–II rapids, possible strainers

Scenery: Good to very good

Highlights: Scenic mountains, rural setting

Fishing: Fishing is limited due to acid mine drainage.

Camping: None available, most land is privately owned.

This section of the Nescopeck is tamer than that upstream, which attracts whitewater kayakers to its Class II and III rapids. Begin at the Hollow Road bridge and float through a gorge-like setting with hemlocks and rhododendrons

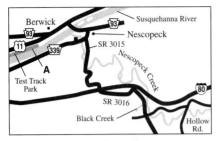

51. Nescopeck Creek

along wooded bluffs, particularly on the left. The setting is very scenic and mostly undeveloped. There are easy rapids and riffles that can reach Class II in higher flows. The creek does braid around a few islands, so keep an eye out for strainers.

The rapids do pick up before the confluence with Black Creek; just keep your boat straight and maintain some speed. At the confluence with Black Creek, the Nescopeck cuts an impressive water gap through Nescopeck Mountain that is almost 1,000 feet deep. The scenery is marred by busy I-80; fortunately, the interstate only straddles the creek through the water gap and briefly thereafter. One mile below the Overlook Road bridge is an abutment that can collect strainers. For the ensuing five miles the creek flows through a pleasant rural setting with easy riffles and no hazards. The banks are often steep and surround the creek with hardwoods and hemlocks. Wooded bluffs rise 100–300 feet above the creek and create a gorge-like setting that is mostly undeveloped. A mile after the SR 3015 bridge the creek flows around an island. The town of Nescopeck is mostly out of sight.

Taking out can be a little problematic. It may be possible to take out at the PA 339 bridge, but expect a steep climb and limited parking. A half-mile below the bridge is a sewage treatment plant on the left, which is probably the most popular take-out, but it is not developed for access. You can continue on to the Susquehanna River, but the creek braids around many islands before reaching the river and there is a high possibility for strainers. An easy take-out is 1.5 miles downriver on the right, at Berwick's Test Track Park.

52. Catawissa Creek

Section: PA 339 to Catawissa

Length: 21 miles

Water level: No online gauge available. The creek is usually runnable in early and mid-spring.

Difficulty: Easy, many easy rapids and riffles

Hazards: Dam at Catawissa, potential strainers

Scenery: Good to very good

Highlights: Mountain scenery, covered bridge

Fishing: Limited due to acid mine drainage; trout in sidestreams

Camping: Primitive camping is possible, but most land along the creek is privately owned.

Catawissa Creek is a moderately sized stream that flows down a winding, narrow valley surrounded by the high ridges of impressive, muscular mountains. Hemlocks and rhododendrons often line the creek, while hardwoods carpet the higher ridges. For the first eight miles, the creek has a surprisingly isolated feel as it is encased in woodlands with

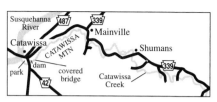

52. Catawissa Creek

a gorge-like setting. Below Shumans, the valley opens a little and fields become more common. However, development along the creek is still light and woods often border the creek.

The creek slices through a ridge before Mainville and leaves the mountains; it then flows along the ridge of Catawissa Mountain through the pastoral and scenic Susquehanna River valley. A corridor of trees lines the creek as fields stretch beyond. A covered bridge before Catawissa highlights this pastoral setting; watch for a lowdam below that must be portaged, and a potentially heavy rapid below the dam. Paddle under the PA 42 bridge and take out at a town park on the right.

Being a moderately sized stream, the Catawissa doesn't run as frequently as other streams in this guide. Do not expect to paddle it in summer unless there has been a heavy rain. Riffles and easy rapids are common along the creek, particularly down to Mainville. There are only a few islands along the Catawissa, but strainers are always a possibility.

53. Penns Creek

Section: Poe Paddy State Park to Susquehanna River

Length: 45 miles

Water level: USGS Penns Creek gauge should be 2.6 feet.

Difficulty: Easy to moderate

Hazards: Strainers along islands and braids; lowdam at Millmont; a few Class II rapids below Poe Paddy

Scenery: Fair to very good

Highlights: Mountain scenery, trout fishing

Fishing: Trout, smallmouth bass, carp, largemouth bass

Camping: Primitive camping is very limited due to private land. Camping is allowed in the state forest land on the right between Poe Paddy and Weikert. There is a commercial campground 3 miles below New Berlin.

Located strategically in the middle of the state, a region of high forested ridges with scars of talus and rolling scenic countryside, Penns Creek, one would think,

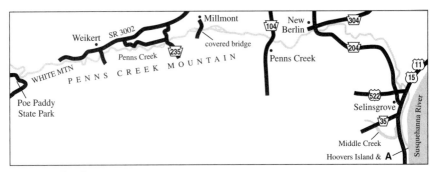

53. Penns Creek

would be very popular with paddlers. But it isn't. While it offers many fine features, it also has drawbacks. First, the beginning part of this section is by far the most scenic, but the shuttle is very long. Second, the lower half of this section can have little current, which can make for a long, tiresome day. Third, expect to see occasional strings of cottages between Weikert and PA 104. And fourth, after all the miles it flows, the creek doesn't grow much wider at its mouth than it was at Weikert or Glen Iron.

While Penns Creek may not be very popular with paddlers, it does attract many trout anglers. Penns Creek is born in a cave and receives a lot of limestone influence from other caves and springs. The creek is world-famous for its trout and green drake hatches. Penns Creek is not a place a paddler wants to be during trout season, particularly between Poe Paddy and Cherry Run.

You must also understand the first few miles do have a few rapids that can reach Class II in difficulty. They are not difficult and can be run by paddlers with experience. This stretch of the creek is somewhat rocky with small boulders. You may even be lucky enough to see an otter, as I once did on a spring day.

The section between Poe Paddy and Weikert is the most scenic. The creek winds through a rugged gorge with impressive talus fields on the towering ridges. White Mountain rises to the south, and Paddy Mountain to the north. An old railroad grade, now harboring the Mid State Trail, is off to the left. The scenery is truly impressive.

As you proceed downstream, the valley opens and the creek widens. Penns Creek likes to braid and it loves islands, and you will encounter both every mile or so. The main channel is usually obvious, but expect that when this creek braids, it does so very well with several intermingling channels. The main risks, of course, are strainers, so approach each braid with caution.

Cottages become more common on the left, but they don't completely inundate the creek. Penns Creek Mountain rises off to the right with a few cliffs. Below Glen Iron, the setting becomes more pastoral with rolling fields and distant ridges. Paddle under a scenic covered bridge near Millmont. Be aware that a mile further is a lowdam; run the chute, or portage, just to the right of the main island; avoid the channel to the left since it doesn't rejoin the creek for about a mile and there is a risk of strainers.

From PA 104 to Selinsgrove, the setting is entirely pastoral with some surprisingly rugged hills. There are also few if any islands and no significant braids. While that may be good news, the bad news is that the current can slow to a crawl, particularly in low water. In sections, the creek resembles a long, narrow pond. Bridges provide the only access; another possible access is the ballfield in New Berlin, on the left below the bridge. New Berlin is a scenic little town that is worth a visit. Three miles below New Berlin is a commercial campground that provides an option for those looking for an overnight trip.

At Selinsgrove, the creek becomes developed with busy highways and commercial development. Below town, the development ends but the highways of U.S. 11/15 remain; otherwise, fields surround the creek, which delays its union with the Susquehanna by five miles. Middle Creek joins from the right, and after two miles, Penns Creek finally joins the Susquehanna. Take out at the PGC Hoovers Island access on the right.

54. Mahantango Creek

Section: Klingerstown to Susquehanna River	
Length: 17 miles	
Water level: No online gauge available. The creek is usually runnable in early and mid-spring.	
Difficulty: Easy	
Hazards: Lowhead dam at Pillow	
Scenery: Good to very good	
Highlights: Mountain scenery	
Fishing: Smallmouth bass, trout	
Camping: None. Creek flows through private land.	

Mahantango Creek provides a scenic tour of east central Pennsylvania's ridge and valley region. As a general rule, this creek features scenic farmlands to the right and the high forested ridge of Mahantango Mountain to the left. In places, wooded bluffs rise along the creek, often on the right. The creek is usually bordered by a corridor of trees, even where it flows among farmlands.

Mahantango has few islands or braids since the creek is usually confined to a single channel. Nevertheless, you must keep an

54. Mahantango Creek

eye out for strainers on this moderately sized stream. The first danger on this creek is a lowhead dam at Pillow, where part of the creek is diverted to a left channel. This dam will require a portage. Below the PA 225 bridge, there are a string of cottages on the left, a rare sight on this creek since it is largely undeveloped.

The high forested ridge of Mahantango Mountain continues to rise above the creek below Pillow, as do wooded bluffs along the outside bends to the right. The end of the creek has two challenging features—a ledge drop, or old dam, about a mile below Kiwanis Farm Road bridge and a broken old dam with rapids about a mile farther. It is possible to run both, but exercise caution and if you feel unsure, portage. More bluffs rise on the right. Take out at PA 147 before the Susquehanna River.

55. Shermans Creek

Section: Bridgeport to Susquehanna River

Length: 23 miles

Water level: USGS Shermans Dale gauge should be 1.5 feet.

Difficulty: Easy. There are a few easy riffles and rapids over gravel bars.

Hazards: Lowhead dam above Dromgold and breached dams; potential strainers

Scenery: Good to very good

Highlights: Covered bridge at Dellville, mountain scenery

Fishing: Smallmouth bass, trout

Camping: No public camping; there are potential primitive campsites along the creek with permission from the landowner.

This trip begins at the PA 74 bridge in Bridgeport, where the creek flows around a large island. Paddle through a farm valley and encounter more islands a little more than a mile downstream. The creek bends to the left and flows through a small, isolated valley between ridges that rise 400 feet. PA 850 joins from the left as the creek cuts through a scenic ridge in a gorge-like setting at Falling Spring. The creek braids around a few islands and then there is a 3-foot lowhead dam that you should portage. A half-mile farther is a breached lowhead dam that should be approached with caution. Shermans Creek alternates between fields, homes, small towns, and isolated woodlands along ridges and bluffs.

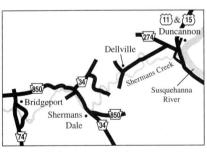

55. Shermans Creek

Below Dromgold, cottages become more frequent, but the creek is still scenic as it meanders through a farm valley. Cross under a covered bridge at Dellville. The ridge of Cove Mountain rises to the right, offering fine mountain scenery. Take out before the creek joins the Susquehanna just south of Duncannon on the right.

56. Conodoguinet Creek

Section: Creekview Park to West Fairview Point

Length: 36.5 miles

Water level: USGS Hogestown gauge should be 1.7 feet.

Difficulty: Easy

Hazards: Possible strainers

Scenery: Good

Highlights: Wildlife

Fishing: Smallmouth bass, muskellunge, rock bass, sunfish

Camping: None; most land along the creek is privately owned.

The Conodoguinet is a long and placid creek that meanders through the bucolic Cumberland Valley. There are no rapids along this section, but expect long pools and easy riffles over gravel bars and long pools. Because the Cumberland Valley from Carlisle to the Susquehanna River is becoming increasingly developed, do not expect this to be a wilderness float.

Below Creekview Park, there are houses on the right, and fields and woods on the left. Below the PA 34 bridge, the creek is undeveloped as it flows

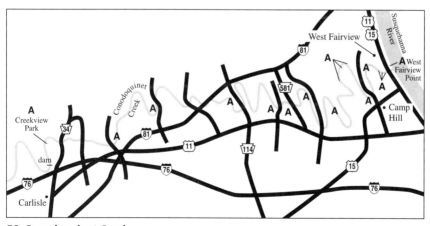

56. Conodoguinet Creek

through a pastoral setting. After a brief brush with development at the juncture of U.S. 11 and North Middlesex Road, the Conodoguinet remains mostly undeveloped and pastoral down to Willow Mill Park and Hustons Mill, where more homes come into view. Below Lambs Gap Road, the creek meanders through residential areas that continue to encompass the creek to the Susquehanna. However, there are a few sections along the creek that are wooded and undeveloped because the terrain is too steep. On other sections, trees often line the creek, obscuring the housing developments that lie beyond. To avoid having to paddle this more developed section, take out at the Fry Tract, Westover Commons Area, or Good Hope access.

The surrounding terrain is rolling, with steep bluffs often on the outside bends. Despite the developed surroundings, expect to see a variety of birds and wildlife. Due to influx from limestone springs upstream, the Conodoguinet features fertile waters and good fishing potential. The creek also has a habit of meandering along exaggerated oxbow loops. For example, Willow Mill Park is only about seven miles from West Fairview Point, but is 23.2 miles away by floating the creek.

The creek also features several access points that can shorten a float trip. For those Harrisburg metro area residents who are looking for a more intimate creek to paddle as compared to the vast Susquehanna, the Conodoguinet is an ideal destination.

57. Swatara Creek

Pine Grove to PFBC Waterworks Access

Length: 22 miles	
Water level: USGS Harpers Tavern gauge should be 2.1 feet.	
Difficulty: Easy	
Hazards: Lowhead dam, possible strainers	
Scenery: Good to very good	
Highlights: Swatara State Park, Appalachian Trail, remnants of Union Canal	
Fishing: Sucker, smallmouth bass, catfish, muskellunge	
Camping: Private campground at Lickdale	

The Swatara is a sizeable stream that offers some fine paddling opportunities. Below Pine Grove, the creek meanders through wetlands and braids around some islands. The stream enters Swatara State Park after crossing under the I-81 bridge; the segment through the state park features thick woodlands that would give a sense of isolation if it wasn't for traffic from the nearby interstate. There are three access areas in the state park. Pass under an iron bridge that serves the Appalachian Trail as the creek flows through an 800-foot-deep water gap in Blue Mountain.

From here to the take-out, the Swatara flows through a pastoral setting with fields and woodlands. There is moderate development around Lickdale. Fortunately, the creek is often shielded by a wall of trees. Private camping is available at the Lickdale Campground. Watch for and portage a lowhead dam a

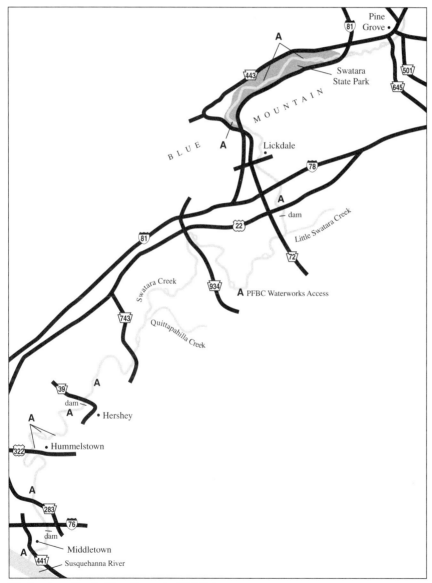

57. Swatara Creek, Pine Grove to Middletown

mile below the U.S. 22 bridge. After a brief touch with development, the creek enters the woods. Little Swatara Creek joins from the left and the Swatara grows to the size of a small river. Below the confluence there is an island and railroad bridge. Strainers become less of a concern. Take out at the PFBC Waterworks Access on the right after several miles of meandering through a pastoral setting.

PFBC Waterworks Access to Middletown

Length: 32 miles

Water level: USGS Harpers Tavern gauge should be 2.1 feet.

Difficulty: Easy; long pools with easy riffles and rapids

Hazards: Lowhead dams

Scenery: Good

Highlights: Limestone outcrops, covered bridge, caves, remnants of Union Canal, local historical sites

Fishing: Sucker, smallmouth bass, catfish, muskellunge

Camping: No primitive camping along the creek; camping is available for a fee at Union Canal Canoe Rentals.

Like the end of the prior section, the Swatara continues its serpentine route through pastoral countryside. This section contains many access points so you can shorten your journey. About 2 miles below the put-in is an interesting limestone rock outcrop on the right. The creek continues its pastoral journey with small islands and easy riffles through a corridor of trees. Old stoneworks along the creek are the remnants of the Union Canal. Watch for a dam below PA 39 at Union Deposit. While there are some cottages and homes, the Swatara is usually bordered by trees.

Development becomes more common starting at Hummelstown. Watch for rapids at a large island below the Hummelstown Borough access; though easy, they can cause problems in high water. Below U.S. 322 are more outcrops, a covered bridge, and small cave openings; Indian Echo Caverns is nearby. Development again increases below PA 283 and the Pennsylvania Turnpike. You must portage a dam below the turnpike bridge to the left since it contains a dangerous hydraulic. Take out at the PFBC Middletown access on the right, just before the Swatara joins the Susquehanna River.

58. Yellow Breeches Creek

Section: South Middleton Township Park to New Cumberland

Length: 31 miles

Water level: USGS Camp Hill gauge should be 1.4 feet.

Hazards: Several dams, strainers

Difficulty: Easy

Scenery: Good

Highlights: Trout fishing, pastoral scenery

Fishing: Trout, smallmouth bass, largemouth bass, rock bass

Camping: Only possible camping is by reservation at Lower Allen Community Park.

Yellow Breeches has increasingly attracted the attention of paddlers over the years because it is an attractive creek that is close to populated areas. It is also a unique creek. First, thanks to the many limestone springs that feed it, Yellow Breeches is a world-famous trout stream. You can expect to share the creek with anglers, particularly along the upper half of this section. Second, it is the definition of a pastoral stream with fields, small towns, bluffs, and woodlots along the creek. Yellow Breeches has been designated as a state scenic river, and parts of it are a water trail. The creek flows by several small community parks and a PFBC access at Spanglers Mills, so there are many put-in and take-out options.

The most important thing to know about this creek is the many dams along it, probably more than any other creek in this guide. These dams are in various states of repair—some are deathtraps, some are breached, and some are runnable. Many dams redirect waterflow into raceways. It is very important to approach each with caution. If the dam is not breached with a clear channel, it

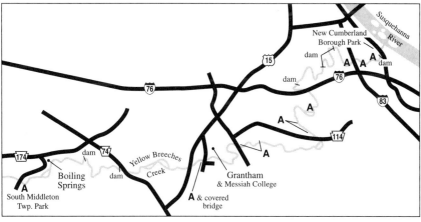

58. Yellow Breeches Creek

is advisable to portage. The majority of the dams require a portage. There is an effort underway to remove some of the dams from the creek. Otherwise, there are no difficult rapids, just riffles over gravel bars and pools.

Most of this creek is undeveloped and pastoral, with views of South Mountain off to the right. After the put-in, pass fields and woods; watch for a dam that appears to feed a canal or raceway to the left. The creek meanders below the dam through the woods, so strainers are a concern. The first town is attractive Boiling Springs, an area that receives intense fishing pressure. There is another lowdam below Boiling Springs.

With the brief exception of Williams Grove, the creek is undeveloped and pastoral down to Grantham. Yellow Breeches flows under a covered bridge through Messiah College's attractive campus, where there is also an access. Below Grantham, the creek becomes pastoral again with attractive farms and well-kept homes as the creek winds between hills with wooded bluffs and small cliffs. This is one of the more scenic sections of the creek. The surroundings become more developed and urban along the final 3.5 miles of this section, although the creek is often bordered by trees. Due to an unrunnable dam downstream, it is best to take out at New Cumberland Borough Park on the left.

59. Conewago Creek

Section: East Berlin to York Haven (Susquehanna River)

Length: 39 miles

Water level: USGS Camp Hill gauge on Yellow Breeches Creek should be 2.2 feet.

Difficulty: Easy

Hazards: Several lowdams, possible strainers

Scenery: Good

Highlights: Pastoral scenery

Fishing: Smallmouth bass, catfish, bullhead, panfish

Camping: No public primitive camping is available; most of the land along the river is privately owned.

This large creek drains more than 500 square miles and offers a pleasant cruise through the countryside of Adams and York counties. Begin in the small town of East Berlin, either at the PA 234 bridge or at a town park just .5 mile downstream. The creek meanders through a setting of farm fields, barns, and occasional homes. Wooded bluffs often rise to about 100–300 feet above the creek. Although there are many bridges, and roads occasionally follow the creek, it is not overdeveloped. Even when there are fields, a corridor of trees often lines the shore. All those bridges provide a number of different trip options.

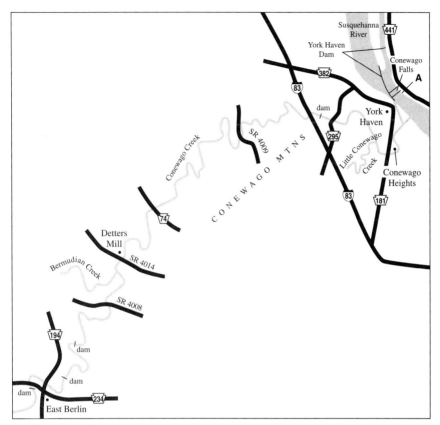

59. Conewago Creek

A particularly scenic part of the creek is a 5-mile section between SR 4009 and the I-83 bridge where the creek cuts through the low, rolling Conewago Mountains, creating a wooded gorge. The creekbanks become developed with homes as the stream curves around the town of Conewago Heights. Soon thereafter, the Conewago reaches the Susquehanna River, and before doing so, splits into two channels. The one to the right, or straight ahead, slices through Brunners Island and goes into the river. Take the one to the left, as it will lead to an access area on the left where the creek joins the Susquehanna River.

There are surprisingly few islands and braids; however, the creek is known for its rather slow current. Expect to paddle a lot, particularly in low water. The Conewago has four dams on this section, and even more upstream, that slow the current even more. Although some of the dams are runnable, approach each with caution. They are located 2 and 5 miles below East Berlin and a half mile below the I-83 bridge.

60. Conestoga River

Section: Brownstown to River Road

Length: 32 miles

Water level: USGS Conestoga Blvd. gauge should be 2.0 feet.

Difficulty: Easy

Hazards: Dams, potential strainers

Scenery: Good

Highlights: Covered bridges, historical points of interest

Fishing: Smallmouth bass, rock bass, carp, trout, bluegill, catfish, bullheads

Camping: No public primitive camping is available; most of the land along the river is privately owned.

Twisting and turning through Lancaster County's famous countryside, the Conestoga River is an enjoyable place to paddle. The river features easy riffles and pools as it passes neat Amish farms, riparian forests, and residential areas. Wooded bluffs and high banks often rise along the way. There are many historical points of interest along the river, including two covered bridges and old mills and taverns. With about fifteen different access points, a variety of different trips can be made on the Conestoga.

A popular place to begin is on Stone Quarry Road in Brownstown. The Conestoga meanders through pastoral farms as Cocalico Creek joins from the right and nearly doubles the Conestoga in size. About 3 miles from the put-in, watch for a dam below Quarry Road Bridge; you can portage to the right. Below is the Pinetown Covered Bridge, and a mile and a half farther is the second covered bridge, Hunsickers Mill Covered Bridge. The creek flows through a golf course and under the PA 23 bridge, after which houses and development become more common.

After you pass under the PA 30 bridge as you near Lancaster, watch for two dams; the first can be portaged on the right, and the second on the left. As the river winds through the city, the setting becomes urbanized, but for the most part, the scenery is pretty good, thanks to a buffer of trees that line the river and Lancaster County's Central and Buchmiller parks on the left.

Below PA 741, the Conestoga returns to its pastoral state as it often flows through a corridor of sycamore, silver maple, river birch, and some oak, maple, ash, and tulip trees. Homes are occasionally seen from the river, as are fields and farms. The river meanders between rock cliffs, wooded bluffs, and hillsides. It is best to take out before the Susquehanna River at River Road on the left.

The Conestoga offers some good opportunities to observe birdlife including great blue herons, black-crowned night herons, yellow-crowned night herons, green herons, great white egrets, snowy egrets, kingfishers, ducks, geese, hawks, ospreys, and bald eagles.

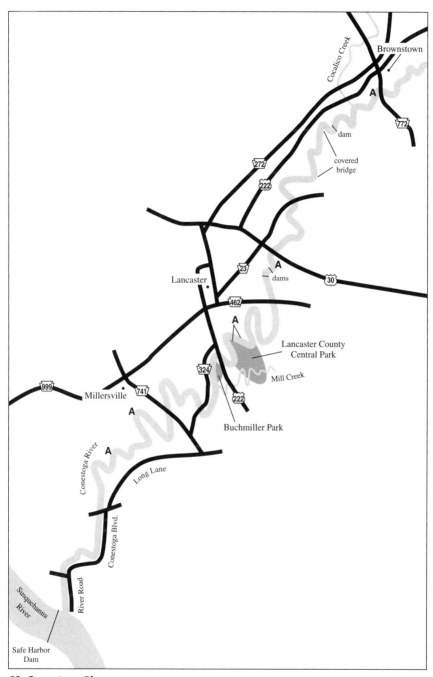

60. Conestoga River

61. Octoraro Creek

Section: Forge Road to New Bridge Road, Maryland

Length: 14.5 miles

Water level: USGS Chadds Ford gauge on the Brandywine Creek should be approximately 2.4 feet.

Difficulty: Easy

Hazards: Potential strainers

Scenery: Good to very good

Highlights: Covered bridge, wooded bluffs, birdlife

Fishing: Smallmouth bass, rock bass, carp, trout, bluegill, catfish, bullheads

Camping: No public primitive camping is available; most of the land along the creek is privately owned.

The Octoraro provides a pleasant, easy cruise through the hilly farmlands of Chester and Lancaster counties. Begin at a covered bridge along Forge Road; just upstream is a lowdam, and farther upstream is a large dam that forms the Octoraro Reservoir. The creek meanders between fields, meadows, and wooded bluffs that grow higher as you proceed downstream. The setting is pastoral and relatively undeveloped. Below Lees Bridge Road, another popular put-in point, the creek enters a scenic gorge-like setting with steep wooded bluffs that rise up to 200 feet. From here to the take-out, easy riffles and rapids become more common.

Although you will not likely notice from the creek, the Goat Hill Serpentine Barrens are located off river left. These barrens are a state natural area and are part of Valley Forge State Forest; the Nature Conservancy also has a preserve protecting the barrens. Serpentine barrens are formed by metals in the bedrock that naturally make the soils inhospitable to most plants. As a result, unique and rare plants grow here that are found in few other places. The "forest" that grows on the barrens is dominated by pitch pine and scrub oak. Besides plants, the barrens are also home to several species of rare moths and many species of birds. These barrens occur in only a few places in the country, and these are some of the largest and most diverse on the East Coast.

Just before entering Maryland, there is a large quarry on the right, the only significant scenic drawback along the creek. The creek is wooded and scenic down to the take-out at New Bridge Road. Besides its bluffs and pastoral scenery, the Octoraro is particularly well known for its birdlife; bald eagles, ospreys, kingfishers, egrets, and herons are commonly seen along the creek.

🛶 Lakes, Ponds, and Reservoirs

62. Beechwood Lake

Size: 67 acres

Ownership: PFBC

Horsepower restrictions: Electric motors

Scenery: Good to very good

Fishing: Walleye, largemouth bass, smallmouth bass, bluegill, crappie, perch, trout, pickerel

Location: From Sabinsville along PA 349, follow SR 4012 for 1.1 miles and turn right; follow signs to the lake.

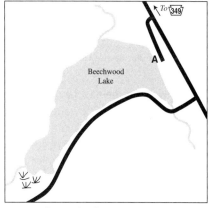

62. Beechwood Lake

This small, lonely lake is nestled among the rolling farm fields and forested hills of northern Tioga County. It is roughly U-shaped with two small inlets. There are wetlands and sedges along the southwestern inlet. Hemlocks adorn a wooded hill along the southern shore. With the exception of a few anglers, you can expect to have Beechwood all to yourself. One launch provides access.

63. Cowanesque Lake

Size: 1,085 acres

Ownership: USACE

Horsepower restrictions: Unlimited

Scenery: Good to very good

Fishing: Walleye, striped bass, muskellunge, white crappie, channel catfish, largemouth bass, smallmouth bass

Location: From Lawrenceville, follow PA 49 west for 3 miles to the lake. The north shore is accessible via Bliss Road from Lawrenceville.

This long, narrow lake stretches for more than 4 miles between the forested hills and rolling fields of northern Pennsylvania. This hilly terrain rises to 500 feet above the lake. The pastoral scenery is attractive. Cowanesque features many small coves, bays, and inlets, as well as two no-wake zones. One zone is

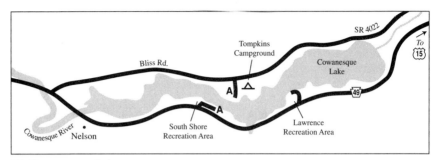

63. Cowanesque Lake

located in the narrow middle section of the lake, the other at the western end at the inlet of the Cowanesque River. It is this zone where paddlers will want to spend most of their time since there are islands, wetlands, sedges, coves, and great opportunities to observe wildlife.

There are boat launches at the South Shore Recreation Area and Tompkins Campground. South Shore provides better access to the western section of the lake. Cowanesque Lake also features a swimming area, campgrounds, hiking trails, playgrounds, restrooms, and picnic facilities. The lake is a flood-control project and the level is variable depending on conditions.

64. Tioga Lake and Hammond Lake

Size: Tioga Lake is 498 acres and Hammond Lake is 685 acres.

Ownership: USACE

Horsepower restrictions: Unlimited

Scenery: Tioga Lake is very good; Hammond Lake is good.

Fishing: Walleye, striped bass, muskellunge, white crappie, channel catfish, largemouth bass, smallmouth bass

Location: Hammond Lake is 12 miles northeast of Wellsboro via U.S. 6 and PA 287, and 6.5 miles from U.S. 15 along PA 287. Follow signs to the Ives Run boat launch.

To reach Tioga Lake from U.S. 6 at Mansfield, follow the Lambs Creek Access Road for 4 miles and follow signs to the launch.

These two large lakes are described together due to their proximity and similarities; they are even connected by a channel. Tioga and Hammond lakes are popular boating and fishing destinations, but there are also great paddling opportunities.

Hammond is the larger lake and likely to have more powerboat traffic. The setting and shoreline are not wilderness and undisturbed, since they are dominated by the massive USACE dam to the east, PA 287 along the north shore, and a large campground on the south shore. Regardless, this is a worthy lake to

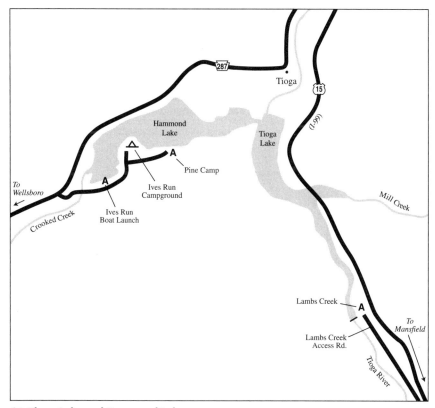

64. Tioga Lake and Hammond Lake

paddle with a no-wake zone at its western end. Also make sure to explore the coves, wetlands, sedges, and inlet of Crooked Creek. Another highlight is paddling along the north shore and looking south to enjoy a very beautiful panorama of mountains that rise 1,000 feet above the lake. Hammond Lake also features a swimming area, campgrounds, hiking trails, playgrounds, restrooms, and picnic facilities.

Tioga Lake is a great place to paddle. First, the scenery is superb and the setting is relatively undisturbed, as impressive mountains rise 1,000 feet above the narrow lake and create a gorge-like setting. The only distraction is that U.S. 15 is high above the eastern shore and crosses Mill Creek Cove via a high bridge. Make sure to visit the two no-wake zones, the first being the long, peaceful inlet of the Tioga River. As you paddle downstream from Lambs Creek Access, the inlet slowly widens into the lake, but you can also paddle upstream from the access. The other no-wake zone is the Mill Creek Cove that is nearly surrounded by steep mountains on the eastern shore.

Both lakes are flood-control projects and water level is variable depending on conditions. If the level is low or drawn down, it may not be possible to access Tioga Lake from the Lambs Creek Access.

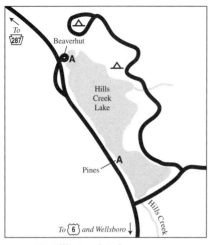

65. Hills Creek Lake

Size: 137 acres	
Ownership: DCNR, Hills Creek State Park	
Horsepower restrictions: Electric motors	
Scenery: Good to very good	

Fishing: Walleye, muskellunge, largemouth bass, smallmouth bass, bluegill, crappie, yellow perch. The lake is well-known as an excellent largemouth bass fishery.

Location: The park is located 7 miles east of Wellsboro along Charleston Ave. and Hills Creek Lake Road. Signs also lead to the park from U.S. 6 and PA 287.

65. Hills Creek Lake

Hills Creek Lake is surrounded by the wooded hills of the northern tier, with a forest of pine and oak and a wall of spruce along the western shore. Many coves and inlets line the lake; interesting places to explore are the small coves near the Beaverhut boat launch. The lake is serene since horsepower is limited to electric motors, although it is popular with anglers. Two boat launches provide access to the lake.

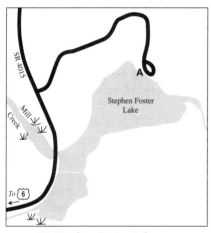

66. Stephen Foster Lake

Size: 75 acres	
Ownership: DCNR, Mt. Pisgah State Park	
Horsepower restrictions: Electric motors	
Scenery: Good to very good	

Fishing: Perch, largemouth bass, crappie, bluegill

Location: From the village of West Burlington along U.S. 6, follow SR 3019 (Wallace Rd.) for 3 miles to State Park Road. Turn right and follow for 1.2 miles; then turn right on an unnamed state park road. Follow the signs to the launch.

66. Stephen Foster Lake

Steep wooded hillsides and fields surround Stephen Foster Lake, which is named after the famous composer of "Camptown Races" and "Oh! Susanna" and who once lived nearby. The small lake is nestled along the steep eastern flank of Mt. Pisgah, a prominent peak in Bradford County; the ridge of this mountain can be seen from the lake. The southern shore features a scenic forest of mature hardwoods, hemlock, and large white pine trees. One launch provides access to the lake. The inlet of Mill Creek is a scenic place to paddle with a deep forest of hemlocks and wetlands.

67. Sunfish Pond

Size: 20 acres

Ownership: Sunfish Pond County Park, Bradford County

Horsepower restrictions: Electric motors

Scenery: Good

Fishing: Largemouth bass, crappie, muskellunge, rainbow trout

Location: From the village of Leroy, along PA 414 between Monroeton and Canton, follow Leroy Mountain Road (SR 3010) straight through an intersection and up the mountain. There is a small green park sign along PA 414. At a T at the top of the mountain, turn right onto Sunfish Pond Road, enter the park and bear left to the pond.

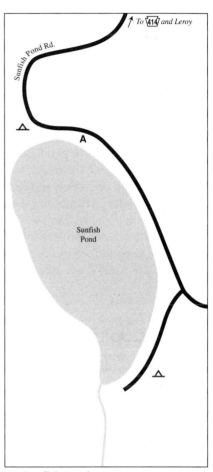

67. Sunfish Pond

This small lake is within a county park located high on the plateau of State Game Lands 12. Boulders adorn its southern shore; the lake is surrounded by low, forested hills with a thick understory of mountain laurel. A beaver lodge is on the western shore. The highlight of Sunfish Pond is its prevailing sense of isolation and serenity since there are no noises from towns or highways. Camping and picnic facilities are available around the pond. Camping here on a clear night will feature an incredible showcase of stars, an experience you will not soon forget.

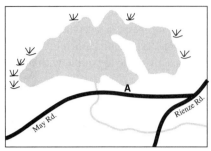

68. State Game Lands 250 Pond

68. State Game Lands 250 Pond

Size: Approx. 50 acres

Ownership: PGC

Horsepower restrictions: Electric motors

Scenery: Very good

Fishing: Largemouth bass, bluegill, crappie

Location: From Wyalusing, follow SR 2010 across the bridge over the Susquehanna River and proceed straight through the intersection with SR 187. After 3 miles, follow SR 2010 as it makes a right turn. After 2.3 miles, turn right onto Rienze Road, SR 2013 and follow for 1.4 miles. Turn left onto May Road and follow for .3 mile; there is a parking area on the right.

I do not know if this pond has a formal name, but it is worth a trip to paddle. It is nestled among the rolling farmlands and wooded hills of southern Bradford County and conveys a surprising sense of isolation. The shoreline is mostly wooded with wetlands and sedges; there are fields to the north, but the shoreline is undeveloped. Lily pads cover parts of the pond in summer and the western shore has dead tree trunks that attract wildlife; duck houses also dot the pond. Expect to see turtles and plenty of waterfowl. A peninsula nearly divides the lake. There is one access area on the southern shore.

69. Cooks Pond

Size: Approx. 40 acres

Ownership: Cooks Pond Association

Horsepower restrictions: Electric motors

Scenery: Very good

Fishing: Largemouth bass, bluegill, crappie

Location: From LeRaysville, follow PA 467 west for 3.6 miles. After passing the Northeast Bradford Junior/Senior High School on the left, turn right onto SR 1051 and follow for 2.1 miles. Turn right onto Manchester Lane and drive down to the parking area at the pond.

This small, hidden gem is nestled among the scenic rolling forested hills and farmlands of northeast Bradford County. The pond is undeveloped and has tree stumps and sedges along the shores, with few significant coves or bays. The setting is serene and peaceful as you are likely to have the pond to yourself. Much of Cooks Pond is surrounded by a thick hemlock forest, with a meadow at the north end. The pond is privately owned by the Cooks Pond Association, but it is open to the public thanks to the Manchester family, who gave it to the association. Donations are appreciated and can be sent to Cooks Pond Association, C & N Bank, 428 S. Main St., Athens, PA 18810.

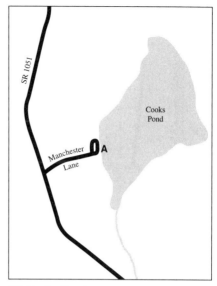

69. Cooks Pond

70. Stevens Lake

Size: 62 acres

Ownership: PFBC

Horsepower restrictions: Electric motors

Scenery: Good

Fishing: Largemouth bass, bluegill, brown bullhead, black crappie, yellow perch, rainbow trout

Location: From Tunkhannock, drive north on PA 29 for 4 miles and turn left onto Lakewood Drive (T491) for .1 mile. Turn right onto a dirt road and follow for .2 mile to a parking lot and boat launch.

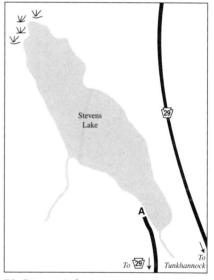

70. Stevens Lake

Stevens Lake is located near popular Lake Carey, but offers more isolation among its woods and farm fields. In summer, Stevens Lake is covered with lily pads, which bloom in early June, and is a great place to view wildlife with a variety of turtles, birds, and amphibians; even otters and ospreys have been observed. The lake is known as an excellent largemouth bass fishery. Paddlers will want to explore the north end of the lake where there are wetlands and a stream inlet. There is one boat launch.

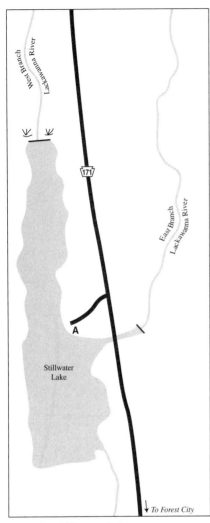

71. Stillwater Lake

71. Stillwater Lake

Size: Approx. 120 acres

Ownership: USACE

Horsepower restrictions: Electric motors

Scenery: Good

Fishing: Bluegill, largemouth bass, trout

Location: From Forest City, follow PA 171 north for about 4 miles to a road on the left that accesses the launch area.

This lake is formed by a large, gray flood-control dam on the Lackawanna River. The north end of the lake features sedges and wetlands, while the inlet of the East Branch Lackawanna River on the eastern shore invites some exploring. Steep mountains rise above the lake to the east; to the west are wooded hills and fields. The western shore is wooded and undeveloped. As a flood-control project, the level of the lake is variable depending on conditions.

72. Merli-Sarnoski Lake

Size: 35 acres

Ownership: Lackawanna County

Horsepower restrictions: Electric motors

Scenery: Good

Fishing: Trout, crappie, bluegill

Location: From Carbondale, follow PA 106 towards Clifford for 3.4 miles. Turn left onto Fall Brook Road and follow for .4 mile. Turn left into the park.

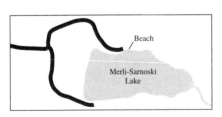

72. Merli-Sarnoski Lake

This small lake is located in a county park of the same name. It is primarily a fishing destination and attracts many anglers when the lake is stocked with trout. Forested hills surround the lake and there is a beach on the northern shore; expect crowds on summer weekends. There are sedges, wetlands, and islets at the western end of the lake. One boat launch provides access. Merli-Sarnoski Park is also a popular destination for mountain bikers.

73. Lackawanna Lake

Size: 198 acres

Ownership: DCNR, Lackawanna State Park

Horsepower restrictions: Electric motors

Scenery: Very good

Fishing: Trout, muskellunge, walleye, pickerel, catfish, largemouth bass

Location: From I-81, take Exit 199 and follow PA 524 west 3 miles. From U.S. 6 and 11, take PA 438 east for 3 miles to PA 407, then turn right to the main park area, or continue straight on PA 438 to a launch at Bullhead Bay.

Lackawanna Lake is a popular paddling destination due to its accessibility, fine scenery, and horsepower restrictions. This scenic lake is surrounded by Lackawanna State Park; forested hills and quaint farmlands also encompass the

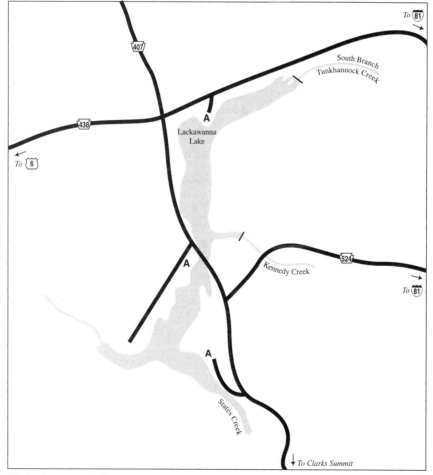

73. Lackawanna Lake

lake. There is access from at least three points in the state park; one near the main entrance into the park along Lake View Drive, another off PA 438, and another at States Creek Inlet off 407.

Some of the most scenic areas are the narrow gorge behind the dam and the South Branch Tunkhannock Creek inlet; the latter features sedges on islands and peninsulas created by sediments deposited by the creek. Do not miss exploring the Kennedy Creek Inlet, where there is a narrow, winding, hemlock-shaded ravine that is exceptionally scenic. The lake is very popular with anglers and there are always a few boats on the lake. However, since horsepower is limited to electric motors, Lackawanna Lake is a serene place to paddle.

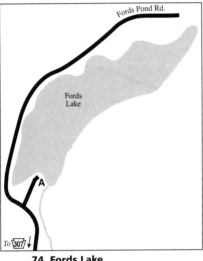

74. Fords Lake

74. Fords Lake

Size: 73 acres

Ownership: PFBC

Horsepower restrictions: Electric motors

Scenery: Good to very good

Fishing: Largemouth bass, bluegill

Location: From Clarks Summit, follow PA 307 north for 3 miles to the small village of Schultzville. Turn right onto Fords Pond Road and follow for .5 mile to an access area on the right.

This small, quiet lake is surrounded by fields and wooded hillsides. When I was small, I would come here to fish for bluegill, anxiously waiting for my bobber to come to life. It is still a popular place for anglers, but also a peaceful lake for local paddlers. There are a few small coves on the northern shore, and the inlet and its wetlands at the eastern end of the lake are worth exploring. The lake is also commonly known as Fords Pond. One launch provides access.

75. Frances Slocum Lake

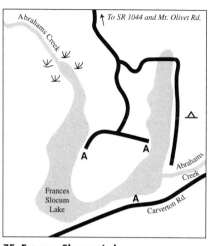

Size: 165 acres

Ownership: DCNR, Frances Slocum State Park

Horsepower restrictions: Electric motors

Scenery: Good to very good

Fishing: Crappie, bluegill, perch, catfish, muskellunge, pickerel, smallmouth bass, large-mouth bass, walleye

Location: From PA 309 at Trucksville, take Carverton Road three miles to a boat launch on the left.

75. Frances Slocum Lake

This U-shaped lake features two boat launches and is surrounded by forested hills. Carverton Road is along the southern shore and can be somewhat busy. The western arm of the lake offers the most isolation, as well as the inlet of Abrahams Creek and its winding inlet of lily pads—the most interesting place to paddle on the lake. It is a great place to view wildlife and wildflowers. The surrounding forest is a mix of pine, hemlock, and hardwoods. The state park offers camping, picnic facilities, and various hiking and mountain biking trails. Frances Slocum Lake is an ideal local paddling destination for those living in the Wyoming Valley.

76. Mountain Springs Lake

Size: 40 acres

Ownership: PFBC

Horsepower restrictions: Electric motors

Scenery: Very good

Fishing: Trout, bluegill, smallmouth bass

Location: From the Lake Jean entrance at Ricketts Glen State Park, follow PA 487 north for 4.1 miles and turn right onto Mountain Spring Road, a dirt road at a PGC sign. Follow this road 5.2 miles to the lake. Avoid a side road to the left that goes to Noxen.

Although it is located just east of famous Ricketts Glen State Park and is well-known by locals, Mountain Springs Lake is largely unknown to the general public. It is a small lake and may not justify a trip on its own, but it is a great lake to paddle in tandem with Lake Jean while visiting Ricketts Glen.

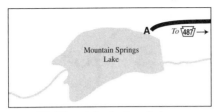

76. Mountain Springs Lake

This oval-shaped lake is set in a wilderness with beautiful forested hills and thick, wild blueberry bushes. The water is remarkably clear and cool, thanks both to its elevation and the mountain streams that feed it. You may even be lucky enough to see the otters that have been known to visit the lake. Mountain Springs Lake is formed by a long, and somewhat dilapidated, concrete dam. There is talk of removing the dam; if it is removed, hopefully it will be rebuilt. Steep wooded mountains rise more than 400 feet above the shore.

Mountain Springs was initially built to provide ice in the late 1800s and early 1900s. Each winter, ice was cut and harvested from the lake and then transported down a railroad to Noxen. The thriving ice industry even supported a town of the same name. With the creation of refrigeration, there was no need for ice and the town and industry disappeared, the forests regrew, and only Mountain Springs Lake remains. Another lake was just downstream but is now drained. Old foundations now lie beneath the canopy of the forests. The old railroad grade to Noxen is now a narrow road that is popular with bicyclists.

77. The Meadows and Beech Lake

Size: The Meadows are approximately 10 acres; Beech Lake is 20 acres.

Ownership: PGC

Horsepower restrictions: Unpowered boats only

Scenery: Very good to excellent

Fishing: Pickerel, largemouth bass

Location: From the Lake Jean entrance at Ricketts Glen State Park, follow PA 487 north for 4.1 miles and turn right onto Mountain Spring Road, a dirt road at a PGC sign. Follow this road 3.3 miles to parking on the left along The Meadows. To reach Beech Lake, hike down Mountain Spring Road a few hundred feet and cross over the outlet of The Meadows. Turn left onto Beech Lake Road, a gated gravel road. After a few hundred feet, where the road turns right, bear left onto a grassy trail marked with yellow blazes. Follow for about 1/5 mile to the north end of the lake.

Of the two lakes in this entry, Beech Lake is the more worthwhile to paddle. It is one of the very few natural, undeveloped lakes in Pennsylvania that can only be reached by hiking. You must follow an old grassy grade to reach the lake. Although it is small, Beech Lake is beautiful and serene; it is surrounded by sedges and a hardwood forest and the terrain is low and rolling. There is beaver activity on the lake. The untouched setting conveys the sense that you are miles from anywhere. Unlike other nearby lakes, the water is relatively clear and free of natural tannin from swamp water. Like Mountain Springs Lake, Beech was once used for ice production and was one of the first lakes used for that purpose due to its higher elevation. The lake was named after the many beech trees that grew around the lake and are still prevalent today. Wood duck houses dot the lake.

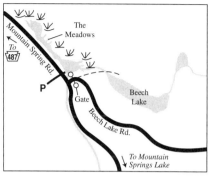

77. The Meadows and Beech Lake

If you are going to visit Beech Lake, you may also decide to paddle The Meadows (also known as Bowmans Marsh), which is located along the road. As its name implies, extensive meadows and sedges surround this pond. Small, narrow inlets on the eastern shore wind into the meadows and sedges. Paddlers will be interested in the couple of beaver lodges that dot the pond. It appears as if The Meadows was once much larger, possibly a pond used for ice production that has since been partially drained. There is an old earthen dam at the outlet.

78. Lake John

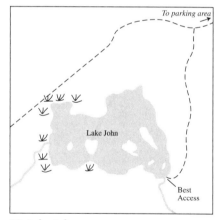

78. Lake John

Size: 75 acres

Ownership: PGC

Horsepower restrictions: Unpowered boats only

Scenery: Excellent

Fishing: Pickerel, largemouth bass

Location: From Dushore, follow PA 487 south through Lopez; after 8 miles, turn left onto Dutch Mountain Road (SR 1002) and follow for 4.2 miles. At McCarroll Corner, turn right onto SR 1001 and follow for .7 mile. Turn right onto Mud Road and follow for .3 mile to a parking area on the right.

You must hike in to reach Lake John; the best access is at the outlet. To reach the outlet, follow the grassy, gated road for almost 2 miles until it reaches the top of a ridge. Before descending, take the unmarked grade to the left down to the outlet.

This is another hidden gem located on the plateaus of North Mountain. You must hike about 2.5 miles along a gated road to reach this beautiful lake set in a wilderness. Being at the top of a plateau, the surrounding topography is low, but thick forests of hardwoods, hemlock, pine, and spruce encompass this lake with bushes of blueberries and mountain laurel. The setting invokes the feeling of being in a place much farther north.

Take time to explore the many islets, extensive wetlands, and sedges with excellent opportunities to observe wildlife, particularly near the outlet. Rock outcrops adorn the western shore. There is a creek inlet at the western end of the lake, and the outlet is at the eastern end, where there is also a beaver dam. The lake is known for its birdlife; when I visited one April I saw kingfishers as they dove into the water after minnows between announcing their presence with a rapid-fire call. I also observed the squabbling of several geese over a mate as timid mergansers kept their distance.

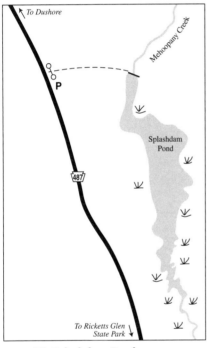

79. Splashdam Pond

79. Splashdam Pond

Size: 86 acres

Ownership: PGC

Horsepower restrictions: Unpowered boats only

Scenery: Excellent

Fishing: Pickerel, largemouth bass

Location: From Dushore, follow PA 487 south for 11.7 miles to a gravel parking lot and wooden PGC sign on the left, with a gate. The parking area is located 5.9 miles north on PA 487 from the Lake Jean entrance at Ricketts Glen State Park.

Splashdam is very similar to its neighbors Lake John and Shumans Lake. Together these lakes offer great paddling opportunities in a wilderness setting far from the crowds that descend on more accessible lakes and rivers. You must hike about .5 mile to reach the northern end of this narrow lake. The setting is untouched and very serene, although an occasional car can be heard on lonely PA 487. This is a shallow lake with extensive sedges, winding channels, bogs, wetlands, and islets; take time to explore the southern end with its meandering channels through wetlands and bogs. Extensive meadows surround the pond. Splashdam is recognized for its superb opportunities to observe wildlife and unique plant life; it is also recognized as an important birding area. To the south, the plateau rises 200–300 feet. The outlet of Splashdam Pond marks the put-in for the Mehoopany Creek, possibly Pennsylvania's finest wilderness whitewater kayaking run.

80. Lake Jean

Size: 245 acres

Ownership: DCNR, Ricketts Glen State Park

Horsepower restrictions: Electric motors

Scenery: Excellent

Fishing: Largemouth bass, muskellunge, bluegill

Location: From Red Rock and PA 118, follow PA 287 north for 4 miles to the park entrance. There are two access areas: one along the park road, immediately after the entrance on the left, and another at the eastern end of the lake accessed by a park road that is 1.7 miles from PA 487.

Like the state park in which it is located, Lake Jean is known for its beauty; it is one of the finest lakes for paddling in Pennsylvania. There are many coves, inlets, and a few small islands. With horsepower restricted to electric motors, Lake Jean is a peaceful place to paddle and is rarely overcrowded. The northern shore and eastern end of the lake provide plenty of isolation. The western shore

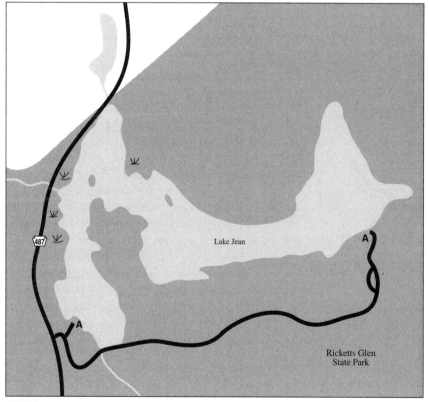

80. Lake Jean

offers many coves, inlets, and wetlands, but PA 287 is close by. Hardwood forests, hemlocks, pine, wetlands, and sedges adorn the shores. Located at an elevation of 2,200 feet, Lake Jean is one of the highest lakes described in this guide in eastern Pennsylvania and offers superb sunsets. Two boat launches, located at the eastern and western ends of the lake, provide access.

I once had the privilege of visiting this lake on a clear, warm October day as the shoreline was engulfed in spectacular foliage of red, orange, and yellow. The still surface perfectly reflected a deep blue autumnal sky that was laced with high cirrus clouds.

81. Lily Lake

Size: 160 acres

Ownership: PFBC

Horsepower restrictions: 60 hp

Scenery: Good to very good

Fishing: Largemouth bass, bluegill, bullhead, perch, pickerel, pike, pumpkinseed, rainbow trout

Location: From Moconaqua, follow PA 239 south for 2 miles. Turn left onto SR 3006 and go 2.6 miles. Bear left onto SR 3005 and follow for .4 mile to the lake. Bear left onto Forest Drive and turn into the parking area.

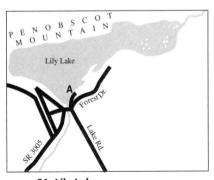

81. Lily Lake

Lily Lake is set at the foot of Penobscot Mountain, a long ridge that stretches east towards Wilkes-Barre. Rolling forested hills also surround the lake, which features a meandering shoreline. There are cottages and docks along the southern shore; the cottages are set back and the lake retains a mostly undeveloped setting. The rest of the shore is undeveloped. Paddlers will want to explore the northern shore along the southern slope of Penobscot Mountain and the coves, wetlands, and sedges at the eastern end of the lake, where there is also a small stream inlet and islets. One boat launch near the dam provides access. Most of the lake is a no-wake zone, except for a section in the western part where 60-horsepower motorboats are allowed.

82. McWilliams Reservoir and Klines Reservoir

Size: McWilliams Reservoir is 184 acres; Klines Reservoir is 31 acres.

Ownership: DCNR, Weiser State Forest

Horsepower restrictions: Unpowered boats

Scenery: Very good to excellent

Fishing: McWilliams Reservoir has bluegill, largemouth bass, pumpkinseed, brown bull-head, and sunfish. Klines Reservoir has pumpkin-seed, bluegill, chain pickerel, yellow perch, and brown bullhead.

Location: Klines Reservoir is located 3.5 miles north of Centralia along PA 42.

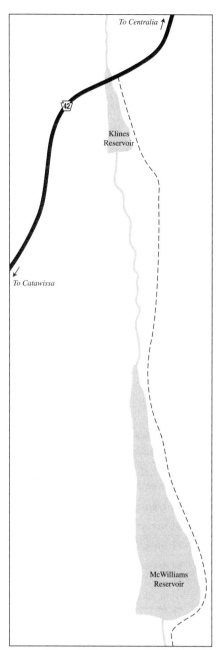

These two reservoirs are described together due to their proximity and similarities. Both are teardrop-shaped and formed by a dam; the widest parts of each are at the dam, and then the reservoirs narrow towards their inlets. What is unique about both is that there is no vehicle access; if you're intrepid and looking for a different paddling experience, you must carry your boat. Klines is located along PA 42, but beautiful Mc-Williams will require a 3-mile hike, one way, along a gated forest road. Both reservoirs are protected by Weiser State Forest and offer beautiful sylvan isolation between the narrow ridges of Little and Big mountains.

Klines is the smaller of the two reservoirs and features a shoreline that meanders gradually. High forested ridges surround the lake, with fine views to the west. A diverse forest, comprised of hemlocks and hardwoods, surrounds the reservoir. There is an inlet that goes under PA 42.

82. McWilliams Reservoir and Klines Reservoir

McWilliams Reservoir is by far the larger and arguably the more scenic. Because of its isolation and inaccessibility, expect to have this peaceful gem all to yourself with glorious views of the forested ridges that rise 800 feet, particularly to the west. Pines and hemlocks border the shoreline. Make sure to visit the winding inlet at the reservoir's eastern end.

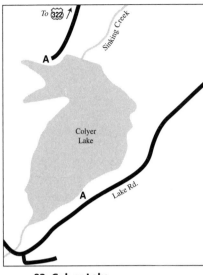

83. Colyer Lake

83. Colyer Lake

Size: 77 acres

Ownership: PFBC

Horsepower restrictions: Electric motors

Scenery: Very good

Fishing: Largemoth bass, bluegill, crappie, pickerel, pumpkinseed

Location: The lake is located 4 miles west of Potters Mills off U.S. 322.

High forested ridges of the Seven Mountains and Rothrock State Forest rise to the south and west of this scenic lake. Colyer offers some of the best, and most convenient, lake paddling near State College. It features coves at its northern end and an inlet at the southern end. Fields lie to the north. Two boat launches provide access. At the time of this writing, the lake had been partially drawn down due to the condition of its dam.

84. Walker Lake

Size: 239 acres

Ownership: PFBC

Horsepower restrictions: Electric motors

Scenery: Very good

Fishing: Largemouth bass, bluegill, bullhead, crappie, northern pike, walleye

Location: From Beaver Springs, follow PA 235 north for almost 5 miles. Turn right onto SR 4018 and follow for a mile. Turn right and follow the road .5 mile, and then turn right again to the access.

Walker Lake is nestled in the ridge and valley region of central Pennsylvania and is a pleasant place to paddle. Walker is a narrow lake that stretches for more than 2 miles along a forested ridge. There is one boat launch, located in the middle of the northern shore. Coves and inlets are located on the eastern half of the lake, where small streams feed the lake at its eastern end and northern shore. Forests surround the lake and a dam is located at its western end. There are fields at the eastern end of the lake. Anglers often try their luck at the lake, which is well-known for its crappie.

84. Walker Lake

85. Faylor Lake

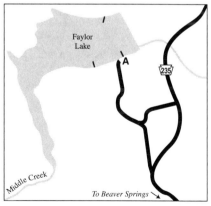

85. Faylor Lake

Size: 140 acres

Ownership: PGC

Horsepower restrictions: No motors permitted

Scenery: Good to very good

Fishing: Bluegill, crappie, pumpkinseed, bullhead, suckers

Location: The lake is located a mile north of Beaver Springs, off PA 239.

This lake is surrounded by low forested hills and several fields. Faylor Lake offers good wildlife watching opportunities with a variety of waterfowl, wading birds, herons, turtles, frogs, and muskrats. Paddlers will want to explore the long inlet of Middle Creek and two smaller inlets along the north shore; there are also a few islets.

86. Memorial Lake

Size: 85 acres

Ownership: DCNR, Memorial Lake State Park

Horsepower restrictions: Electric motors

Scenery: Good

Fishing: Largemouth bass, muskellunge, northern pike, perch, crappie, trout, bluegill, bullhead, catfish, carp, suckers

Location: The state park is located off Exit 85 of I-81. Take Fisher Avenue north and then turn left onto Asher Miner Road and follow for a quarter-mile. Turn left onto Boundary Road and follow into the park.

Memorial Lake lies at the foot of Blue Mountain adjacent to Fort Indiantown Gap. Rolling woodlands and fields surround the lake; the park features the typical amenities of picnic areas, parking, and restrooms. There are a few small coves, particularly on the northern and western shores, where small streams feed the lake. Two boat launches provide access.

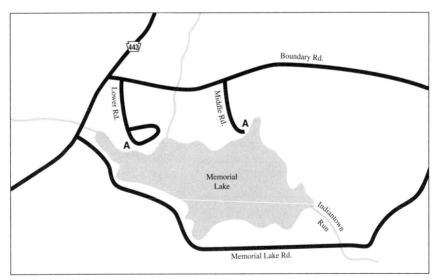

86. Memorial Lake

87. Opossum Lake

Size: 59 acres

Ownership: PFBC

Horsepower restrictions: Electric motors

Scenery: Very good

Fishing: Largemouth bass, crappie, muskellunge, rainbow trout

Location: The lake is 4 miles northwest of Carlisle off McClures Gap Road.

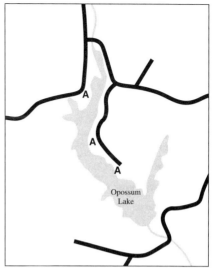

87. Opossum Lake

Opossum Lake is popular with anglers and is a designated big bass lake. Nestled between forested hills and fields, the lake offers pleasant pastoral scenery; the west shore is wooded. The forested ridge of Blue Mountain rises to the north.

The northern end of the lake features many inlets and bays; there is a long inlet near the dam that invites exploration. Three launches provide access to the lake. At the time of this writing, the lake was partially drawn down due to the condition of the dam.

88. Letterkenny Reservoir

Size: 58 acres

Ownership: PFBC

Horsepower restrictions: Electric motors

Scenery: Very good

Fishing: Largemouth bass, crappie, muskellunge, rainbow trout

Location: From Roxbury, follow PA 641 towards Spring Run for 2.3 miles. Turn left onto Lower Horse Valley Road and follow for .5 mile. Turn left and then make a second left down towards the reservoir.

88. Letterkenny Reservoir

This small, hidden gem is nestled between the steep forested ridges of Blue and Kittatinny mountains in northern Franklin County. The lake is a water source for the nearby town of Shippensburg, so the water quality here is very good. Paddlers will particularly enjoy the beautiful mountain scenery and the lake's isolated, undeveloped surroundings. The view of the ridges and water gap to the north is very scenic; these ridges rise to about 1,000 feet above the lake. The lake's southern end features the long inlet of Conodoguinet Creek, coves, and sedges.

89. Pinchot Lake

Size: 340 acres

Ownership: DCNR, Gifford Pinchot State Park

Horsepower restrictions: Electric motors

Scenery: Very good

Fishing: Largemouth bass, catfish, carp, muskellunge, walleye, crappie, sunfish

Location: From I-83, take Exit 35 and follow PA 177 south 7 miles to the park. Alpine Road leads to Boat Mooring No. 3; PA 177 leads to Boat Mooring Nos. 1 and 2.

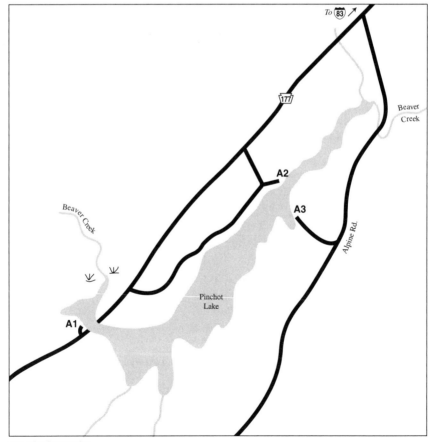

89. Pinchot Lake

Pinchot Lake offers some of the best lake paddling in this part of the state. The lake is surrounded by wooded hillsides; horsepower is limited to electric motors; and there are many bays and coves that invite exploration. There are three public access areas onto the lake. Good places to paddle are in the inlet at boat mooring No. 1 and behind the dam, where the lake narrows. The winding inlet of Beaver Creek is also a good place to paddle.

Like the state park that surrounds it, Pinchot Lake is named after Gifford Pinchot, who served as governor of Pennsylvania and also as a chief forester under President Theodore Roosevelt in what would later become the U.S. Forest Service.

90. Speedwell Forge Lake

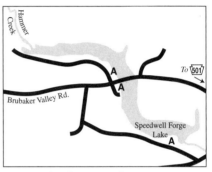

90. Speedwell Forge Lake

Size: 106 acres

Ownership: PFBC

Horsepower restrictions: Electric motors

Scenery: Good

Fishing: Largemouth bass, bluegill, carp, crappie, catfish

Location: From Lititz, follow PA 501 north for 4 miles. Turn left onto West Brubaker Valley Road and follow 1 mile to the lake.

Speedwell Forge Lake attracts many paddlers from the Lancaster area, and for good reason. This narrow lake winds through a scenic countryside of farms and forested hills. The northwestern half of the lake is more wooded, while the southeastern half has more fields and woodlots. Some homes and farms are also in view from the lake. The lake features the inlet of Hammer Creek where the creek has deposited sediments to create a meandering peninsula and islets. The two small coves on the north shore also invite exploration. Speedwell Forge is also known as a fine fishery for bass and panfish. Three launches provide access.

91. Lake Williams and Lake Redman

Size: Lake Williams is 220 acres; Lake Redman is 290 acres.

Ownership: York Water Co. (Leased by York County)

Horsepower restrictions: Electric motors

Scenery: Good

Fishing: Largemouth bass, muskellunge, crappie, catfish, bluegill

Location: The lakes are 3 miles south of York near Jacobus. Access areas can be reached from Water Street and Hess Farm Road.

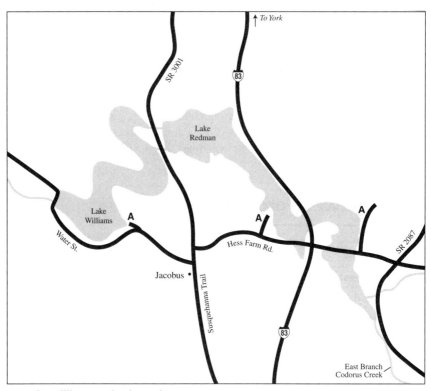

91. Lake Williams and Lake Redman

These lakes, both formed by dams on the East Branch Codorus Creek, are described together because they are located next to each other. Lake Williams is located immediately downstream from Lake Redman. Both lakes are owned by the York Water Company, but York County has a fifty-year lease and the lakes are surrounded by 1,637 acres of William H. Kain County Park. The park features picnic areas, hiking trails, playgrounds, restrooms, parking areas, and a concessionaire. Lake Williams has one boat launch and Lake Redman has two.

Despite being located immediately south of York, the lakes feature fine scenery. Lake Williams is the more secluded of the two and is mostly undeveloped, as it twists between forested hills that rise 220–300 feet. Boating is not permitted at the northern end of Lake Williams.

Lake Redman is narrow and stretches for more than 2 miles between forested hills; it features a variety of coves and inlets. Redman is not as serene since I-83 traverses part of the northern shore and crosses the lake; other roads cross the lake and are near the shore. However, Redman does have a long, narrow inlet at its southern end.

92. Lake Marburg

Size: 1,275 acres

Ownership: DCNR, Codorus State Park

Horsepower restrictions: 20 hp

Scenery: Good to very good

Fishing: Yellow perch, bluegill, northern pike, crappie, largemouth bass, catfish, muskellunge

Location: Codorus State Park is 3 miles southeast of Hanover, via PA 116 and PA 216.

Lake Marburg offers some of the best flatwater paddling in southern Pennsylvania. Rolling hills of forests and fields surround Marburg. The lake features 26 miles of shoreline with numerous coves and inlets, and Round and Long

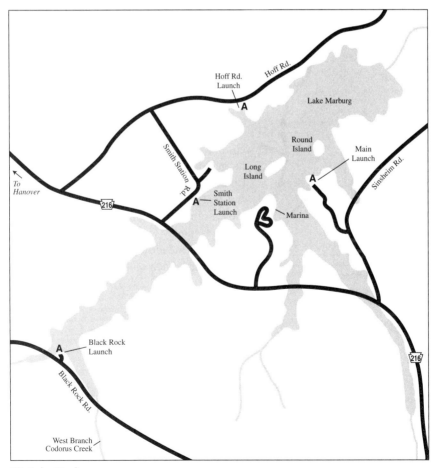

92. Lake Marburg

islands. Paddlers will want to explore the largest coves, known as Wildasin and Marburg Flats. Seven boat launches provide access and there is a marina at the center of the lake. Lake Marburg is surrounded by forested hills and rolling fields. The lake is popular with anglers, but rarely feels overcrowded due to its numerous coves and large size.

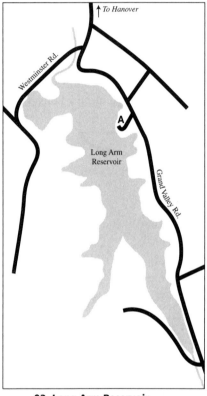

93. Long Arm Reservoir

93. Long Arm Reservoir

Size: Approx. 350 acres

Ownership: Local government

Horsepower restrictions: Electric motors

Scenery: Good to very good

Fishing: Bluegill, brown bullhead, yellow bullhead, black crappie, chain pickerel, pumpkinseed, yellow perch, largemouth bass

Location: From Hanover, follow Westminster Road south for 2.5 miles. Bear left onto Grand Valley Road and follow .5 mile to an access on the right.

This overlooked gem offers scenic pastoral countryside and a winding shoreline with many coves and inlets. Long Arm is in the Conewago Creek watershed, just north of the Maryland border. Paddlers will spend most of their time along the western shore, which is mostly wooded with several coves. Fields and meadows dominate the eastern shore. One launch on the eastern shore provides access.

94. Muddy Run Recreational Reservoir (Muddy Run Lake)

Size: 100 acres

Ownership: Exelon Corporation

Horsepower restrictions: Electric motors

Scenery: Good to very good

Fishing: Largemouth bass, crappie, catfish, carp, muskellunge, bullhead

Location: The access is off Bethesda Church Road West about a mile east of Bethesda.

Set among rolling forested hills and fields, Muddy Run is a fine paddling destination. The lake features a large island and two long, narrow arms that reach to the north and east. The southern shore is forested, while the remainder of the shore features a mixture of woodlands and fields. At the end of the northern arm, there are fields and a campground. Power lines cross over the end of the

94. Muddy Run Recreational Reservoir (Muddy Run Lake)

eastern arm. A fee is required to paddle on the lake, and there is one launch on the western shore.

The setup for this lake is unique; it is formed by a dam that is immediately adjacent to the 1,000-acre Muddy Run Reservoir, which is not open to the public. Muddy Run Reservoir was at one time the largest pump storage facility in the world and is an engineering feat. During off-peak hours, water is pumped up from the Susquehanna River into the reservoir. The water is then discharged back into the river to generate electricity during peak hours.

Muddy Run offers good opportunities for birdwatching, with herons, ospreys, bald eagles, waterfowl, and various songbirds visiting the lake.

95. Octoraro Reservoir

Size: Approx. 750 acres

Ownership: Chester Water Authority

Horsepower restrictions: Electric motors

Scenery: Very good

Fishing: Largemouth bass, crappie, catfish, carp, muskellunge, bullhead

Location: From Oxford, follow PA 472 for 4.3 miles towards Quarryville and turn left onto Spruce Grove Road. Follow for a mile to the fishing headquarters on the left.

Octoraro Reservoir offers some of the best lake paddling in southeastern Pennsylvania. The reservoir is located in a secluded, rural area of farmlands and rolling wooded hills. Octoraro is shaped like a Y where the east and west branches of Octoraro Creek feed the reservoir, which is narrow and meanders in a shallow valley. The reservoir has many coves and inlets, and it is worthwhile to explore the inlets of both branches of Octoraro Creek, where wetlands and sedges adorn islands and sinuous peninsulas were formed by sediments deposited by the creeks. Expect to see many herons, egrets, waterfowl, and osprey as you paddle.

Because the reservoir is privately owned, there are several regulations you must follow. Paddling is prohibited behind the dam and some sections of shoreline are also restricted. Boats must be at least ten feet in length and can only be launched from the fishing headquarters on the western arm of the reservoir. As a result, exploring the northern arm—which is fed by the East Branch Octoraro Creek—requires several hours of paddling. Before paddling, you must pay a fee and receive a pennant. Boating is only allowed between the months of April and October. For more information, contact Fishing Headquarters, 212 Spruce Grove Road, Kirkwood, PA 17536; (717) 529-2488.

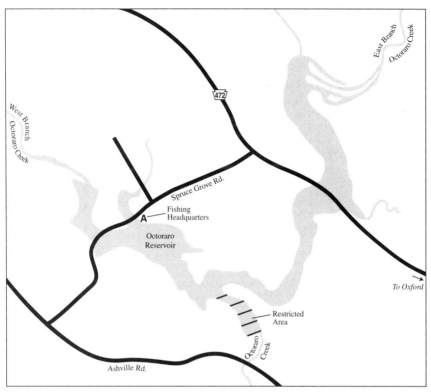

95. Octoraro Reservoir

West Branch Susquehanna River Watershed

The famous West Branch Susquehanna River drains almost 7,000 square miles of north-central Pennsylvania and is widely considered a premier paddling destination. This is a region defined by towering plateaus, through which the river and its tributaries have carved grand canyons and glens. With so much isolation, expansive forests, and plentiful wildlife, this region offers some of the finest paddling in the state.

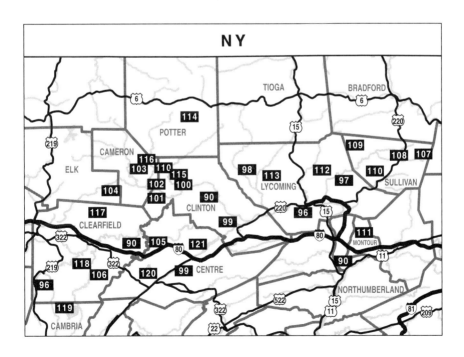

 Rivers and Creeks

96. West Branch Susquehanna River
Cherry Tree to Shawville

Length: 66 miles	

Water level: USGS Bower gauge should be 3.5 feet; USGS Curwensville gauge should be 4.4 feet.

Difficulty: Easy to moderate

Hazards: Various class I–II rapids, dams, possible strainers

Scenery: Fair to good

Highlights: Pastoral scenery, rapids

Fishing: Limited due to acid mine drainage

Camping: Primitive camping is possible but limited due to private land. There is a campground at Chest Falls Campground and Curwensville Lake.

The village of Cherry Tree marks the beginning of the West Branch Susquehanna River Water Trail, and here the river is more like a large creek. The river meanders down a shallow valley with wooded hills and fields; its setting is largely undeveloped, with steep banks and forested lowlands. Burnside provides an access area, and by the time the West Branch reaches Mahaffey, where Chest Creek joins, it grows into a small river.

Paddlers must be aware of Chest Falls, a Class II-plus rapid 2.5 miles below Mahaffey that has the greatest drop of any rapid on the river. Run it center, or use a tough portage on the right. Approach with caution; high flows can swamp or flip a canoe or kayak. Below on the left is Chest Falls Campground, with camping and a private access.

Down to Curwensville Lake, the river is pastoral and attractive. Rhododendrons and forests line the river and the current tends to keep moving amid boulders and cobblestones. Six miles below the Curry Run bridge are Spencer's Rocks and Sheep's Pen, tricky Class II rapids where the river bends right. During the logging era, rafts had difficulty here and would sometimes lose control. In high water, you must avoid these rapids since they become Class IV. Two miles farther marks the backwater of Curwensville Lake, which is described separately in this guide. The lake is attractive and contains hiking trails, a beach, and a campground; it also becomes popular with motorboats in summer. A vehicle portage around Curwensville dam via Lake Drive (T447) and PA 453 to Curwensville is required. In Curwensville, put in at the Irvin Park access, below the Curwensville Timber Dam; it is possible to run the dam, but avoiding it is probably best.

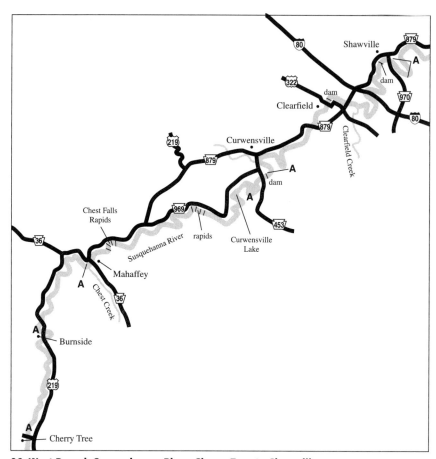

96. West Branch Susquehanna River, Cherry Tree to Shawville

The float down to Clearfield is easy as the river broadens and the current slows. Development becomes a little more common, and the river is straddled by the Clearfield–Grampian Rail Trail. Clearfield is an attractive town with some beautiful old Victorian and colonial homes. You must take out below the Market Street Bridge on the right at the Lower Witmer Park Borough access because of the dangerous Dudley Tonkin Raftsmen's Memorial Dam; this will require a .7-mile vehicular portage. You can also take out at the Nichols Street Bridge downstream for a 200-yard carry around the dam, but you must not use this option in high water since the dam is immediately downstream.

There is development below Clearfield and Clearfield Creek joins from the right. You will notice the beginnings of a canyon, reaching about 400 feet deep, with rising wooded bluffs, cliffs, and steeper terrain. Pass under the high I-80 bridge. Four miles downstream is the dam at the Shawville Electric Generation Plant that must be portaged to the left; a .5-mile portage to the Shawville Grocery, below the PA 970 bridge, is required.

Shawville to Renovo

Length: 66 miles

Water level: USGS Karthaus gauge should be 2.0 feet.

Difficulty: Easy to moderate

Hazards: Moshannon Falls, various Class I–II rapids

Scenery: Very good to excellent

Highlights: Isolation, wilderness canyons

Fishing: Limited due to acid mine drainage

Camping: Numerous primitive campsites, usually where streams and creeks join the river

This section of the West Branch Susquehanna River is one of the finest paddling trips in Pennsylvania, if not the eastern United States. It has many unique qualities. First, it is a sizeable river that flows through a deepening canyon. Second, there is little development, providing a pervasive sense of wilderness and isolation. Third, there are many excellent campsites. The primary drawback is that the river is affected by acid mine drainage, the effects of which become gradually less noticeable as you paddle downstream—so do not expect good fishing. A lonely railroad also follows the river through the canyon. It is unusual to paddle a river of this size without encountering dams, locks, towns, and cities. The river's primary use was as a logging run during the lumbering

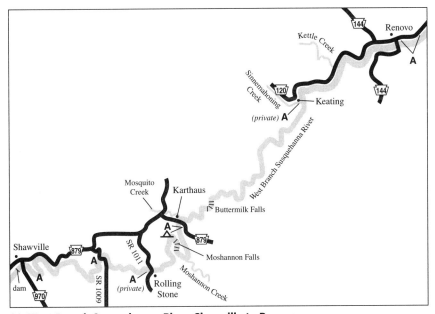

96. West Branch Susquehanna River, Shawville to Renovo

era, but after the forests were decimated, this grand river was largely ignored. It is now enjoying a revival thanks to paddlers; there is even a concerted effort from governmental agencies and nonprofit groups to resolve the acid mine drainage problem.

In my humble opinion, the West Branch Susquehanna River should become a National River, similar to Arkansas's Buffalo River and West Virginia's New River Gorge.

Most paddlers begin at Shawville or the PFBC Millstone Run access. This marks the beginning of this wilderness voyage and avoids a dam upstream. The canyon is initially fairly shallow but grows deeper. Expect a few cottages, usually near the few bridges. Side streams emerge from glens and rush into the river. Down to Karthaus, there are roughly eleven easy rapids. However, the one significant rapid is the ominously named Moshannon Falls, located 1.5 miles upstream from the river's juncture with Moshannon Creek. This Class II rapid is not particularly difficult but can flip a poorly handled canoe. To run this rapid, begin on the right and move into the center. Moshannon Creek, sometimes known as Red Moshannon Creek, joins from the right; on the left are some cottages. Continue 4 miles to Karthaus, where you can take out, or put in, at a DCNR access on the right before the bridge. Primitive camping is also permitted here; Karthaus is a small town but can serve as a resupply point.

The 22-mile stretch from Karthaus to Keating is the true gem of this beautiful river as it winds through an impressive canyon and deep gorges join from either side, carved by clear mountain streams. The canyon reaches a depth of almost 1,000 feet. This section is known for its birdlife and the possibility, although slim, of seeing the wild elk that inhabit the region. There are also many beautiful campsites set in this wilderness. If you have to choose one section of the West Branch, this is it. Be aware of Buttermilk Falls, a Class II rapid, 5 miles below Karthaus.

At Keating, the Sinnemahoning Creek joins from the left. This massive creek is a great float trip in its own right and increases the size of the river. PA 120 follows the river along the left, but there is still little development. The canyon scenery continues to be impressive as the plateaus tower over the river and steep gorges carved by tributaries join from the right and left. Kettle Creek joins from the right and small islands occasionally dot the river. Much of the canyon rim and the side gorges on the right are protected state natural and wild areas that are being managed to become old growth forests. Take out at Renovo, at the PA State Flaming Foliage access on the left below the PA 144 bridge or at PFBC North Bend access, 3 miles farther downstream, also on the left.

Renovo to PFBC Linden Access

Length: 50 miles

Water level: USGS Karthaus gauge should be 2.0 feet.

Difficulty: Easy

Hazards: Lowhead dam at Lock Haven

Scenery: Good to excellent

Highlights: Isolation, canyon scenery

Fishing: Limited due to acid mine drainage

Camping: Primitive campsites possible, but less frequent than the previous section and likely to be on private land

From Renovo to Lock Haven, the valley opens a little, but the West Branch continues to flow through a beautiful canyon carved into a plateau that rises as much as 1,400 feet above the river. The setting is relatively undisturbed since much of the canyon is protected by the Bucktail State Park Natural Area and Sproul State Forest. PA 120 follows the river and you can expect to see more cottages than in the previous section, but development is still scant. As you pass under the PA 120 bridge, look up to the left to see the famous Hyner View. Small islands dot the river with more frequency. Fishing is somewhat poor, but water quality gradually improves as you proceed downstream and the acid mine drainage is diluted.

At Lock Haven, the river leaves the canyon and enters a broad pastoral valley with high forested ridges to the right. The current slows behind a lowhead dam below Jay Street; portage to the right. This dam creates a 3-mile-long pool that is popular with motorboats in summer. The Lock Haven Municipal access is across the river, on the left. Below Lock Haven, the West Branch divides itself

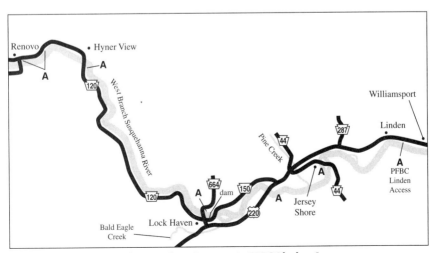

96. West Branch Susquehanna River, Renovo to PFBC Linden Access

as it flows around Great Island and Bald Eagle Creek joins from the right. Continue down the broad valley framed by forested hills to the north and the impressive ridge of Bald Eagle Mountain to the south.

Famous Pine Creek joins from the left. Thanks to the limestone waters of Bald Eagle Creek and the clean waters of Pine Creek, the acid mine drainage in the West Branch is neutralized and water quality improves, making the river superb for smallmouth bass, catfish, and other fish.

Encounter another large island at Jersey Shore as the river winds back and forth across the valley; take the left channel to use the Jersey Shore Borough access, on river left. The river is still scenic as it is encased with a riparian forest of sycamore and silver maple. Below Larrys Creek is the Susquehanna Campground on the left, with camping and a private access. The current slows into the 12-mile-long pool created by the Hepburn Street Dam in Williamsport; motorboats may be common in summer. Take out at the PFBC Linden access above Williamsport.

PFBC Linden Access to Sunbury

Length: 46.5 miles

Water level: USGS Williamsport gauge should be at least 0.0 feet.

Difficulty: Easy

Hazards: Hepburn Street Dam at Williamsport

Scenery: Good to very good

Highlights: Mountain scenery, wildlife

Fishing: Smallmouth bass, muskellunge, catfish, rock bass, trout near side streams

Camping: Primitive campsites are possible, but most land along the river is privately owned.

This section begins as the river passes a long, narrow island and reaches the development of the Williamsport metro area. You will pass Susquehanna State Park with access on the left, and the outlet of Lycoming Creek that can be paddled from the river. The current slows behind the Hepburn Street Dam that you must portage to the left at Williamsport. Pass under a bridge and some old bridge abutments. Upon leaving Williamsport, the PFBC Greevy access is on the left, as well as the Loyalsock Township Riverfront Park, featuring a thick riparian forest. The famous Loyalsock Creek joins from the left, marked by several small islands; the Montoursville Municipal access is a mile farther downstream on the left. The river flows around Racetrack Island; to the right is the imposing forested ridge of Bald Eagle Mountain and to the left is a floodplain with a thick riparian forest with meandering stream outlets.

The West Branch begins to curve to the right as it journeys south. On river left, the Muncy Hills rise over the river below the town of Muncy. On the right,

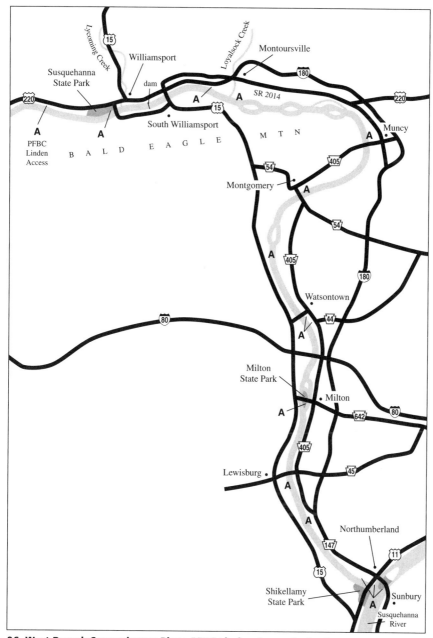

96. West Branch Susquehanna River, PFBC Linden Access to Sunbury

below Montgomery, is a towering forested bluff. The river continues down a pastoral valley and through a corridor of riparian woodlands with distant ridges and occasional islands. Milton State Park is an ideal resting spot and access point; this state park is comprised of two islands in the river. To reach the access area, take the river left channel. The next major town is elegant

Lewisburg, on the right just below the outlet of Buffalo Creek. Lewisburg is a scenic Victorian town with shops and restaurants that is worth exploring. The St. George Street Municipal access is on the right, about a half mile below the PA 45 bridge.

About a mile farther, the current slows in the backwaters of Lake Augusta, an 8-mile pool formed by the Sunbury Fabridam from Memorial Day to late September, when the dam is inflated. Motorboats are very common in the summer. The West Branch passes between the low ridges of Shamokin Mountain and Montour Ridge, flows around a series of islands, and ends at its confluence with the Susquehanna River at Sunbury. The cliffs of Shikellamy State Park rise to the right. Take out at the Pineknotter Park or Northumberland Point access areas on the left; they are located just above and below the U.S. 11 bridge. When Lake Augusta is formed by the fabridam, you can also use the Shikellamy State Park Marina access on Packers Island.

97. Loyalsock Creek

Section: Forksville to Montoursville	
Length: 38 miles	
Water level: USGS Loyalsockville gauge should be 3.5 feet.	
Difficulty: Easy with many riffles (some are long) and a few rapids that can approach Class II in difficulty	
Hazards: A few rapids with large waves in high water; dam below covered bridge upstream of Hillsgrove	
Scenery: Very good to excellent	
Highlights: Beautiful mountain scenery	
Fishing: Smallmouth bass and trout	
Camping: Yes, but limited; many potential campsites are on private land.	

The Loyalsock is one of Pennsylvania's most scenic streams. It begins in western Wyoming County and flows west into Sullivan County. The section from Lopez to Forksville is famous for its incredible scenery and challenging whitewater rapids. The remaining section from Forksville to the creek's mouth at Montoursville is an excellent float stream with impressive scenery. Although it is not nearly as challenging as the upper section, this part of the Loyalsock still contains many riffles and easy rapids that can be long, and at least two rapids that can approach Class II in high water. This creek also has many deep pools that are ideal for fishing or swimming.

Below Forksville, the Little Loyalsock joins from the right, and the creek grows into a small river as it flows up against a steep mountainside on the

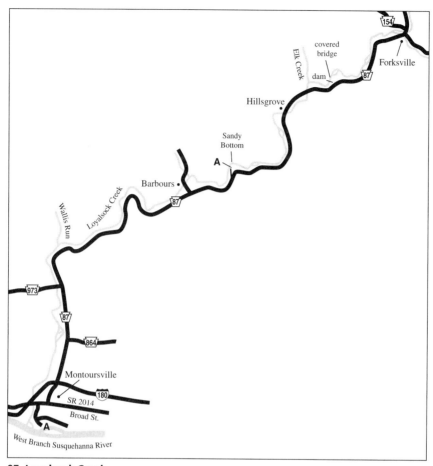

97. Loyalsock Creek

right and fields on the left. Encounter an island 2 miles below the Little Loyal-sock; a mile below the island, the creek makes a sharp right where there is a rapid with large waves in high water. Two miles farther is the beautiful Hills-grove Covered Bridge; immediately below is a low dam that must be portaged. Enjoy some easy rapids before another major tributary, Elk Creek, joins from the right.

Below Hillsgrove, the Loyalsock flows between impressive mountains that rise more than 1,000 feet above the creek. Access, but not camping, is permit-ted at Sandy Bottom on river left, which is part of the Loyalsock State Forest. Below Barbours, development becomes more common along the creek with homes and cottages, although it is not overwhelming and the scenery is still very good. At the juncture with Wallis Run on the right, watch for a large wave that forms in high water that whitewater kayakers enjoy surfing; an easy portage is available to the left. The Loyalsock then leaves the plateau and the remaining 9 miles are through farmlands, wooded hillsides, and occasional homes. Almost a mile below the PA 973 bridge the Loyalsock braids and there are wooded bluffs on the right. Reach the West Branch Susquehanna River and take out a mile farther, at the Montoursville Municipal access on the left. Another possible take-out is a mile below the I-180 bridge where there is a ballfield on the left.

98. Pine Creek

Ansonia to Blackwell

Length: 17 miles

Water level: USGS Cedar Run gauge should be 2.1 feet.

Hazards: Mild whitewater rapids

Difficulty: Easy to moderate

Scenery: Excellent

Highlights: Pine Creek Gorge, Pine Creek Trail, incredible canyon in a wilderness setting, sidestream waterfalls, excellent camping

Fishing: Trout and smallmouth bass

Camping: Public camping available; permit required.

Pine Creek is one of the most popular and beautiful streams in Pennsylvania, boasting breathtaking scenery, excellent camping, and good fishing. It was one of the few rivers in the country to be initially recommended as a national wild and scenic river in 1968. Pine Creek is presently a state scenic river.

This is an excellent trip through a spectacular canyon with sheer cliffs and sidestream waterfalls. Pine Creek is famous for its scenery, and rightfully so. This section is now protected as a state natural area and the Pine Creek Trail, one of the nation's finest rail trails, runs the length of this section on the left.

As you float from Ansonia, the canyon walls rise on both sides. The most spectacular cliffs are above Owasee Rapid, the most difficult, and famous, rapid on the creek. This rapid's reputation is far worse than its bite; it is a strong Class II that can be easily portaged, or avoided, on the left. Avoid the right shore. Just downstream is Split Rock Rapid, another Class II rapid that is best run to the left. The remainder of the trip features easy rapids and riffles. In high water, expect big wave trains that can swamp a canoe. Primitive camping is allowed at Tiadaghton, about halfway down the section on the left. As you continue downstream, the canyon reaches 1,000 feet in depth. Take out at the PA 414 bridge in Blackwell, on the left.

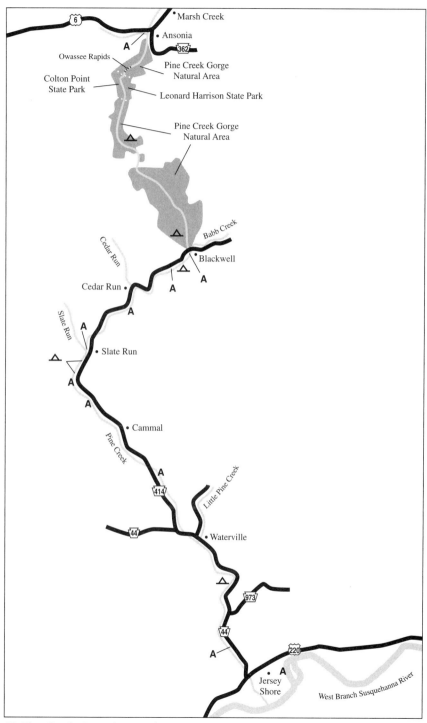

98. Pine Creek, Ansonia to Torbert Canoe Access

Blackwell to Torbert Canoe Access

Length: 36 miles

Water level: USGS Cedar Run gauge should be 2.4 feet.

Difficulty: Easy

Hazards: Swift current and easy rapids

Scenery: Very good to excellent

Highlights: Impressive canyon scenery, Pine Creek Trail, cliffs, good primitive campsites

Fishing: Smallmouth bass and trout

Camping: Public camping is available; a permit is required.

At the scenic village of Blackwell, Babb Creek joins from the left and the canyon opens up to a narrow valley surrounded by towering mountains and plateaus. Fields and a few homes are on the left, while the right has very steep terrain. Pine Creek grows into a small mountain river with many fast currents and riffles. In high water, large waves can swamp a canoe. Fishing is very good with trout and smallmouth bass; the insect hatches, particularly near Slate Run, are famous. The Pine Creek Trail follows the creek and crosses it via railroad bridges. With sublime scenery and good access, this section is an excellent float trip. Occasional homes and cottages are seen, usually on the left.

Public access points are at Rattlesnake Rocks, Gamble Run, Slate Run, Black Walnut Bottom, and Ross Run. Campsites are available a mile below Blackwell and a mile or two below Slate Run. Private land does abut Pine Creek, and there are occasional clusters of homes and cottages, but the creek does not suffer from overdevelopment. The canyon grows most impressive at Waterville, where it reaches 1,400 feet in depth. There are also several islands below Waterville. Camping is available about 6 miles below Waterville, on the right. Homes become more common as you near the end of this section. Pass Torbert Island Natural Area, which protects a rich riparian forest on an 18-acre island. The creek leaves the mountains and gorge and enters an agricultural valley with wooded hills and homes along the shore. Take out on the left at the Torbert Canoe Access, or continue down to the West Branch Susquehanna River and take out at Jersey Shore.

99. Bald Eagle Creek

Sections: Milesburg to Upper Greens Access at Bald Eagle State Park; Eagleville to West Branch Susquehanna River

Length: Milesburg to Upper Greens Access is 8.2 miles; Eagleville to West Branch Susquehanna River is 14.3 miles.

Water level: USGS Milesburg gauge should be about 1.5 feet; USGS Beech Creek Station gauge should be about 6.8 feet.

Difficulty: Easy

Hazards: Lowhead dam below PA 150, strainers

Scenery: Good to very good

Highlights: Wildlife, fishing

Fishing: Trout, smallmouth bass, catfish

Camping: Primitive camping is possible but most land along the creek is privately owned.

This description is separated into two sections since the Foster Joseph Sayers Lake (see page 169) lies along this creek. At Milesburg, Spring Creek joins from the right and Bald Eagle Creek grows into a small river; put in at the park. Spring Creek is a famous trout stream and you can expect superb trout fishing along Bald Eagle Creek. This section is often boatable into June. Paddlers can

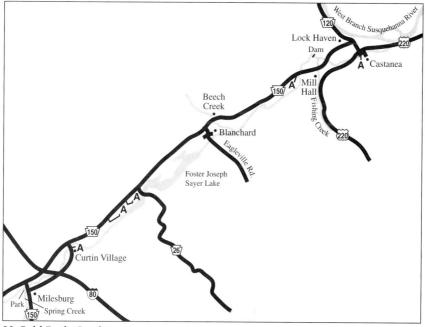

99. Bald Eagle Creek

begin as far up as Port Matilda, but the creek is much smaller and the paddling season is shorter.

The creek flows down a valley with riffles over gravel bars and pools. It marks the dividing line between the plateaus to the north and the narrow forested ridges to the south. It is hard to get a view of either due to the trees that encase the creek. Bald Eagle Creek keeps its distance from U.S. 220 and PA 150, but you can still hear traffic from both; the creek also passes underneath busy I-80. The setting, however, is mostly undisturbed with thick riparian forests.

After passing under I-80, you will pass an island, and soon thereafter, a railroad bridge. To the right is the Curtin Village, a site owned by the Pennsylvania Historical and Museum Commission featuring a restored ironworkers settlement. There is also access at the village on the right below a one-lane bridge, but the current is swift. The creek widens as it enters Foster Joseph Sayers Lake, which offers great views of the surrounding mountains and ridges. Take out at the Upper Greens Run Access on the left.

Below the dam, paddlers begin at the Eagleville Road bridge; the surroundings are pastoral and scenic. The creek often runs in the late fall as the dam begins to draw down the lake. Beech Creek joins from the left and increases the size of Bald Eagle Creek. Two and a half miles downstream from Beech Creek is a large island; watch for strainers in both channels, but particularly the right. Another island lies a mile downstream. The creek slowly bends to the left and passes a series of equidistant islets with trees growing on them; they appear to be old abutments of some kind. Most paddlers take out at the PFBC access on the left before the PA 150 bridge.

If you continue, the scenery is the same, but there is a lowhead dam 1.5 miles below the PA 150 bridge that you should portage. Below the dam the creek braids around a series of islands where there is a risk of strainers. The creek becomes more industrialized and built-up as it flows south of Lock Haven. The best take-out is a developed access at Castanea on the left, or continue down the West Branch Susquehanna River to the PFBC Pine Creek access on the right near Pine Station.

100. Kettle Creek

Section: PA 144 to PA 120	
Length: 18 miles	
Water level: USGS Cross Fork gauge should be about 1.9 feet; USGS Westport gauge should be 2.8 feet.	
Difficulty: Easy	
Hazards: Dam at state park swimming and camping area, possible strainers	
Scenery: Very good to excellent	
Highlights: Canyon scenery, wilderness, isolation	
Fishing: Trout and smallmouth bass. Creek does suffer from mild acid mine drainage in its lower section.	
Camping: Available at Kettle Creek State Park Lower Campground	

This is an excellent float trip through a deep canyon. Put in at the PA 144 bridge as the creek meanders around several islands through a valley surrounded by towering mountains; the terrain on the left becomes particularly steep as the creek curves along the ridge of a plateau. Islands are common on this upper section, so be aware of strainers. In the first 3 miles there are some cottages, but once Kettle Creek enters the state park, the scenery is unspoiled, although there are fields and meadows on one side of the creek or other. This upper section is very popular for trout fishing, so be courteous. The creek enters the Kettle Creek Reservoir (see page 163) with access on the right. This is a relatively small and narrow reservoir bordered by steep mountains. It offers pleasant paddling and a chance to view bald eagles.

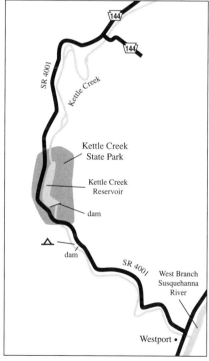

Put back in at the 4001 bridge below the Alvin R. Bush Dam. You will bounce down easy riffles as SR 4001 follows closely to the left and hemlocks and rhododendron adorn the right bank. A mile below the put-in is a dam at the state park's lower campground; portage on the left. SR 4001 follows the creek but usually stays out of sight as the creek flows through a deepening, 1,000-foot canyon that resembles a wilderness. A few boulders are in the creek, but there are no significant rapids. There are several riffles

100. Kettle Creek

and the confines of the canyon inhibit braiding, resulting in a healthy current. The creek flows past thick hemlocks, rhododendrons, and hardwoods. Pass a few homes and take out at the PA 120 bridge before the creek joins the West Branch Susquehanna River.

101. Sinnemahoning Creek

Section: Driftwood to Keating

Length: 15.6 miles

Water level: USGS Sinnemahoning gauge should be 3.3 feet.

Difficulty: Easy

Hazards: None

Scenery: Very good to excellent

Highlights: Impressive canyon

Fishing: Smallmouth bass, trout

Camping: No established, recognized sites, but there is potential for camping.

This creek is formed where its two branches, Bennett Branch and Driftwood Branch, join at the small village of Driftwood. The Sinnemahoning, and the three tributaries that form it, flows through the canyon country of Pennsylva-

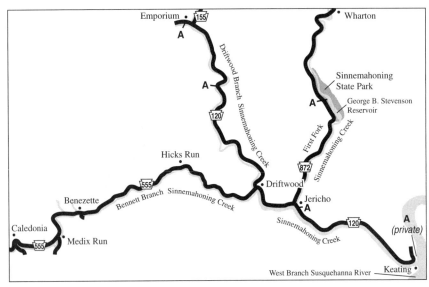

101. Sinnemahoning Creek
102. First Fork Sinnemahoning Creek
103. Driftwood Branch Sinnemahoning Creek
104. Bennett Branch Sinnemahoning Creek

nia, with scenery that easily rivals the more famous Pine Creek Gorge. The canyon formed by the Sinnemahoning reaches 1,200 feet in depth with incredibly steep canyon walls, particularly along river right where there are thick forests of hemlock and pine. Much of this canyon below Jericho is protected by the Bucktail State Park Natural Area, comprising the more scenic section of this creek. While there are occasional cottages and small villages, development is scant. PA 120 stays along river left while a lonely railroad is on the right. The First Fork Sinnemahoning Creek joins at Jericho on the left and swells the huge Sinnemahoning even larger.

A half-mile below Jericho is a large island; islands are not very common on this creek. Down to Keating there are three more islands and a cluster of small islands a few miles before the West Branch Susquehanna River. Much of this section is forested, although there are a few fields and meadows, usually on the left.

The Sinnemahoning is a massive creek and would easily qualify as a river. There are no rapids, but there are several easy riffles formed by the cobblestone bottom. This tends to be a shallow creek so be sure you paddle with enough water. Take out at Keating where there is a private access, or continue down the West Branch Susquehanna River to Renovo.

102. First Fork Sinnemahoning Creek

Section: Wharton to Sinnemahoning

Length: 20 miles (including George B. Stevenson Reservoir)

Water level: USGS gauge at Stevenson Dam should be 1.0 foot.

Difficulty: Easy

Hazards: Strainers

Scenery: Very good

Highlights: Impressive canyon, isolation

Fishing: Trout, smallmouth bass

Camping: Primitive sites are possible, but most of the land along the creek is privately owned.

At Wharton, the East Fork joins the First Fork and the latter grows into a sizeable mountain stream worthy of your canoe or kayak. As you will soon notice, this creek likes to braid around islands, so you must keep an eye out for strainers. There are no significant rapids; just cobblestone riffles and occasional deep pools. PA 872 stays mostly on the right and that is where you'll typically see cottages; however, most of the creek is undeveloped and isolated. Meadows are common and the creek often abuts the steep forested slopes of mountains; there are also several islands. The creek is particularly scenic and isolated for the last 4 or 5 miles before reaching George B. Stevenson Reservoir, which essentially divides the creek in two sections—a 10.5-mile segment from Wharton to the reservoir and an 8-mile section from the reservoir to Sinnemahoning. The reservoir, located in Sinnemahoning State Park, is described on page 164. There is an access to take out on the right on the reservoir.

Below the dam, the impressive canyon grows deeper, reaching 1,300 feet in depth. Cottages are more common; there is even a long footbridge that crosses the creek. The First Fork becomes very wide and potentially shallow depending on flows from the dam. There isn't as much flat bottomland as above the dam since the canyon is deeper and narrower, but there are still a few meadows and fields. Take out at the PA 120 bridge in Sinnemahoning.

103. Driftwood Branch Sinnemahoning Creek

Section: 19.6 miles

Length: Emporium to Driftwood

Water level: If Sinnemahoning Creek is running, so should Driftwood Branch.

Difficulty: Easy

Hazards: Possible strainers

Scenery: Very good to excellent

Highlights: Impressive canyons

Fishing: Trout, smallmouth bass

Camping: Primitive camping is possible, although most land along the creek is privately owned.

At Emporium, the West Creek and Portage Creek join to swell the Driftwood Branch into a canoeable mountain stream. Upon exiting the town you immediately enter an impressive, twisting canyon that is partially protected by Elk State Forest and Bucktail State Park Natural Area. The canyon reaches a depth of approximately 1,200 feet as you near Driftwood and smaller gorges carved by the numerous side streams add to the scenery. About two-thirds of the way down, the creek bends around an oxbow loop with an impressive arching canyon wall along river right.

This is an easy creek with gravelly bends and no significant rapids. Watch for strainers at islands and where the creek braids. PA 120 crosses the creek twice, but mostly stays along the left shore. Most of the creek is forested, although there are a few fields and homes, particularly below Hunts Run. Driftwood Branch is probably the most scenic of the Sinnemahoning's primary tributaries and it has largely escaped the ravages of acid mine drainage. Take out at Driftwood.

The Driftwood Branch is the site of the popular Cameron County Canoe and Kayak Classic, a race held every April for the past thirty-five years.

104. Bennett Branch Sinnemahoning Creek

Section: Caledonia to Driftwood

Length: 24 miles

Water level: If Sinnemahoning Creek is running, so should Bennett Branch.

Difficulty: Easy

Hazards: Possible strainers

Scenery: Good to very good

Highlights: Isolation, canyon

Fishing: Limited due to acid mine drainage

Camping: Primitive camping is possible, although most land along the creek is privately owned.

Bennett Branch begins high on the abused plateaus of Clearfield County where there are strip mines. Not surprisingly, the creek suffers from acid mine drainage. But don't let this deter you from paddling this hidden sojourn—below Caledonia, the creek grows more and more beautiful as it meanders down a canyon that reaches 1,200 feet in depth. The canyon walls are incredibly steep along river right, particularly between Grant and Driftwood.

This is an easy creek with riffles and no difficult rapids; there are also occasional islands. Much of the shore is undeveloped and forested, except for some cottages and fields. PA 555 follows on the left shore, but it is lightly traveled. Bennett Branch also flows through Pennsylvania's elk country, so you may be lucky enough to see one of the animals as you paddle.

105. Moshannon Creek

Section: Peale Bridge to West Branch Susquehanna River

Length: 12 miles, and an additional 3 miles on the West Branch Susquehanna River to Karthaus

Water level: No online gauge available. The creek is generally running from early to mid-spring.

Hazards: Rapids that can reach Class II above PA 53 bridge, numerous riffles, possible strainers

Difficulty: Easy to moderate

Scenery: Excellent

Highlights: Isolated gorge with hemlocks and rhododendron

Fishing: Limited due to acid mine drainage

Camping: Although primitive camping is possible along Moshannon Creek, most land is privately owned or on state game lands where camping is not permitted.

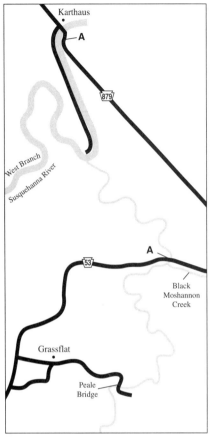

105. Moshannon Creek

The Moshannon Creek drains a vast portion of Pennsylvania's central plateau. Below Philipsburg, it begins to cut a gorge and offers fun Class II whitewater between the Peale Bridge near Grassflat and PA 53. This section is very scenic as the creek flows through an isolated, 400-foot-deep canyon; it is also home to the popular "Red Mo," canoe and kayak race every March. If you paddle this stretch, expect many riffles that grow into relatively straightforward Class II rapids as you near the PA 53 bridge. The section between Peale Bridge and PA 53 requires paddlers with experience; a sprayskirt is strongly recommended.

Otherwise, begin at the PA 53 bridge, a popular put-in. This last stretch of the Moshannon features riffles and easy rapids, plus extra flow from Black Moshannon Creek, which joins at the put-in. This beautiful creek winds its way through an impressive wilderness gorge with steep wooded bluffs of hemlock and pine. The banks are often overgrown with jungles of rhododendron.

The Moshannon is affectionately known as the "Red Mo," or Red Moshannon, and it is easy to see why. Thanks to acid mine drainage, the creek has an orange-red tint, although the clean waters of the Black Moshannon offer some alleviation by diluting the mine drainage. At its terminus, the creek abruptly joins the far larger West Branch Susquehanna River. Here, the Moshannon's canyon is more than 600 feet deep. There is a private take-out across the river on the left. But if the Moshannon is high enough to paddle, the West Branch should have enough current to easily take you down to Karthaus, and it makes for an easier shuttle.

106. Clearfield Creek

Section: Madera to PA 153

Length: 22 miles

Water level: USGS Dimeling gauge should be 3.7 feet.

Difficulty: Easy

Hazards: Possible strainers

Scenery: Good to very good

Highlights: Isolated gorge

Fishing: Limited due to acid mine drainage

Camping: Primitive camping is possible, but private land borders most of the creek.

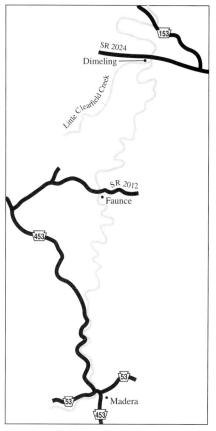

106. Clearfield Creek

The Clearfield drains the high Allegheny Plateau, and like many streams in the area, it is affected by acid mine drainage. If it weren't for such drainage, Clearfield Creek would make an excellent paddling stream that would be a great regional tourist asset. Nevertheless, the section from Madera to PA 153 is a surprisingly scenic and isolated paddle that makes the Clearfield worthy of your attention. The creek burrows into a shallow gorge that reaches 500–600 feet in depth; the mining scars common in the area are largely out of view. The forest is often comprised of hemlock, pine, rhododendrons, and, of course, various hardwoods. For most of this section, no roads follow the creek—only a lonely railroad keeps it company and there are only three bridges between the put-in and take-out.

The creek meanders frequently, but there are relatively few islands or braids. Clearfield is an easy paddle with riffles over gravel bars and long pools. Strainers are always a possibility.

The isolation ends where the Little Clearfield Creek joins from the left. The gorge opens up to a rolling valley with more development and mining activity. Take out at the PA 153 bridge or the SR 2024 bridge just below the juncture of Little Clearfield Creek.

⛵ Lakes, Ponds, and Reservoirs

107. Shumans Lake

Size: Approx. 55 acres

Ownership: PGC

Horsepower restrictions: Electric motors, non-powered boats

Scenery: Excellent

Fishing: Largemouth bass, pickerel

Location: From Dushore, follow PA 487 south through Lopez; after 8 miles, turn left onto Dutch Mountain Road (SR 1002) and follow for 2.6 miles. Turn right onto Rouse Pond Road and follow .1 mile to a gate on the left. There is no parking area, so park off the road the best you can. Hike along the gated road down to the lake.

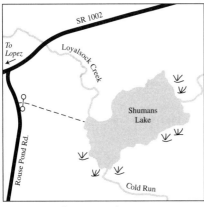

107. Shumans Lake

Shumans is hidden in a wilderness, protected by State Game Lands 66. To reach the lake, you must hike in .3 mile along a gated forest road to a gravel launch at the outlet, where there is also a small beaver dam. The setting is completely untouched and is very scenic; the lake is located on top of a plateau of rolling forest lands. Spruce, hemlock, and pine grow along the shore and evoke the feeling of a lake you would expect to find farther north. Wetlands and sedges line the shore, particularly along its eastern end where the Loyalsock Creek enters. Large meadows of grass and sphagnum moss are along the western and southwestern shores. Cold Run enters from the south. This is a shallow lake with beaver activity, tree stumps, and lily pads. Not surprisingly, Shumans offers great fishing for largemouth bass and excellent wildlife and birdwatching opportunities.

I will never forget standing on the shore and watching a majestic bald eagle circle above the lake before it pivoted and dove to the surface, where it caught a fish. This is a sight you would never see on a lake crowded with cottages, docks, and motorboats.

108. Sones Pond

Size: 20 acres

Ownership: DCNR

Horsepower restrictions: Electric motors

Scenery: Very good

Fishing: Largemouth bass, crappie, muskellunge, rainbow trout

Location: From Laporte, follow PA 154 north for 1.8 miles and turn right onto Rock Run Road. Follow this road for 2 miles and bear left at a Y; the pond is .1 mile farther.

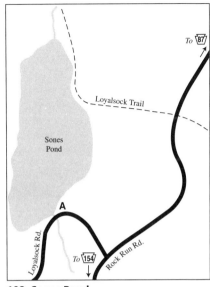

108. Sones Pond

Sones Pond is a serene place to paddle; it is located on top of the plateau, surrounded by the Loyalsock State Forest. Wetlands and sedges are located at its northern end, and the pond is surrounded by a scenic forest of hemlock, pine, and hardwoods. The water is often so calm it provides a perfect reflection of the forest and sky. There is one launch and picnic facilities at the pond's outlet. The Loyalsock Trail follows the northeast shore of the pond.

109. Bearwallow Pond

Size: Approx. 30 acres

Ownership: DCNR

Horsepower restrictions: Electric motors

Scenery: Very good to excellent

Fishing: Largemouth bass, crappie, muskellunge, rainbow trout

Location: From Hillsgrove, follow Mill Creek Road for 3.9 miles and turn right onto Camels Road. Follow for 1.9 miles and bear right onto Bear Wallow Road; the pond is .4 miles farther.

Like Sones Pond, Bearwallow is a peaceful gem set high on the plateau in the Loyalsock State Forest. Paddling here gives the impression that you are miles from anywhere, and in some sense you are; to reach the pond you must follow dirt forest roads for several miles. This small pond features towering white pine and hemlock trees. The northern end features wetlands and sedges where small streams feed the pond. Dead tree stumps dot the lake and lily pads float on the

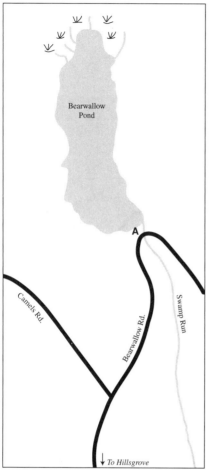

109. Bearwallow Pond

surface. This combination, along with clear water, makes Bearwallow Pond perfect for wildlife and fish. There are picnic tables and a parking area at the pond's outlet.

110. Hunters Lake

Size: 119 acres

Ownership: PFBC

Horsepower restrictions: Electric motors

Scenery: Excellent

Fishing: Bluegill, chain pickerel, pumpkinseed, brook trout, rainbow trout, yellow perch

Location: From U.S. 220, turn left onto PA 42 north at Muncy Valley towards Eagles Mere. After almost 3 miles, reach the top of the plateau and turn left on Brunnerdale Road and follow .75 mile to a parking area at the dam, or .5 miles farther to a boat launch on the right.

Hunters Lake is a best-kept paddling secret in Pennsylvania. It is one of the most scenic lakes in the state, with clear water and a sense that you are miles from civilization. The beauty invokes a serene wilderness. The lake is surrounded by forested hills and mountains; the shoreline is undeveloped with the exception of the boat launch and dam. There is an excellent view to the southeast of North Mountain's summit. The lake is popular with anglers and it's best to paddle elsewhere during the beginning of trout season.

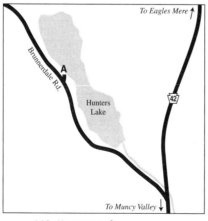

110. Hunters Lake

111. Lake Chillisquaque

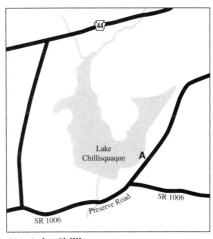

Size: 165 acres

Ownership: Pennsylvania Power and Light (PP&L)

Horsepower restrictions: Electric motors

Scenery: Good to very good

Fishing: Northern pike, largemouth bass, channel catfish, bullhead, perch, walleye, crappie, muskellunge

Location: The lake is located 4 miles northeast of Washingtonville and is accessible from PA 54 and PA 44.

111. Lake Chillisquaque

This scenic lake is set among wooded hills and farmlands; to the north are the Muncy Hills. The lake was built to provide a backup source of cool water for a power plant. Chillisquaque offers many small coves and bays that invite exploration. Boating into Goose Cove is not permitted, nor is boating permitted from March 15 to April 30 due to waterfowl migrations. The lake is known for its incredible diversity of waterfowl, with more than fifty species visiting the lake. Two hundred species of birds have been documented at the lake and surrounding preserve. There is one boat launch located at Heron Cove.

112. Rose Valley Lake

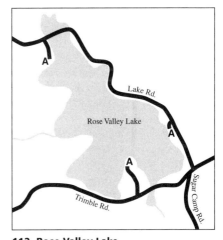

Size: 389 acres

Ownership: PFBC

Horsepower restrictions: Electric motors

Scenery: Good to very good

Fishing: Muskellunge, crappie, largemouth bass, bluegill, bullhead, perch, pickerel, walleye, pumpkinseed

Location: From U.S. 220/I-180, follow PA 87 north for 4 miles and turn left onto PA 973. Follow for 2 miles to Warrensville, where you turn right onto SR 2022 and follow for 2 miles before turning right onto Sugar Camp Road. Follow this road for 3.2 miles to Trimble Road on the left, which you can follow for .4 mile to the south

112. Rose Valley Lake

access. To reach the east and north accesses from Sugar Camp Road, turn left onto Lake Road; the east access is .3 mile on the left and the north access is 1.3 miles on the left.

Rose Valley Lake is nestled in a beautiful mountain valley surrounded by farms and forested hills. It is hard to imagine Williamsport is located only 10 miles to the south. To the north, south, and west of the lake, mountains rise to almost 1,000 feet above the water and enhance the scenery of the lake. The meandering shoreline features large bays with a few small coves and inlets. The northern cove and the western and southern shores are the most scenic. Rolling farm fields and a few houses are also in sight of the lake. Rose Valley Lake is fairly wide and open, so wind can be a problem. Rose Valley is known for its fine fishing, particularly for largemouth bass. Three boat launches provide access.

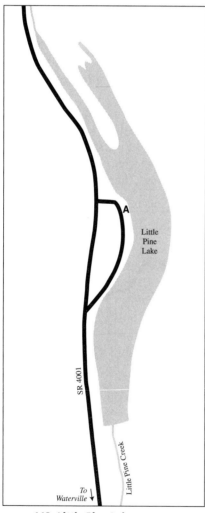

113. Little Pine Lake

Size: 94 acres

Ownership: DCNR, Little Pine State Park

Horsepower restrictions: Electric motors

Scenery: Very good to excellent

Fishing: Smallmouth bass, pickerel, sunfish, catfish, perch, brook trout, brown trout, rainbow trout

Location: From Waterville and PA 44, follow SR 4001 for 4 miles to the park; from PA 287 at English Center, follow SR 4001 7 miles to the park.

The surrounding plateaus that rise more than 1,200 feet are the highlight of Little Pine Lake. The beautiful mountain scenery makes this lake an excellent place to paddle during fall foliage. Like several other lakes in north-central Pennsylvania, Little Pine is formed by what appears to be an oversized dam. The best places to paddle are the coves and the inlet of Little Pine Creek at the northern end of the park.

113. Little Pine Lake

114. Lyman Lake

Size: 45 acres

Ownership: DCNR, Lyman Run State Park

Horsepower restrictions: Electric motors

Scenery: Good to very good

Fishing: Trout

Location: From U.S. 6 at Galeton, turn onto SR 2002 (West Street) and follow for 5.4 miles. Turn right onto Lyman Run Road and follow 2.7 miles to the boat launch and mooring area on the left.

114. Lyman Lake

Lyman Run State Park is nestled in the vast Susquehannock State Forest. With beautiful mountain scenery and superb water quality, small Lyman Lake is a hidden gem for paddlers. The surrounding mountains rise almost 700 feet above the lake and the clean, cool mountain water makes the lake an excellent trout fishery. Paddlers will want to explore the western end of the lake, where there are spruce trees, wetlands, and sedges along the inlet of Lyman Run. One boat launch provides access.

115. Kettle Creek Reservoir

Size: 167 acres

Ownership: DCNR, Kettle Creek State Park

Horsepower restrictions: Electric motors

Scenery: Very good to excellent

Fishing: Trout, largemouth bass, brown bullhead, crappie, bluegill, smallmouth bass, pickerel

Location: The park is along SR 4001, 7 miles north of Westport and PA 120.

This reservoir is formed by the Alvin R. Bush Dam, a USACE flood-control project that seems oversized for the lake. As a result, be

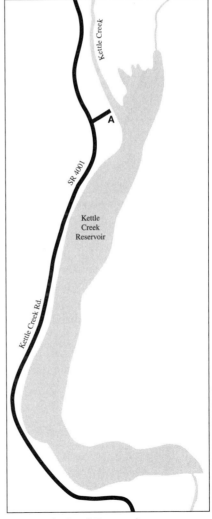

115. Kettle Creek Reservoir

aware that the lake level is changeable. DCNR manages the reservoir and surrounding state park, which features picnic areas, a beach, and a playground. Kettle Creek Reservoir is a narrow L-shaped lake that offers excellent scenery as steep mountains rise more than a thousand feet above the shore. The eastern shore is undeveloped and paddlers will want to explore the inlet of Kettle Creek, a famed trout stream (see page 151). One boat launch provides access.

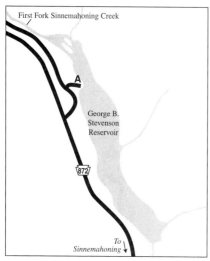

116. George B. Stevenson Reservoir

Size: 142 acres

Ownership: DCNR, Sinnemahoning State Park

Horsepower restrictions: Electric motors

Scenery: Excellent

Fishing: Trout, crappie, bass, sunfish, bluegill, pickerel, perch, muskellunge

Location: From PA 120 at Sinnemahoning, follow PA 872 north for 8 miles to the state park.

116. George B. Stevenson Reservoir

Like Kettle Creek Reservoir to the east, this reservoir is formed by a USACE flood control dam; as a result, the lake level is changeable. DCNR manages the reservoir and surrounding state park, which features picnic areas. The reservoir is almost 2 miles long and offers small coves along its undeveloped eastern shore. The scenery is superb as the surrounding mountains rise to almost 1,200 feet above the reservoir. Do not miss an opportunity to explore the inlets of First Fork Sinnemahoning Creek and Lushbaugh Run at the northern end of the reservoir, where there are wetlands and sedges. The prime attraction, however, is the magnificent bald eagles that visit and nest at the reservoir. Please keep your distance from the nests. One boat launch provides access.

117. Shaggers Inn Shallow Water Impoundment

Size: Approx. 30 acres

Ownership: DCNR, Moshannon State Forest

Horsepower restrictions: Unpowered boats only

Scenery: Good to very good

Fishing: Smallmouth bass, largemouth bass, bluegill, crappie

Location: The impoundment is 4 miles east of Parker Dam State Park, near the intersection of Caledonia Pike and Shaggers Inn Road.

117. Shaggers Inn Shallow Water Impoundment

Set in the vast Moshannon State Forest, Shaggers Inn is a hidden gem offering superb opportunities to observe wildlife in an isolated setting. The surrounding topography is low and rolling with forests and extensive meadows. Sedges and wetlands lie along the shore, and there are islets that are worth exploring. The impoundment also has dead trees still standing in the water that are bleached white, creating a surreal appearance. As the name implies, Shaggers Inn is shallow; as a result, it is a good warmwater fishery. It was built to provide habitat for migrating waterfowl and is also home to beavers and ospreys.

The state forest has another similar impoundment at Beaver Run, but kayaking is discouraged there since it is a wildlife viewing area.

118. Curwensville Lake

Size: 790 acres

Ownership: USACE

Horsepower restrictions: Unlimited horsepower

Scenery: Good

Fishing: Smallmouth bass, largemouth bass, muskellunge, bluegill, crappie, walleye, northern pike

Location: From Curwensville, follow PA 453 south towards Madera for 3.2 miles and turn right onto Lake Drive; follow signs to the boat launch.

Curwensville Lake is formed by a flood-control dam on the West Branch Susquehanna River. Even though the lake is owned by the USACE, it is managed and operated by the Clearfield County Recreation and Tourism Authority.

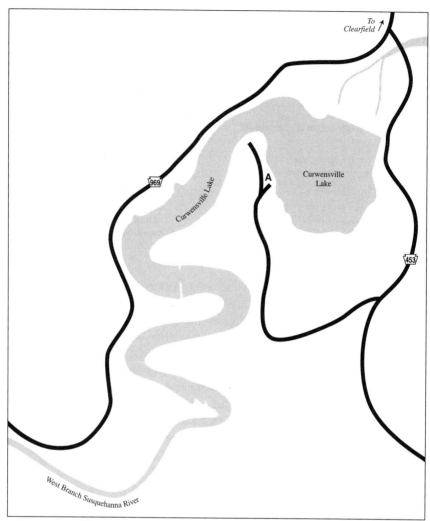

118. Curwensville Lake

The surrounding land features a beach, picnic facilities, campgrounds, and hiking trails; the shoreline is mostly undeveloped as wooded bluffs rise to 300–400 feet above the lake. There are fees to paddle on the lake. Curwensville receives heavy powerboat traffic in the summer.

The lake meanders underneath rolling fields and forested bluffs and widens at the massive dam. The northern section of the lake behind the dam tends to receive the most powerboat traffic. Paddlers will want to explore the southern end of the lake as it narrows to the West Branch Susquehanna River's inlet. Here you will find the most isolation and best opportunities to view wildlife.

119. Glendale Lake

Size: 1,600 acres

Ownership: DCNR, Prince Gallitzin State Park

Horsepower restrictions: 10 hp

Scenery: Good to very good

Fishing: Smallmouth bass, largemouth bass, crappie, muskellunge, bluegill, perch, pike

Location: From U.S. 219 at Carrolltown, follow SR 4015 to Patton. At Patton, follow SR 1021 (Beaver Valley Road) to the state park. Most of the access areas to Glendale Lake are located off SR 1021. From PA 53, follow SR 1026 at Frugality, or SR 1021 at Flinton.

Glendale Lake is located high on the Allegheny Plateau and is surrounded by low wooded hills and fields. This large lake also features eight public access areas. Due to horsepower restrictions, Glendale Lake is rarely overcrowded with powerboats, although fishing and pontoon boats are popular. High winds can cause some problems for paddlers.

With miles of undeveloped shoreline and numerous bays and inlets, Glendale is an excellent paddling destination. The bays and inlets associated with Wyerough Run, Killbuck Run, Mud Lick, and Slate Lick Run are prime places to

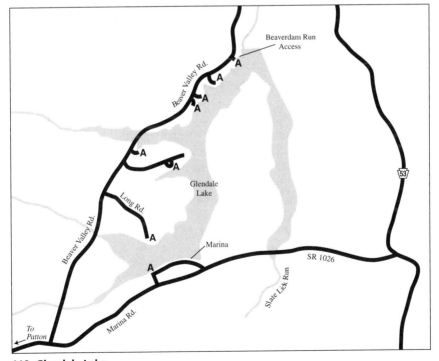

119. Glendale Lake

paddle. Slate Lick and Wyerough in particular offer winding inlets and wetlands that are home to plentiful plant and animal life; both are isolated. Slate Lick represents a large arm of the lake that offers isolation and wilderness along its forested slopes. The best ways to access Slate Lick are from the Beaverdam Run and McKee's Run launch areas.

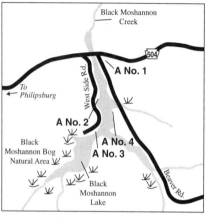

120. Black Moshannon Lake

120. Black Moshannon Lake

120. Black Moshannon Lake

Size: 250 acres

Ownership: DCNR, Black Moshannon State Park

Horsepower restrictions: Electric motors

Scenery: Excellent

Fishing: Largemouth bass, sunfish, bluegill

Location: The park is located along PA 504, 11.5 miles west of Unionville and 9 miles east of Philipsburg.

Black Moshannon Lake is one of the premier paddling destinations in Pennsylvania. This exceptional lake offers some of the finest opportunities to observe wildlife and unique plant life; much of the lake is protected as the Black Moshannon Bog Natural Area. Thanks to the lake's altitude and northern exposure, it is home to many plants and animals that are typically found in more northern climates. The lake is visited by ospreys, tundra swans, wood ducks, and great blue herons. Turtles often relax on the tree stumps that adorn the surface; lily pads cover much of the lake. Water lilies, watershield, bladderwort, sundew, and pitcher plants are also common. Expansive wetlands and sedges border the lake; the southwestern arm of the lake, at the inlet of Black Moshannon Creek, features an extensive sphagnum moss bog. Pine, spruce, hemlock, and hardwoods comprise the forests that surround the lake, bogs, and marshes. Four boat launches provide access.

121. Foster Joseph Sayers Lake

Size: 1,730 acres

Ownership: DCNR, Bald Eagle State Park

Horsepower restrictions: Unlimited horsepower

Scenery: Good to very good

Fishing: Crappie, bluegill, largemouth bass, smallmouth bass, catfish, walleye, yellow perch

Location: The lake is accessed from PA 150, from Exit 158 of I-80, or from Mill Hall along U.S. 220.

This large lake is 8 miles long, has 23 miles of shoreline, and features seven access areas. There are many inlets and small bays that invite exploration; of particular interest to paddlers are Hunters Run Cove and Bald Eagle Creek's inlet. The southwestern part of the lake offers many small coves and a line of

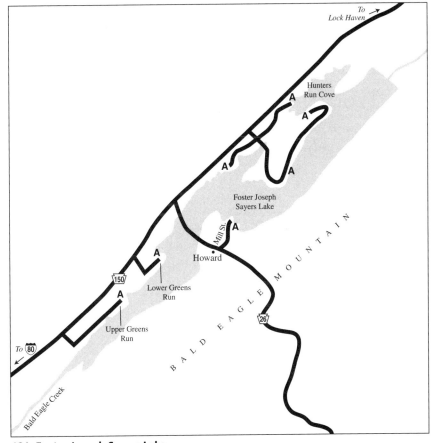

121. Foster Joseph Sayers Lake

long, narrow islands. You'll notice roads have a tendency to just disappear into the lake, since they were submerged by the dam. The small town of Howard can also be seen from the lake.

The lake is popular with anglers and powerboats, so expect traffic on summer weekends. Rolling wooded hills and fields rise more than 400 feet above the lake to the north; in the distance are high plateaus and ridges that add to the beauty of the lake. The towering ridge of Bald Eagle Mountain rises 1,000 feet above the lake along its southern shore. Foster Joseph Sayers Lake is located on the boundary between the ridge and valley region to the south and the Allegheny Plateau to the north.

The lake is a flood-control project, so it is drawn down every November, and is raised to summer pool by the middle of May. When the lake is drawn down, expect exposed shorelines with rock and mud. The level of the lake may vary throughout the year depending on conditions.

Juniata River Watershed

The Juniata drains southcentral Pennsylvania from the Allegheny Front to the Susquehanna River at Duncannon. Along the way it slices through the high, linear ridges and broad valleys that characterize this region. Some of the most impressive water gaps in the state are located along this river.

Not surprisingly, the Juniata was a great transportation asset to early settlers since it provided convenient access to the west. First a canal was built, remnants of which still lie along the river. Next came the railroad, which remains to this day. Thanks to the route provided by the Juniata through the mountains, the Allegheny Portage and the famous Horseshoe Curve were built to cross over the Allegheny Front.

For the paddler, the Juniata is an excellent river to explore with rural scenery, high forested ridges with rock outcrops, deep water gaps, fine camping, and great fishing.

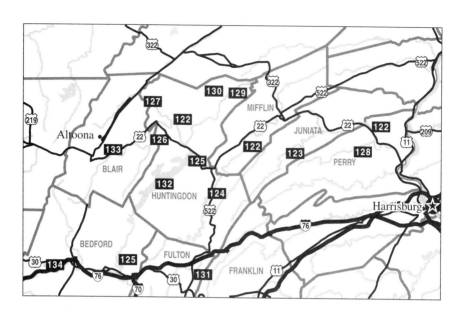

 Rivers and Creeks

122. Juniata River
Huntingdon to Lewistown

Length: 47.1 miles

Water level: USGS Huntingdon gauge should be 1.5 feet; USGS Mapleton gauge should be 2.5 feet; USGS Lewistown gauge should be 3.1 feet.

Difficulty: Easy

Hazards: None. Several riffles and a few old eel weirs; watch for a railroad trestle two miles below Mill Creek with tricky currents.

Scenery: Very good

Highlights: Jacks Narrows, wildlife, bald eagles, good fishing, mountain scenery

Fishing: Smallmouth bass, muskellunge, trout

Camping: Several islands are open to primitive camping. There are other potential sites, though they are likely to be on private land. A few commercial campgrounds border the river.

The beautiful Juniata holds a special place in my heart. I lived for two years in Lewistown and I spent countless hours fishing and paddling the "Blue Juniata" with my friend Steve Davis. The river offers some of the best paddling and primitive camping in the state. It is unique in that it showcases incredible mountain scenery, precipitous water gaps, river-friendly towns, and a phenomenal diversity of plants and animals. I'm a rather poor angler, but even I could catch more than my share of smallmouth and rock bass on the Juniata. Take the time to get to know this wonderful river—it is well worth it.

The Juniata actually begins 6 miles above Huntingdon, at the confluence of the Little Juniata and Frankstown Branch, but Huntingdon is the most convenient access since it avoids the Warrior Ridge Dam upstream. After leaving Huntingdon, paddle through rural scenery where the river is largely surrounded by forest. The Raystown Branch joins from the right at a PFBC access, swelling the river. The Juniata becomes more isolated with steep forested slopes and thick riparian forests. The river is surprisingly secluded despite the adjacent railroad and U.S. 22. The river is bordered by forests and a few fields; several islands also dot this stretch. Impressive Jacks Mountain rises downstream like a wall with talus slopes.

Be aware of the railroad trestle about 2 miles below Mill Creek which can create eddies and swells that can flip a canoe—take the middle span. Pass

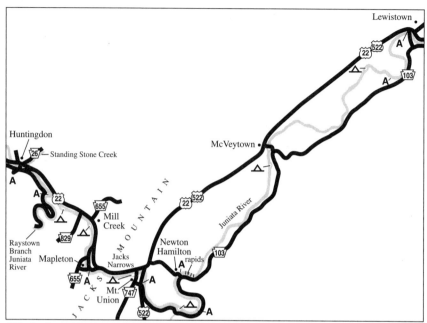

122. Juniata River, Huntingdon to Lewistown

Mapleton to the right, with access on the left below the SR 2020 bridge at a municipal park. The Juniata now enters the incredible Jacks Narrows, one of the most impressive water gaps in the state at nearly 1,400 feet in depth. Massive talus slopes adorn the steep mountain buttresses. On the left slope is the Standing Stone Trail and the famous Thousand Steps offering awe-inspiring views.

As you leave the gap, Mt. Union is on the right and Aughwick Creek also joins from the right; the PFBC Shawmut access is below on the right. At Newton Hamilton, there is a PFBC access on the left; below are easy ledge and cobblestone rapids. From here to Lewistown, the Juniata flows through a broad valley bordered by distant ridges. A string of riparian forests frame the river; also expect to see fields and cottages. The river is broader and the current slower with riffles that will require dragging in low water. The Juniata is divided by a large island at McVeytown. There is a PFBC access on the right about 7 miles above Lewistown, and access in Lewistown on the left below the PA 103 bridge.

Pine Creek below Slate Run

Shohola Lake

Shumans Lake, above; Raystown Branch Juniata River, below.

Beaverdam Run Reservoir, above; Splashdam Pond, below.

Beltzville Lake

Bearwallow Pond

Brady's Lake, above; Tobyhanna Lake, below.

Tunkhannock Creek, above; Sones Pond, below.

Lake Jean, Ricketts Glen State Park, above; Raystown Lake, below.

Susquehanna River at Vosburg Neck

Stephen Foster Lake, Mt. Pisgah State Park

Lewistown to Duncannon

Length: 44 miles

Water level: USGS Lewistown gauge should be 3.1 feet.

Difficulty: Easy to moderate

Hazards: Occasional ledge rapids

Scenery: Good to very good

Highlights: Wildlife, good fishing, the Narrows, easy rapids below Newport

Fishing: Smallmouth bass, rock bass, muskellunge, walleye

Camping: Private campgrounds are along the river and several small islands are open to primitive camping.

Below Lewistown, Kishacoquillas and Jacks creeks join from the left. Many fertile limestone streams like these empty into the Juniata, creating some of the best fishing opportunities in the state. The river then flows through the Narrows, a beautiful canyonlike section with high ridges, vast talus slopes, and rock outcrops. The Narrows are nearly 1,600 feet deep, making them one of the deepest gorges in the state. Busy U.S. 322 is on the left, but the scenery is still very good. Despite the rugged terrain, the river is generally mild, except for one riffle that bends into the left bank near the beginning of the Narrows.

After flowing through the Narrows, the Juniata enters a broad valley; in the distance Tuscarora Mountain stands like a giant wall. A PFBC access is on the left at Arch Rock and there is a large island above Mifflintown. Tuscarora Creek joins from the right at Port Royal. Another PFBC access is on the left at Mexico. Sections are broad as the river flows over grass, so expect to do some extra paddling. Between the Mexico and Thompsontown PFBC accesses the river flows

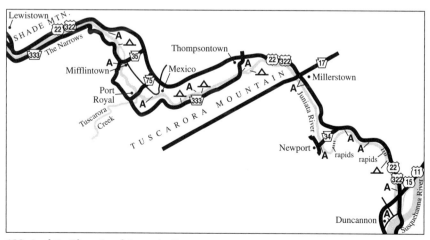

122. Juniata River, Lewistown to Duncannon

along Tuscarora Mountain and features several small islands that are open to primitive camping.

The Juniata flows through a small water gap as it turns south into Perry County. A highlight of this river is its diversity of wildlife; on one late-summer trip I saw countless herons, egrets, turtles, and waterfowl; I also saw otters, muskrats, bald eagles, ospreys, and red-tailed hawks. Paddle through another valley with low hills and ridges. There is an access below the PA 34 bridge at Newport, on the right. The river bends to the left and encounters its first ledge rapid with a rock in the middle; run it to the left. Development also increases along the river. From here to the take-out at Amity Hall, the Juniata cuts through low ridges with several short ledge-formed rapids that are fairly easy to run, but can tip a canoe in high water, so scouting is advisable. The rugged riverbed is scenic and the swift water and deep pools make for some great fishing, so take your time.

The best take-out is at the Amity Hall PFBC access on the left. The river continues on for 2 miles to the massive Susquehanna River, where the transition from the moderately sized Juniata is impressive. The private Riverfront Campground is on the right at the mouth of the Juniata. You can also continue a mile down the Susquehanna River to Duncannon on the right where there is an unestablished access under the railroad trestle in town.

123. Tuscarora Creek

Section: PA 850 to Juniata River (Port Royal)

Length: 23 miles

Water level: USGS Port Royal gauge should read approximately 200–250 cfs.

Difficulty: Easy

Hazards: Strainers

Scenery: Very good

Highlights: Academia-Pomeroy Covered Bridge, excellent pastoral scenery

Fishing: Trout, smallmouth bass, rock bass

Camping: Primitive camping may be possible, but almost all land along the creek is privately owned.

This creek may be among the state's finest for pastoral and farmland scenery. The creek curves and winds incessantly through a manicured valley bordered by the towering ridges of Tuscarora Mountain to the south and Shade Mountain to the north. Many of the farms in this beautiful valley are owned by Amish. Lower ridges and rolling wooded hills rise within this valley and border the creek, creating steep wooded bluffs.

The first thing you must know about Tuscarora Creek is that it likes islands, and it loves to braid. As a result, you must pay extra careful attention for strainers. Between PA 850 and Academia, there are many islands, and at least three significant braids. The first is immediately below the put-in as the creek wraps around a large island; the main channel is to the right. The next is two miles farther where the creek divides around a long island, and braids between smaller islands thereafter. Three miles farther the creek flows around another large island. There are several smaller islands in between.

123. Tuscarora Creek

One of the creek's highlights is the Academia-Pomeroy Covered Bridge, the longest in the state at 278 feet, 9 inches. Below the bridge is another island and braid; the left channel may have an old dam or small ledge, so use caution. Below here, the creek stays in a single channel with few islands.

The scenery is dominated by well-maintained farms and wooded bluffs and hills, with few cottages or homes crowding the shore. Giant beech and sycamore trees often rise over the creek. There are many bridges to shorten your trip. The creek does have some limestone influence from caves and springs, so you may have luck fishing for trout.

Below the PA 75/PA 333 bridge in Port Royal there are a few old bridge abutments. Pass under a railroad bridge and take out at Port Royal (at the Juniata River) or continue down the river for 2 miles to the PFBC Walker Access, on the left.

124. Augwhick Creek

Section: SR 2004 to PA 103 (Juniata River)

Length: 24.6 miles

Water level: As an approximate correlation, USGS Saxton gauge on the Raystown Branch Juniata River should read 3.0 feet.

Difficulty: Easy

Hazards: Strainers

Scenery: Good to very good

Highlights: Pastoral scenery, wooded bluffs

Fishing: Trout, smallmouth bass

Camping: Primitive camping is possible, but most land along the creek is privately owned.

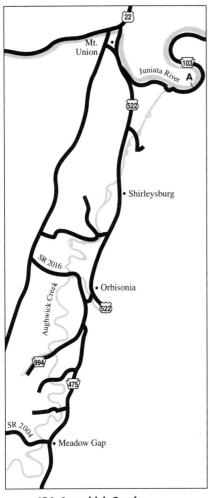

124. Augwhick Creek

Aughwick Creek offers a pleasant cruise among the rugged hills and high ridges of Huntingdon County. This creek meanders around hills, among farm fields, and between steep forested slopes. In places, the ridges rise to about 300 feet above the creek and there are also shale cliffs and outcrops like those found along the Raystown Branch Juniata River.

Despite flowing among farms, this is a surprisingly undeveloped creek as it is usually bordered by trees, and the steep slopes are completely forested. The water quality is fairly good, with the biggest pollution culprit being agricultural runoff. Aughwick does have some limestone influence, so you may have luck fishing for trout.

There are no significant rapids, just riffles over gravel bars and cobblestones. The creek is unique for its size in that there are many islands; some of them are quite large. There are islands every 1 to 3 miles and it is here you can expect the greatest likelihood of strainers. One place to keep an eye out is near Shirleysburg where there may be strainers at the beginning of a large island that partially blocks the main channel to the right. Overall, Aughwick does not have major strainer problems.

SR 2004 is the first bridge crossing below the juncture of Little Aughwick Creek and Sideling Hill Creek, which combine to form Aughwhick Creek. Other possible places to put in are PA 994 at the bridge, or a school after the bridge on the right, and SR 2016 near Orbisonia. PA 103 is the last possible take-out before the Juniata River, or you can continue 2 miles down the river to the PFBC Shawmut access on the right.

125. Raystown Branch Juniata River

Section: Bedford to Juniata River

Length: From Bedford to Weaver Falls access at Raystown Lake, the distance is 58 miles. Below the dam, Corbin's Island access to the Juniata River is 9 miles.

Water level: USGS Saxton gauge should be 1.7 feet.

Difficulty: Easy

Hazards: Two lowdams in Bedford, easy rapids, possible strainers

Scenery: Fair to very good

Highlights: Shale cliffs and ledges, good fishing, Warriors Path State Park, bald eagles

Fishing: Smallmouth bass, muskellunge, trout, rock bass, walleye

Camping: There are potential campsites, usually on private property, and a few private campgrounds along the first half of this section.

The Raystown Branch is the largest tributary of the Juniata River. This river meanders wildly through the ridges and valley of southcentral Pennsylvania, featuring oxbow loops, deep pools, and shale cliffs. The put-in is at the Fort Bedford Park in Bedford where there is a lowdam; another is .25 miles downstream. It is best to portage both dams. This section has both commercial and residential development, and traffic from the busy Pennsylvania Turnpike and U.S. 30 do detract from the sense of isolation.

Dunning Creek is a relatively large tributary that joins from the left under the turnpike bridge. U.S. 30 crosses just a short distance downstream. Here the river flows into a 900-foot-deep water gap through Evitts Mountain; there are rock outcrops and talus slopes above on the left. Residential areas follow on the left, and then the right, sides of the river. Below the SR 2019 bridge, the river is undeveloped, wooded, and scenic for several miles. The Raystown Branch slices through Tussey Mountain via a 1,200-foot-deep water gap at Everett before development returns. There is access on the left in Everett. Below Everett there are some homes on the left, while the right is wooded and attractive. U.S. 30 then returns on the left, while the right features 200-foot bluffs cloaked with hemlocks and hardwoods.

Below the U.S. 30 bridge, the river meanders between farmlands and steep wooded bluffs that rise a few hundred feet. Occasional strings of cottages begin to appear on one shore or the other, but most of the river is undeveloped. The Raystown Branch becomes very attractive, with a mosaic of farms, fields, distant ridges, and wooded bluffs along the bends. As you proceed downstream, the scenery improves. As the river flows against some ridges, there are shale bluffs with rare plants and animals. Below Cypher, the river enters a scenic gorgelike setting as it squeezes between two ridges. PA 26 joins along the left below Hopewell and occasional cottages return. The surrounding terrain is steep with 600-foot-high ridges. About three miles below Hopewell is Riddles-

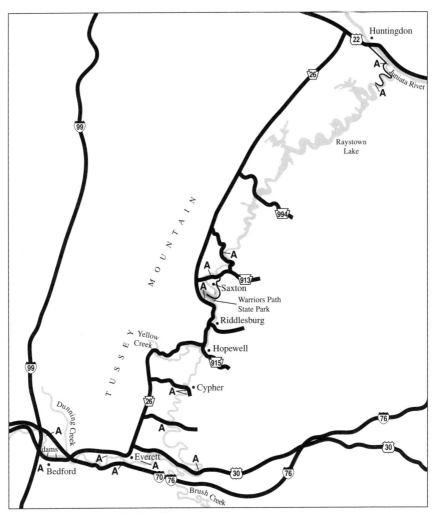

125. Raystown Branch Juniata River

burg; make sure to visit the Riddlesburg Coke Ovens on the right. There are forty-eight beehive brick coke ovens that were built in 1868. Below Riddlesburg, the mountain scenery grows even more impressive as the steep forested ridges rise more than 1,000 feet above the river.

The first take-out is at Warriors Path State Park, where there are towering shale cliffs. Four miles further is the Saxton VFW Park on the right; this is probably your last and best take-out option. If you continue on to the Weaver Falls access, you will pass an old dam that is breached and the current then slows as the river enters Raystown Lake.

The remaining section below Raystown Dam is an excellent one-day float or an extension of a trip on the Juniata River. There is great access at both the put-in and take-out. Put in at the Corbin's Island access, where there is also camping. This section of the river is relatively untouched and is very scenic with high ridges, particularly rugged Terrace Mountain, which rises on the right almost 1,300 feet. Bluffs and cliffs along the bends of the river rise more than 300 feet. The rugged terrain is impressive. Expect the river to be broad with easy riffles and occasional pools. Bald eagles are also a common sight. Take out on the left at the PFBC Point access, which is located at the juncture with the Juniata River.

126. Frankstown Branch Juniata River

Section: Flowing Springs to Juniata River

Length: 26 miles

Water level: USGS Williamsburg gauge should be 3.5 feet.

Difficulty: Easy

Hazards: Possible strainers

Scenery: Very good to excellent

Highlights: Mountainous terrain, isolation, Indian Chief Rock

Fishing: Smallmouth bass, trout, catfish, muskellunge

Camping: Camping is possible on a few islands; most land along the river is privately owned.

The Frankstown Branch, sometimes encompassed by a forest canopy, offers the intimacy of paddling a small river. This is an easy river with riffles over gravel bars and long, peaceful pools. The surrounding mountainous terrain is often impressive. Between the put-in and Williamsburg, the river has cut an impressive 1,000-foot-deep water gap through Lock and Canoe mountains. Huge rock outcrops and talus slopes adorn the water gap on the left. Two-and-a-half miles farther on the left is Indian Chief Rock, a towering precipice said to resemble an Indian chief in a headdress.

There is access at Williamsburg on the right and a small island half a mile downstream is suitable for primitive camping. The scenery improves below Williamsburg as the river flows down a narrow, isolated valley with the towering forested ridge of Tussey Mountain to the right; Canoe Mountain rises in the distance on the left. Bluffs and cliffs rise 200–400 feet above the river around the bends. Between Williamsburg and Water Street, the Lower Trail, a superb rail trail, follows the river and is often in sight. The Mid State Trail, Pennsylvania's longest hiking trail, also follows this rail trail. Don't miss the Etna Furnace about 7 miles downstream from Williamsburg on the left; an access is also located near the furnace.

After a long oxbow loop, the river becomes more isolated since no roads follow; only the Lower Trail provides company. The river enters a canyonlike set-

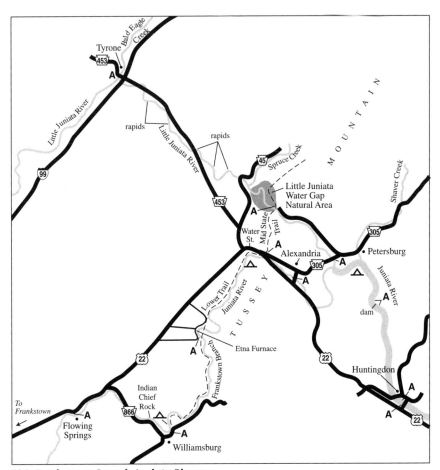

126. Frankstown Branch Juniata River
127. Little Juniata River

ting as Tussey Mountain steeply rises 1,000 feet on the right with talus slopes. Four miles downstream is another small island that is suitable for primitive camping. As you near U.S. 22 at Water Street, the noise of traffic becomes apparent. The Frankstown Branch bends right and slices through another water gap in Tussey Mountain. The surrounding terrain is rugged with huge talus slopes and another access on the left. The river now enters a more pastoral setting with distant forested mountains and ridges. The access at the PA 305 bridge in Alexandria is the last on the river. You can continue onto the Juniata and take out at Petersburg or Warrior Ridge Dam.

127. Little Juniata River

Section: Tyrone to PA 305

Length: 15 miles

Water level: USGS Spruce Creek gauge should be 3.0 feet.

Difficulty: Moderate

Hazards: Class II rapids, possible strainers

Scenery: Very good to excellent

Highlights: Little Juniata Water Gap Natural Area, superb fishing, mountain scenery, railway stone viaducts

Fishing: Trout, smallmouth bass

Camping: There is possible primitive camping on several islands downstream from Spruce Creek. Camping is not permitted in the Little Juniata Water Gap Natural Area.

The Little Juniata, affectionately known as the "Little J," is a very special river. It offers world-class trout fishing, beautiful scenery, enjoyable rapids and riffles, and fine water quality. Be aware that this river is very popular with trout anglers, so be sure to share the water. Ironically, the Little Juniata was once heavily polluted by a paper mill in Tyrone, but the mill closed and the river became clean, making it an ideal paddling destination. A fairly busy railroad follows the river and there are several impressive stone viaducts that cross it.

The Little Juniata has more rapids than most rivers in this guide, so you should have some paddling experience and a spray skirt is recommended. There are approximately seven Class I–II rapids, depending on flows. These rapids are simple and are formed by cobblestones and small ledges. Watch for strong eddy lines where the river makes sharp bends and tricky currents underneath the viaducts. Strainers are always a potential problem. Do not try to paddle this river in high water in a recreational kayak or canoe. In summer, people enjoy floating down the river in inner tubes.

At Tyrone, Bald Eagle Creek joins from the left and the river passes through an 800-foot-deep water gap between Brush and Bald Eagle mountains. Two miles below the put-in, at Ironville, there is a rapid with a strong hydraulic that can be scouted on the right. The river enters a shallow gorge that is set below the pastoral farmlands. There are some homes around Ironville, but most of the creek is wooded and undeveloped. Down to Birmingham, enjoy the isolation as the Little Juniata flows through a canyon more than 600 feet deep. The isolation continues down to Spruce Creek, where there are a few homes and fields.

Where Spruce Creek joins from the left, the highlight of the river begins as it winds through the impressive Little Juniata River Water Gap Natural Area. This 1,300-foot-deep water gap slices through Tussey Mountain with superb scenery as massive talus slopes adorn the mountains. This is one of the few water gaps in the state without a road or highway. The Mid State Trail passes through the gap and climbs Tussey Mountain to the north with phenomenal views. It was in this gap that I caught my first trout on a fly.

Expect to see a lot of wildlife, particularly herons, egrets, mergansers, kingfishers, and the occasional bald eagle or osprey. As you paddle across the pools, countless trout will be rising to the surface for their next meal.

As you near the end of the gap, there is a primitive access and parking area on the left. The river leaves the water gap and passes through pastoral farms with easy rapids and riffles. Islands become more common and wooded hills and many fields comprise the scenery. There are occasional homes and cottages along the river. Take out at the PA 305 bridge.

Access is often a major concern for paddlers; after all, if you can't access a river or lake, you can't paddle it. Several years ago, the Little Juniata was the center of a landmark court battle when a private fishing club decided to close off a section of the river from public use by posting "no trespassing" signs and claiming it was private property. Wealthy private clubs take their trout streams seriously and nearby Spruce Creek, another famous trout stream that is a tributary to the Little Juniata, has long been cordoned off by private clubs. The club was sued by state agencies and thankfully the court ruled against it, finding the Little Juniata River was a historically navigable waterway that is held in public trust by the state of Pennsylvania for the enjoyment of all. And the "Little J" is surely a river you should take the time to enjoy.

🛶 Lakes, Ponds, and Reservoirs

128. Holman Lake

Size: 88 acres

Ownership: DCNR, Little Buffalo State Park

Horsepower restrictions: Electric motors

Scenery: Good to very good

Fishing: Largemouth bass, catfish, bluegill, walleye, muskellunge, trout

Location: From Newport, follow PA 34 south for a mile and turn right onto Little Buffalo Road and follow into the park. The access is off State Park Road.

This small lake is set in a narrow valley between low, forested ridges that rise approximately 500 feet above the lake. The terrain is surprisingly varied, particularly to the north where several small streams have carved ravines that descend towards the lake. A diverse forest of hemlock, pine, and hardwoods covers the hills above the lake. A good place to explore is the inlet of Little Buffalo Creek; there are few other coves and bays on

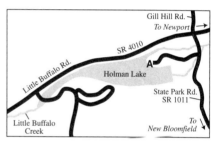

128. Holman Lake

this mile-long lake. Because of limestone influence, Holman Lake offers fine opportunities for fishing. One boat launch near the dam provides access.

129. Whipple Lake

Size: 22 acres

Ownership: DCNR, Whipple Dam State Park

Horsepower restrictions: Electric motors

Scenery: Good

Fishing: Trout, largemouth bass, crappie, bluegill

Location: From the junction of PA 46 and PA 26 at Pine Grove Mills, follow PA 26 south for 6 miles and turn left at the park sign. Follow the road 1 mile into the park. The boat launch is at the northwest shore.

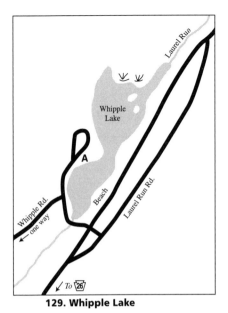

129. Whipple Lake

This small lake is surrounded by Whipple Dam State Park in the Rothrock State Forest. A forested ridge rises to the south and north. The lake features a few small islets and wetlands and the inlet of Laurel Run at its eastern end, where paddlers will want to spend most of their time since the western section can become very busy in summer. Much of the southern shore is comprised of a beach and picnic facilities. There is one boat launch on the northern shore.

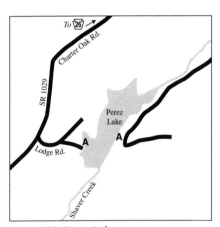

130. Perez Lake

130. Perez Lake

Size: 72 acres

Ownership: Pennsylvania State University

Horsepower restrictions: Electric motors

Scenery: Good to very good

Fishing: Largemouth bass, crappie, bluegill, yellow perch, pumpkinseed

Location: From the juncture of PA 46 and PA 26 at Pine Grove Mills, follow PA 26 south for 4.1 miles to SR 1029 on the right. Follow for 3.1 miles to the east entrance and turn left onto Lodge Road. Bear right at the Y to reach the boat launch.

This placid lake is located within the Stone Valley Recreation Area, home to the Shavers Creek Environmental Center and Penn State University's Experimental Forest. Low, rolling forested hills surround the lake, while the towering ridge of Tussey Mountain is to the north. The inlet of Shaver Creek is at the eastern end of the lake and the northern shore features small coves and bays. There is a fee to launch a canoe or kayak on the lake. At the time of this writing, Perez Lake was drawn down for repairs to its dam.

131. Cowans Gap Lake

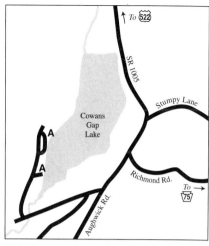

131. Cowans Gap Lake

Size: 42 acres

Ownership: DCNR, Cowans Gap State Park

Horsepower restrictions: Electric motors

Scenery: Good to very good

Fishing: Trout, smallmouth bass, largemouth bass, perch, bluegill

Location: From U.S. 30 at Fort Loudon, follow PA 75 north to Richmond Furnace; turn left onto Richmond Road and follow to the park.

This small lake is located at a gap in a narrow valley between two ridges. This gap in Tuscarora Mountain provided access for frontier paths and roads, including the Forbes Road, a historic path built by British general John Forbes in 1758 during his campaign to seize Fort Duquesne (now Pittsburgh) during the French and Indian War.

Much of the shoreline is forested with pine, hemlock, and hardwoods. Steep ridges rise more than 800 feet above the lake. The fine mountain scenery, best viewed to the north, is the highlight of this lake.

132. Raystown Lake

Size: 8,300 acres

Ownership: USACE

Horsepower restrictions: Unlimited horsepower

Scenery: Very good to excellent

Fishing: Striped bass, muskellunge, largemouth bass, walleye, crappie, smallmouth bass, trout

Location: The lake is south of Huntingdon; follow signs from PA 26 and PA 994 to a variety of access areas.

Raystown Lake is an exceptional paddling destination combining several qualities found in few other Pennsylvania lakes. First, it is huge; it is the largest lake completely within Pennsylvania. Raystown stretches 28 miles, covers 8,300 acres, and has 118 miles of shoreline. The shoreline of this lake is almost completely untouched since it is protected by federal lands, as well as Rothrock State Forest and Trough Creek State Park. The mountain scenery is impressive. To the east Terrace Mountain rises almost 1,000 feet above the lake, forming an impressive ridgeline. To the west are steep wooded hills separated by deep bays

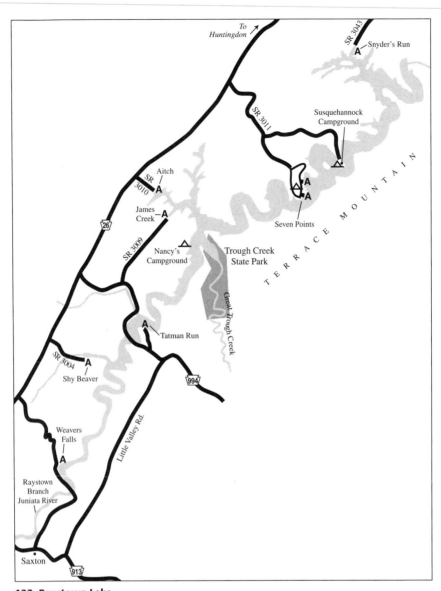

132. Raystown Lake

and countless coves. Towering shale cliffs with cedar trees rise above the lake at various places from Seven Points Recreation Area north to the dam.

There are countless bays and coves that are a pleasure to explore. Some highlights are Shy Beaver Run and Coffee Run inlets; the maze-like coves and bays of James Creek inlet; the shale cliffs a mile north of Seven Points Recreation Area on the west shore; the islands near Susquehannock Camp peninsula; and the islands, coves, and shale cliffs in the vicinity of Hawns Run and Ridenour Overlook. It is also worth exploring the inlet of Trough Creek, where you can get out of your boat and explore the Ice Mine, Balanced Rock, and Rainbow Falls. Bald eagles are also an increasingly common sight at Raystown and they are often seen near the dam. Not surprisingly, Raystown is very popular with powerboats and anglers; summer weekends often bring a lot of powerboat traffic.

As a flood-control project, the water level and shoreline of Raystown are variable. Dry periods can result in exposed shorelines of mud and rock.

Raystown is also only one of three places in the state where kayakers can make an overnight trip and stay at primitive campsites on a lake. Nancy's Camp is open to boat-in camping. Susquehannock Camp is accessible by vehicles, but it is also a fine camping option for paddlers. Seven Points features several campgrounds and sites along the lake, but it tends to be both popular and busy. Paddlers will prefer the Snyder Run, Aitch, or James Creek boat launches since they are closer to the more scenic areas of the lake and are not as heavily used by powerboats.

133. Canoe Lake

Size: 155 acres

Ownership: DCNR, Canoe Creek State Park

Horsepower restrictions: Electric motors

Scenery: Very good

Fishing: Walleye, muskellunge, largemouth bass, smallmouth bass, trout, chain pickerel, catfish, crappie, bluegill

Location: The park is located along U.S. 22 8 miles east of Hollidaysburg. Turn left onto Turkey Valley Road and follow for .5 mile to Canoe Creek Road on the right. Make the first right at Picnic Pavilion No. 1 to a boat launch. Another launch can be reached by taking Huntingdon Pike off of U.S. 22 and turning left onto Beaver Dam Road.

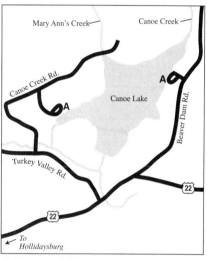

133. Canoe Lake

Located in the ridge and valley region, star-shaped Canoe Lake is surrounded by wooded hills and towering ridges. If you're paddling during a summer evening, expect to see a lot of bats. Canoe Creek State Park is famous for having the largest nursery colony of bats in Pennsylvania with a hibernaculum of 30,000 bats of six species. These bats live in an old church sanctuary and on summer evenings thousands of bats leave in search of bugs in the forests and over the lake. The park is also known for its biodiversity, with over 200 species of birds and mammals.

The Mary Ann's Creek and Canoe Creek inlets are nice places to paddle. The lake's southern shore is forested and there is a beach on the western shore. Two boat launches provide access.

134. Shawnee Lake

Size: 451 acres

Ownership: DCNR, Shawnee State Park

Horsepower restrictions: Electric motors

Scenery: Very good

Fishing: Smallmouth bass, largemouth bass, northern pike, walleye, muskellunge, sunfish, perch, bluegill, carp, pickerel, catfish

Location: From Bedford, follow U.S. 30 west for 10 miles to Shawnee State Park. At Schellsburg, you can also follow PA 96 south into the park.

Shawnee is a superb place to paddle, with a great combination of coves, bays, and three islands, the largest of which divides the lake into three sections. Horsepower is restricted to electric motors, so the lake is never overrun with powerboats. When paddling at Shawnee, explore the three islands and the inlet of Kegg Run. Wooded hills surround the lake; the Allegheny Front rises 5 miles to the west, and high ridges rise 3 miles to the east. Three launch areas provide access to the lake.

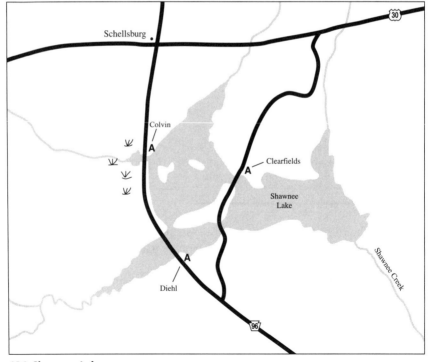

134. Shawnee Lake

Potomac River Watershed

The famous Potomac River drains more than 1,500 square miles of Pennsylvania, but it never enters the state; instead, streams drain pastoral valleys bordered by towering ridges and flow south into Maryland. This section of the state is also home to some beautiful lakes that more than justify a reason to visit.

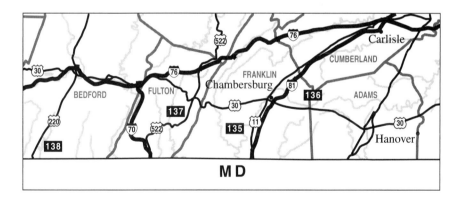

 Rivers and Creeks

135. Conococheague Creek

Section: Chambersburg to MD 58

Length: 30 miles

Water level: USGS Fairview, Maryland, gauge should be 2.5 feet.

Difficulty: Easy

Hazards: Possible low fences and strainers

Scenery: Good to very good

Highlights: Pastoral scenery, covered bridge

Fishing: Smallmouth bass, trout

Camping: Primitive camping is possible, but most land along the creek is privately owned.

The Conococheague is another of Pennsylvania's fine pastoral creeks. It drains the Cumberland Valley, an area with a multitude of neat farms and orchards. To the east, South Mountain rises, and to the west, Broad and Cove mountains form a distant ridge.

Begin in Chambersburg where the creek is fairly small. The stream quickly leaves the town and flows between farms and wooded bluffs that rise about 100 or 200 feet. These bluffs are usually located on the outside bends. The Conococheague likes to meander, and it does so frequently as it twists and turns around and between bucolic farms and fields. A string of trees often borders the creek. Although farms predominate the setting, the creek occasionally flows among forests and woodlots. Despite this being a farm valley, the creek is rarely, if ever, crowded with homes, a quality that simply adds to its appeal. Attractive barns and homes built of timber and limestone are often in view from the creek.

For the most part, the creek stays in a single channel with few islands. Islands and braids are located below Chambersburg and at the juncture with Back Creek. With the additional flow of Back Creek, the Conococheague grows larger and offers more water if the section above is too low.

Another feature of this creek is the impressive Martins Mill Bridge on Weaver Road. This 225-foot-long covered bridge was built in 1949 and renovated in 1973. It is now closed to traffic. The creek also passes several beautiful stone arch bridges along this section.

A little over a mile below Martins Mill Bridge is the SR 3005 bridge, the last in Pennsylvania. If you'd like, you can continue 6 miles to the MD 58 bridge.

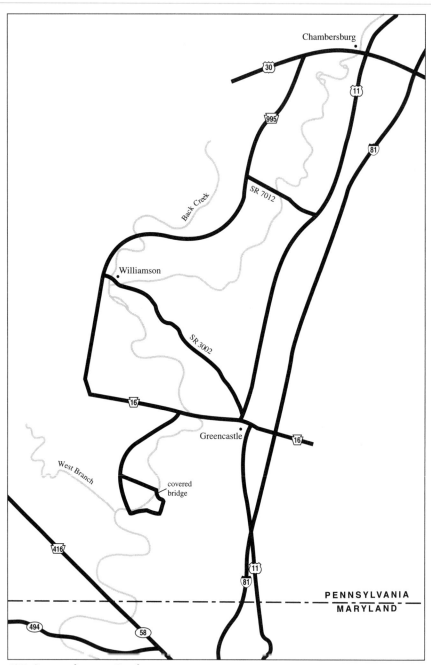

135. Conococheague Creek

Lakes, Ponds, and Reservoirs

136. Long Pine Run Reservoir

Size: 200 acres

Ownership: PFBC

Horsepower restrictions: Electric motors

Scenery: Excellent

Fishing: Largemouth bass, crappie, muskellunge, rainbow trout

Location: From Caledonia State Park at the intersection of U.S. 30 and PA 233, proceed north on PA 233 for 1.8 miles. Turn left onto Milesburn Road and follow for 1.5 miles to the reservoir on the right.

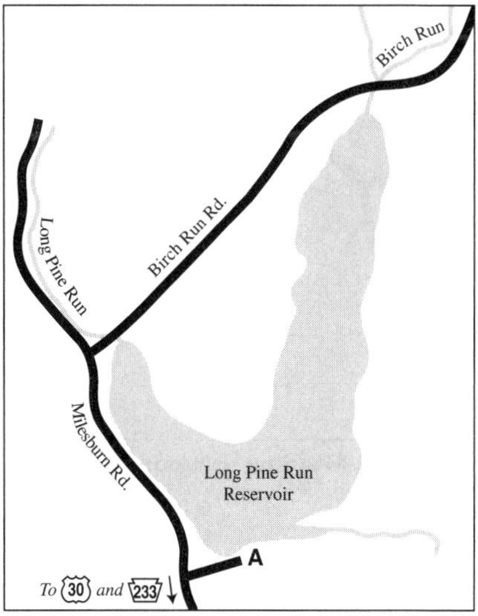

136. Long Pine Run Reservoir

This beautiful lake is located among the forested ridges of South Mountain. With the exception of the dam that forms the lake, the shore and rugged surroundings are completely untouched. Despite being located relatively close to Chambersburg and I-81, you feel you are in the middle of a wilderness when paddling Long Pine Run Reservoir. The lake is U-shaped and features one launch; there are small inlets at the northern ends of the lake and a few small coves along the shore.

137. Meadow Grounds Lake

Size: 204 acres

Ownership: PFBC

Horsepower restrictions: Electric motors

Scenery: Excellent

Fishing: Largemouth bass, northern pike, walleye, muskellunge, sunfish, perch, bluegill, carp, pickerel, catfish

Location: The lake is 3 miles west of McConnellsburg.

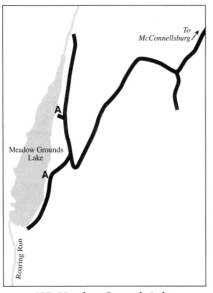

137. Meadow Grounds Lake

Nestled in a narrow mountain valley surrounded by high ridges, Meadow Grounds Lake is one of the state's most scenic lakes. Scrub Ridge rises to the west and Meadow Grounds Mountain to the east; the beautiful natural setting is protected by state game lands. In fact, just to get to the lake you must drive up and over Meadow Grounds Mountain. The lake is nearly 2 miles long and features many small coves and bays on the western shore. Fishing is a popular activity, but horsepower restrictions limit boat traffic. An added bonus is a hiking trail from the dam that follows the creek downstream to beautiful waterfalls in a rugged glen.

138. Lake Koon and Lake Gordon

Size: Lake Koon is 268 acres; Lake Gordon is 120 acres.

Ownership: Evitts Creek Water Co.

Horsepower restrictions: Electric motors

Scenery: Very good to excellent

Fishing: Bluegill, perch, crappie, bullhead, largemouth bass, pumpkinseed

Location: The lakes are located 10 miles north of Cumberland, Maryland, off U.S. 220. Use SR 3003 and SR 3009 to access the lakes.

Lakes Koon and Gordon are two of the state's best-kept secrets. The lakes are formed by dams on Evitts Creek; Lake Gordon is located immediately downstream from Lake Koon. The lakes serve as water sources for the city of Cumberland, Maryland. Although privately owned, both lakes are open to public use through the cooperation of the owner and the PFBC. Paddlers should be appreciative that private lakes are made available to the public.

To the west there are rugged wooded ridges that rise up to 600 feet above the lakes; to the east Evitts Mountain rises more than 1,300 feet above the lakes. The wooded isolation and mountain scenery that surround the lakes is very scenic.

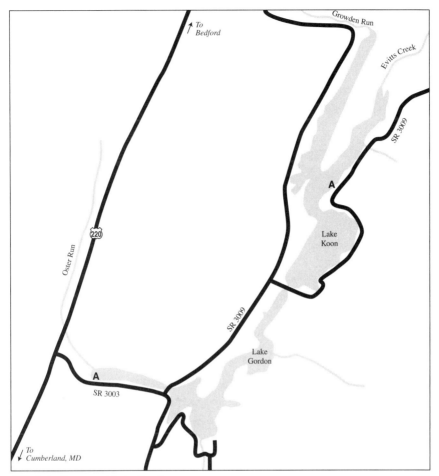

138. Lake Koon and Lake Gordon

Lake Koon features many coves and long, narrow bays at its northern end where Growden Run and Evitts Creek enter. Like Lake Koon, Lake Gordon is narrow and sinuous with a variety of coves and bays. The longest inlet is that of Oster Run. Both lakes offer fine fishing and are particularly well-known for their panfish.

Allegheny River Watershed

The mighty Allegheny River begins as a rivulet in the highlands of Potter County, gathers waters as it flows west, and then curves north into New York. It reenters Pennsylvania as the Allegheny Reservoir, and from the bottom of the Kinzua Dam emerges a river long-loved by paddlers.

But this watershed is much more than just the Allegheny River—it is a wonderland for paddlers. Here you will find countless impeccable lakes, wetlands renowned for their wildlife, and many scenic rivers and creeks that meander through shallow gorges. The sublime Clarion River, one of the crown jewels of Pennsylvania paddling, is in this watershed, as is French Creek, one of the most biodiverse streams in the state. With so many quality paddling destinations, you may find yourself spending more time in this beautiful corner of the state.

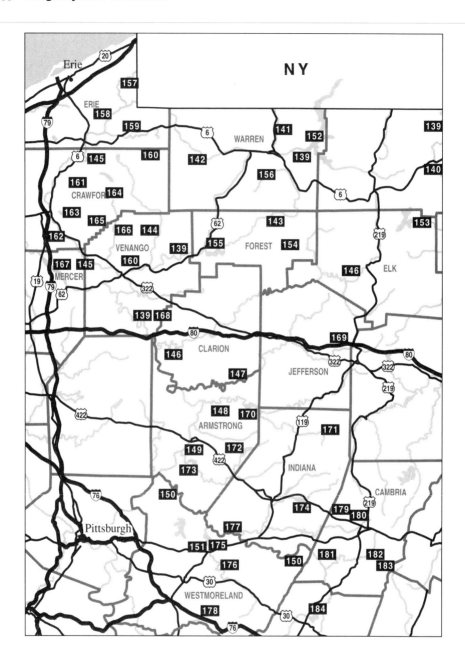

 # Rivers and Creeks

139. Allegheny River
Port Allegany to Eldred

Length: 28 miles	
Water level: USGS Eldred gauge should be 4.6 feet.	
Difficulty: Easy	
Hazards: Possible strainers	
Scenery: Very good to excellent	
Highlights: Wildlife, thick riparian forests, isolation	
Fishing: Smallmouth bass, catfish, trout	
Camping: No public primitive camping available; most land is privately owned.	

At Port Allegany, the Allegheny is a small river; it could also be characterized as a large creek. The river meanders down a valley with a rich floodplain forest of silver maples and sycamores. Because the river is encased in this junglelike forest, it retains an isolated feel. Expect a few islands and islets, which are primarily located along the first half of this section. Development is very limited along the river, and there are only occasional fields because the soil is so wet; the river twists incessantly through a forest-bog environment.

This river is somewhat unique in that it has created oxbow lakes, or ponds, as its channel has shifted over the centuries—similar to the Mississippi River. This is one of the few rivers or creeks in Pennsylvania to exhibit such features. This scenery continues to Eldred with scant development and relatively few fields. The current can slow to a crawl, but the river usually retains enough water to float a boat most of the year. Expect to see wood collected along the river; there is always the possibility of strainers. Thankfully, the current is so slow they are usually easy to avoid. This section offers excellent opportunities to observe wildlife and wildflowers.

Potato Creek joins from the left, providing more elbow room, and the Allegheny flows under PA 446. The river continues to meander heavily downstream. Take out at the PA 346 bridge at Eldred.

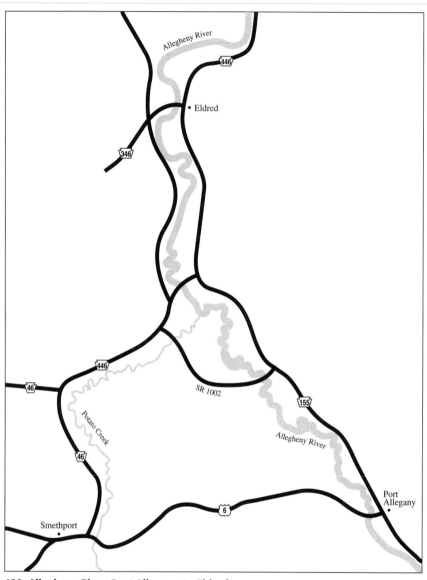

139. Allegheny River, Port Allegany to Eldred

Kinzua Dam to Tionesta

Length: 45 miles

Water level: USGS Franklin gauge should be 1.7 feet; flow should be below 5,000 cfs. The river is usually runnable all year.

Difficulty: Easy

Hazards: A few easy whitewater rapids and riffles

Scenery: Fair to very good

Highlights: Kinzua Dam, Allegheny National Forest, Allegheny Islands Wilderness Area, bald eagles

Fishing: Smallmouth bass, walleye, trout, rock bass, muskellunge, catfish, carp

Camping: Primitive camping is available on several islands; Buckaloons features a developed campground.

After its sojurn into New York and the Allegheny Reservoir, the Allegheny re-emerges below the impressive Kinzua Dam and flows down a beautiful 800-foot-deep canyon with occasional large boulders and several islands. These islands would be perfect for camping if they weren't so close to the put-in. As you continue, development increases on the right shore, and then the left. After passing under the Business Route 6 bridge in Warren, there is a large oil refinery on the right. The river narrows into an easy rapid, although the waves can get high enough to swamp a canoe. Below the rapids is an island with a flare that is part of the refinery; do not trespass on the island or approach the flare.

The large Conewango Creek joins from the right at Point Park, which is also an access area and a good rest stop. The Allegheny flows through Warren and under the PA 62 bridge. Good fishing can often be found along the bridge abutments. Pass under the U.S. 6 bridge. Clifford Betts Park is on the right with access and parking. A mile and a half ahead is large Mead Island; the right channel is the typical route since it usually has sufficient water to paddle. Be careful of the long, easy rapid over cobbles at the beginning of the island. Thereafter the Allegheny enters a large slow pool with hardly any current that will require a lot of paddling. At the end of Mead Island, on the right, is the Starbrick PFBC access. Pass Leek and Grass Flat islands and reach the PA 62 bridge. On the right after the bridge is the Buckaloons Recreation Area with developed camping and access; Brokenstraw Creek also joins from the right.

Below Buckaloons, the Allegheny flows down a narrow valley with forested plateaus that rise more than 600 feet on both sides. Cottages and homes are common along the river in sections, but much of the scenery is forested with occasional fields. The highlight of this section is the Allegheny Islands Wilderness Area, the nation's smallest federal wilderness area. These islands are home to impressive riparian forests and superb primitive campsites. This section also

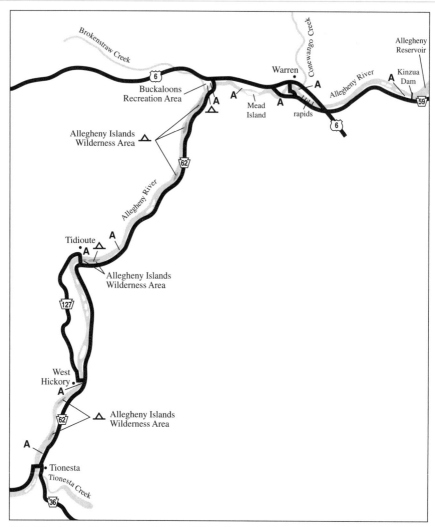

139. Allegheny River, Kinzua Dam to Tionesta

features twenty-four other islands that are part of the Allegheny National Forest and open to camping.

Access areas are at Bonnie Brae, Tidioute Borough, and West Hickory. Take out at the Tionesta PFBC access on the left, a mile before the PA 36 bridge.

Tionesta to Emlenton

Length: 62 miles

Water level: USGS Franklin gauge should be 1.7 feet; flow should be below 5,000 cfs. The river usually is runnable all year.

Difficulty: Easy

Hazards: Oil City Rapids (Class II)

Scenery: Good to very good

Highlights: Allegheny River Canyon, Indian God Rock, good camping, Samuel Justus Recreational Trail, Allegheny River Trail, good fishing

Fishing: Smallmouth bass, walleye, trout, rock bass, muskellunge, catfish, carp

Camping: Public primitive camping is available.

This section features more limited access and fewer camping possibilities than the previous, but it is still a beautiful float trip. From Tionesta to President, the scenery is similar with steep, wooded plateaus, several islands, and some cottages and other residential development. There is access at President, on the left. From here to Oil City, the river becomes more secluded as it meanders through a shallow forested canyon.

Oil City is near the birthplace of the oil industry, which began with the discovery of Drake's Well in 1859. Be aware of the Oil City Rapids, a Class II rapid with big waves just before Veterans Bridge, the first road bridge as you approach Oil City. The rapid is uncomplicated, but the big waves, particularly in high water, can swamp canoes. It is best to portage or avoid the rapids on the shallower river banks; there is an access area on the right, just above the confluence with Oil Creek. Below the U.S. 62 bridge on the left is a PFBC access area.

The 7 miles to Franklin offers similar scenery; on the left is the Samuel Justus Recreational Trail, a bike trail. You will pass a cluster of islands as you near Franklin. The largest is Hoge Island, where primitive camping is permitted. At Franklin, French Creek, a main tributary, joins from the right. Immediately below the U.S. 322 bridge on the left is an access and trailhead to the Allegheny River Trail, another bike trail; camping is also permitted. On the right shore is a PFBC access.

From here to Emlenton, the river flows through the Allegheny River Canyon, complete with steep mountainsides and boulders. No highways or primary roads follow the river, but there are cottages and other residences along the water in sections. The Allegheny regains its National and Wild Scenic River status along this stretch. The Allegheny River Trail is on the left. A popular feature is Indian God Rock, a large boulder on the left that features 800-year-old carvings. Eleven miles downstream from Franklin, a particularly wild and scenic section is encountered as the river abuts a state forest where primitive camping

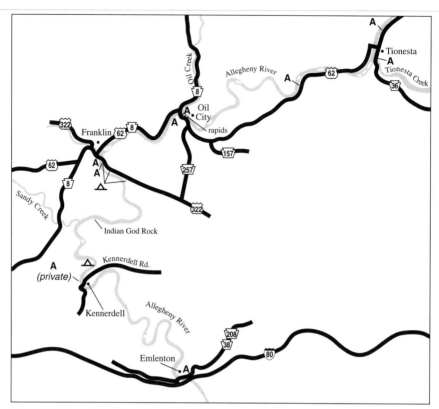

139. Allegheny River, Tionesta to Emlenton

is permitted at Danners Rest. The surrounding forested plateaus rise 400 feet, and in places, close in on the river.

After passing under the Kennerdell bridge, there is a private campground a quarter-mile on the right. This is last available camping before Emlenton, 17 miles away. Take out at an undeveloped access at the first bridge in town, on the left.

The Allegheny continues south from Emlenton towards Pittsburgh, but along the way there are nine locks and dams that slow the river's current considerably, essentially creating a series of long, narrow lakes. As a result, the remaining section of the river is not popular with paddlers. Expect both commercial and powerboat traffic. The scenery is good, but as you proceed south towards Pittsburgh there is increasing commercial, industrial, and residential development.

140. Potato Creek

Section: Smethport to PA 446

Length: 13.4 miles

Water level: There is no online gauge. If the Allegheny River between Port Allegany and Eldred is running, so should Potato Creek.

Difficulty: Easy

Hazards: Possible strainers

Scenery: Good to very good

Highlights: Isolation, thick riparian forest, wildlife

Fishing: Smallmouth bass, trout

Camping: Almost the entire creek flows through private land. Primitive camping is possible with permission.

Potato Creek offers similar scenery as the Allegheny River between Port Allegany and Eldred. Like the Allegheny, this creek has formed oxbow ponds as its course has shifted. The creek constantly meanders and curves through a rich riparian forest that gives a sense of isolation. Dirt banks often rise 3 to 5 feet above the creek. Development is very limited with the most noticeable being a wax factory at Farmers Valley. There are great opportunities to view wildlife as this placid creek carries you downstream. Strainers are always a possibility and occasionally adorn the shore, but the current tends to be slow. Islands are not common. The creek is usually enveloped within a thick forest, but there are an occasional fields and views of distant forested hills. There is no access at the juncture with the Allegheny River, so you can take out at SR 1002 or continue down the Allegheny to PA 446.

141. Conewango Creek

Section: SGL 282 to Warren

Length: 14 miles

Water level: USGS Russell gauge should be 2.0 feet.

Difficulty: Easy

Hazards: Possible strainers, lowdam in Warren

Scenery: Good

Highlights: Good fishing, wildlife

Fishing: Smallmouth bass, catfish, muskellunge

Camping: None

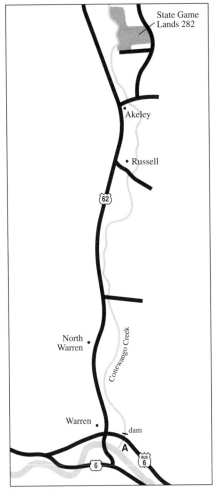

141. Conewango Creek

The Conewango drains a large portion of western New York, including Chautauqua Lake. By the time it enters Pennsylvania, it is a sizeable stream reaching the size of a small river. Putting in at State Game Lands 282 is difficult, as there is no established access and you have to walk up an old railroad grade to reach the Conewango, but it does enable you to experience the most isolated and scenic part of the creek. The Conewango meanders through thick riparian forests and wetlands within a broad farm valley bordered by wooded hills. U.S. 62 is off to the right and is often heard, but usually out of sight. There are a few riffles but surprisingly few braids, as the creek is usually confined to a single channel. There are occasional islands.

Most paddlers begin at the Akeley bridge. Homes and cottages appear on the right, while the left is more wooded. There are occasional islands and islets. Below Russell, the creek is undeveloped for a short section, but homes return on the right, followed soon thereafter by a shopping center. As the creek nears Warren, islands become more common and residential development increases on both sides of the creek.

Beware of a lowhead dam just above the Business Route 6 bridge that you must portage; most people take out at a school on the left just above the dam. However, if you want to paddle to the Allegheny River, you can continue and take out at Point Park on the left, at the creek's juncture with the Allegheny.

142. Brokenstraw Creek

Section: Columbus to Buckaloons

Length: 30 miles

Water level: USGS Youngsville gauge should be about 3.0–3.5 feet.

Difficulty: Moderate

Hazards: Strainers, Class I–II rapids in higher water

Scenery: Good to very good

Highlights: The section from Columbus to Garland is scenic and isolated with a lot of wildlife.

Fishing: Trout

Camping: Primitive camping is possible, but most land along the creek is privately owned.

The Brokenstraw is a popular springtime paddling trip. With good water quality, Brokenstraw Creek is also very popular with anglers. The creek is known for its strong, fast current in places, as well as its islands and braids. There are no difficult rapids, but expect many riffles and easy wave trains over gravel bars.

Most people begin at the PA 27 bridge at Garland and take out 12 miles later at Buckaloons. However, you can also put in at Columbus and the Cemetery Road bridge at Spring Creek. From Columbus, the creek is small and meanders among farms, meadows, woodlots, and rolling hills. Below the PA 426 bridge, the creek becomes more isolated as it meanders heavily through a thick riparian forest. Watch out for strainers. Hare Creek joins from the right and provides more elbow room before you pass under a railroad a short distance farther.

The creek continues to meander through a seemingly isolated forested valley down to Spring Creek. Below Spring Creek, the creek meanders less, but there are several braids and islands where you must watch for strainers. Expect to have to get out of your boat and portage strainers in shallow sections. Much of

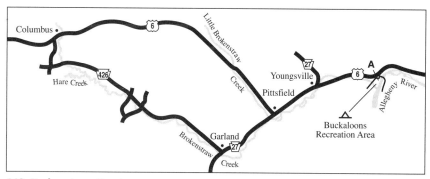

142. Brokenstraw Creek

this section is undeveloped; there are a few clusters of homes on the left, while the right is often wooded with thick hemlocks along steep hillsides.

The section down to Garland is scenic and mostly undeveloped. Wildlife abounds with bald eagles, herons, osprey, muskrats, hawks, waterfowl, and kingfishers. PA 426 is off to the left, but usually out of sight. Forests encompass the creek, with only a few fields. The Brokenstraw continues to braid around islands regularly.

Below Garland, the creek flows down a pastoral valley with wooded hills. Fields abut the creek, which is usually lined with trees. The Little Brokenstraw Creek joins from the left at Pittsfield and the Brokenstraw grows into a small river. The creek usually stays confined to single channel, except for islands and braids every few miles. When the creek does braid, it does so with a vengeance as it meanders around long sinuous islands and several islets.

The surroundings become developed through Youngsville, where there is a small dam; approach with caution. Below are wooded hills that rise 400 feet on the left. Fields are near the creek, as well as a factory on the right before the take-out. Take out at the SR 3022 bridge or at Buckaloons Recreation Area at the Allegheny River. If you continue to the river, take the left channel on the Brokenstraw. A possible primitive take-out is where the creek joins the river, or you can paddle a half mile up the Allegheny to a boat launch. Please note there is a fee to access Buckaloons.

143. Tionesta Creek

Section: Sheffield to Nebraska Bridge

Length: 34 miles

Water level: USGS Tionesta gauge should be about 3.0 feet. Note this gauge is below the Tionesta Dam.

Difficulty: Easy

Hazards: Occasional strainers

Scenery: Very good to excellent

Highlights: Good fishing, superb camping, isolated scenery

Fishing: Smallmouth bass, trout

Camping: Many potential campsites are available in the extensive areas of public land along the creek.

The Tionesta is one of northwest Pennsylvania's finest paddling trips. The creek is largely untouched by development as it flows down a narrow wooded valley with steep hillsides. Put in at the canoe launch in Sheffield, where there is the most development along this creek. Here the Tionesta is small; if there

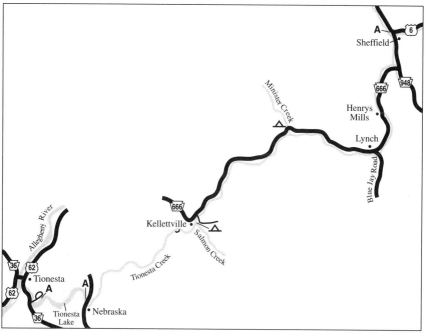

143. Tionesta Creek

isn't enough water, begin at Henrys Mills. Below Sheffield, the creek flows through scenic woodlands as forested slopes rise more than 400 feet. The creek grows to the size of a small river near Barnes, where the South Branch Tionesta Creek joins from the left. PA 666 follows the creek, but it isn't a busy road and is usually out of sight; even cottages are infrequent. The terrain to the right is particularly steep and the creekbed is adorned with boulders. Pass some islands and cottages on the left as the creek nears Henrys Mills, an alternate put-in. No rapids exist on the Tionesta, though there are several riffles with deep pools in between. Below Lynch the valley opens up, but the scenery is still rural and islands are fairly common. The creek passes some cottages at Mayburg and then Kellettville; otherwise, the creek is mostly undeveloped and is surrounded by forests.

Good camping can be found on the right at Minister Creek; a campground is also at Kellettville on the left. Numerous other potential campsites are along the creek and much of the shore is within the Allegheny National Forest, where primitive camping is permitted. Below Kelletville, depending on the water levels, you may enter the backwater of Tionesta Lake. The creek enters a beautiful 700-foot-deep canyon. Take out at Nebraska Bridge, which can be underwater when the lake levels are high. You can continue onto Tionesta Lake (see page 230) and take out at the spillway to the right of the dam. This lake features several primitive backcountry campsites along its shores.

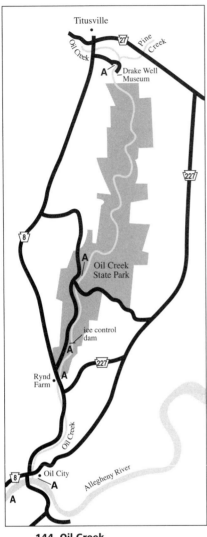

144. Oil Creek

144. Oil Creek

Section: Drake Well Museum to Rynd Farm

Length: 10 miles

Water level: USGS Rouseville gauge should be 2.5 feet.

Difficulty: Easy

Hazards: Possible strainers

Scenery: Very good

Highlights: Oil Creek Gorge, Oil Creek State Park, historic areas

Fishing: Smallmouth bass, trout

Camping: None

This wonderful float trip takes you through beautiful Oil Creek State Park as the creek meanders through the 500-foot-deep Oil Creek Gorge. The put-in is at the Drake Well Museum, where the world's first commercial oil well was established. The sites of old farms and towns also lie along the creek. Steep wooded bluffs rise above the creek and the setting is completely protected by the state park. A paved bike trail is on the right, and then left, side of the creek. This is an easy float with riffles, gravel bends, small islands, and possible strainers. Watch for a lowdam near the take-out. Because this section is entirely within the state park, no primitive overnight camping is available.

145. French Creek

Section: Union City Dam to Franklin	
Length: Approx. 85 miles	
Water level: USGS Meadville gauge should be 2.0 feet.	
Difficulty: Easy	
Hazards: Possible strainers, which become less likely as you head downstream	
Scenery: Good to very good	
Highlights: Wildlife, biodiversity, isolation below Cochranton	
Fishing: Smallmouth bass, trout	
Camping: Primitive camping is possible, but most land is privately owned.	

French Creek is one of Pennsylvania's most beloved waterways and a worthy visit for paddlers. While it doesn't offer soaring canyons, large boulders, or untouched wilderness, it does offer something that is less noticeable, but just as rewarding—incredible biodiversity. In fact, French Creek is one of the most biodiverse rivers in the United States. The creek is home to sixty-six species of fish (almost as many as found in the entire Adirondacks) and almost thirty species of mussels. The creek is particularly famous for its numerous species of mussels and darters, and is also home to the shy and elusive hellbender, a large salamander. Bald eagles, ospreys, egrets, herons, hawks, and countless waterfowl and songbirds also frequent the creek. French Creek is a treasure that everyone should enjoy and protect.

French Creek is also somewhat of a misnomer, since it is a large stream that grows into the size of a river. Between Union City Dam and Cambridge Springs the creek meanders heavily through fields, farmlands, and woodlots. The creek is easy with riffles over gravel bars and cobblestones interspersed with pools; you must keep an eye out for any strainers. The creek is often encased by a riparian forest, but expansive fields are common. There are surprisingly few homes or cottages along the creek.

After the U.S. 6 bridge, the creek meanders through an undeveloped pastoral setting. The creek is in the process of creating oxbow ponds similar to the upper Allegheny River and Potato Creek. Low wooded hills abut the creek as it swings back and forth across the valley. Downstream from the SR 1016 bridge, the French begins to meander wildly; in places it almost loops back on itself. A pleasant mosaic of meadows, fields, and woods continues to surround the creek, with only a few homes near the shore.

Below Cambridge Springs, French Creek grows into a small river and meanders less frequently; even islands are not that common. The creek is still easy with riffles and simple rapids over gravel bars. The setting is still pastoral and pleasant, but you can expect to hear traffic from U.S. 6/19 as it follows the creek's corridor. Strings of homes and cottages are sporadic, but the creek is

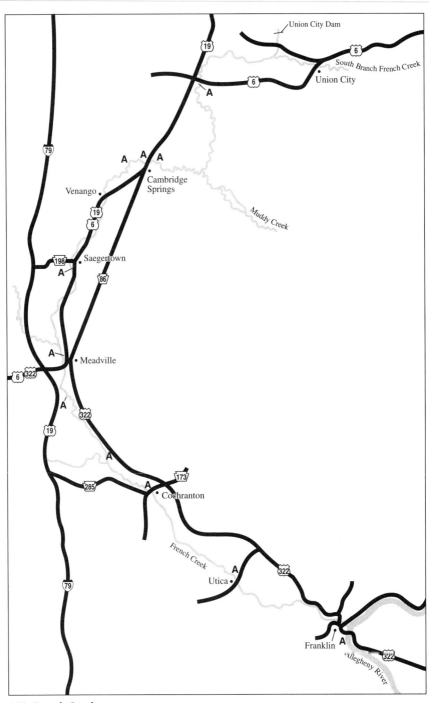

145. French Creek

still largely undeveloped. The creek does encounter some development at Saegertown on the left. Islands become more common between Saegertown and Meadville.

Meadville brings commercial and residential development along the creek, but it is relatively brief. The creek soon leaves Meadville and briefly resumes its meandering ways through thick forests and along fields. Thereafter, the creek meanders less. The setting remains pastoral as forested hills begin to rise. There are cottages on the right before Cochranton and the creek braids around two islands after passing through town.

Between Cochranton and Franklin, the creek enters a deepening wooded gorge that reaches about 600 feet in depth with occasional fields and islands. This is a very scenic paddle trip thanks to the gorge, isolation, and a lack of any busy road near the creek.

Eleven areas provide access to the creek. Many people begin at U.S. 6/U.S. 19 or Cambridge Springs and float down to Saegertown or the access areas near Meadville. Cochranton or Utica are ideal access areas for the lower section of French Creek. Take out on the Allegheny River at Franklin, below the U.S. 322 bridge on the right.

146. Clarion River

Ridgway to Irwin Access

Length: 16 miles

Water level: USGS Ridgway gauge should be 3.0 feet.

Difficulty: Easy to moderate

Hazards: Rapids and riffles that can reach Class II

Scenery: Excellent

Highlights: Rapids, excellent camping, isolation, scenery

Fishing: Trout, smallmouth bass, rock bass

Camping: Available at many places along the river, usually on the right shore.

This section of the Clarion is one of the finest paddling trips in the eastern United States. It offers everything—riffles emptying into deep pools bordered by large boulders, scenic isolation, and excellent primitive campsites.

The best access at Ridgway, a beautiful town, is at Love's Canoe Rental along PA 948. Here the river is small and hurries away from the town, passing a factory on the right. The Clarion soon enters an isolated setting with boulders and long pools; on the right is a railroad. Pass under the railroad trestle and paddle through Idewild Cut Rapids, which are easy at normal water levels. Below there are several fine campsites on the right; PA 949 is on the left shore.

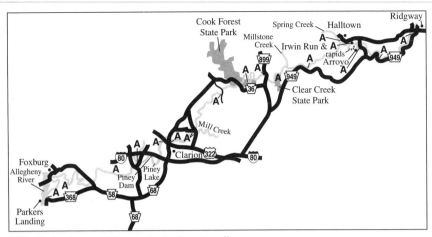

146. Clarion River, Ridgway to Parkers Landing

Toby Creek, a primary tributary, joins from the left and the Clarion grows into a moderately sized river. Below this juncture is a series of riffles that empty into a pool. Pass a few islands before Bear Creek joins from the right. PA 949 leaves the river to the left at Portland Mills and the Clarion enters a particularly scenic section as it flows through a spectacular wilderness canyon about 400–600 feet deep. There is virtually no development until you reach Arroyo. Along this section, occasional campsites are on the right in the Allegheny National Forest. As you near Arroyo, there is a large island with many white pines that offers several excellent campsites. There is access below the bridge at Arroyo, on the left.

The section from Arroyo to Irwin is absolutely exceptional. The scenery becomes more beautiful as the river flows down easy rapids framed by boulders. First is W Rapid or Chassie Rapid. Soon thereafter are X, Y, and Z rapids. Run X Rapid left, Y Rapid right, and Z Rapid right. At normal levels they are easy to moderate; at higher levels they can easily flip or swamp a canoe or kayak. Excellent camping is found near Z Rapid, on the right. Downstream is another easy rapid with superb camping on the right where large boulders surround a deep pool. As you near Irwin access there are more fine campsites and large boulders on the right. The access is also on the right.

Irwin Access to Clarion

Length: 38 miles

Water level: USGS Ridgway gauge should be 3.0 feet.

Difficulty: Easy

Hazards: None

Scenery: Good to excellent

Highlights: Clear Creek State Park, Cook Forest State Park, isolation, good camping

Fishing: Smallmouth bass, trout, rock bass, walleye

Camping: Available, but sites are not as common as in the previous section

Below Irwin the Clarion grows wider and the current slows; westerly winds coming up the river can make paddling a chore. The scenery is rural with occasional houses and cottages, unlike the wilderness of the previous section. Most of the development is on the right shore; the left is relatively untouched and is where you are most likely to find campsites. The surrounding hills and ridges are forested and rise more than 600 feet. At Belltown is an easy rapid formed by an old pipeline. Clear Creek State Park is ideal for access and camping, with riverside campsites and cottages.

The section between Clear Creek and Cook Forest state parks is very popular with canoeists. The scenery is similar as before, with the left shore being relatively untouched. As you near Cook Forest State Park, hills and ridges rise more steeply above the river as it meanders through the landscape. Boulders adorn the shore. Cook Forest is one of Pennsylvania's most popular parks and features an incredible old-growth forest that is a short distance from the Clarion. The steep plateaus create a canyonlike setting.

Below Cook Forest the Clarion flows through beautiful, isolated scenery. The North Country and Baker trails are on the right. There is access on the left along Gravel Lick Road about a mile below the bridge. From here to Mill Creek access, the Clarion flows through a beautiful untouched canyon where most of the land is protected by State Game Lands 283. This is an excellent wilderness float with good fishing and the best scenery since the segment from Ridgway to Irwin access. At Mill Creek the river slows behind the backwaters of Piney Reservoir; expect powerboat traffic. The Mill Creek access is on the left; this is probably the most ideal access for paddlers. The narrow, deep reservoir continues 10 miles to the final access at U.S. 322. If you paddle this section, explore the inlet of Toby Creek on the right; a short hike upstream is Rapp Run Falls. Take out at the Clarion or 322 bridge access areas.

Deer Creek Access to Parkers Landing

Length: 25 miles

Water level: Dependent on releases from Piney Dam

Difficulty: Easy

Hazards: None

Scenery: Very good to excellent

Highlights: Isolated canyon

Fishing: Limited; river is affected by acid mine drainage.

Camping: Potential campsites are infrequent and likely to be on private land.

In this section, the river resumes similar scenery as encountered between Gravel Lick Road and Mill Creek access. The flow of this section is entirely dependent on releases from Piney Reservoir, so be aware of any release schedule. Here the Clarion flows through a beautiful, meandering canyon that is 200–400 feet deep. Roads do not follow the river for any length, so this section is mostly undeveloped and forested. There are easy riffles and many deep pools; the slower current will require additional paddling.

Fields and a few homes return at Callensburg, where PA 58 crosses the river and there is an access. Below Callensburg, the Clarion resumes its meandering ways through a shallow, forested canyon that resembles a wilderness, although there are farms and fields adjacent to the canyon. Access is not available at the mouth of the Clarion, so paddle a mile down the Allegheny River to Parkers Landing on the left, at the PA 368 bridge.

147. Red Bank Creek

Brookville to New Bethlehem

Length: 26.4 miles

Water level: USGS St. Charles gauge should be 3.8 feet.

Difficulty: Easy

Hazards: Dam above PA 28 bridge in New Bethlehem; possible strainers

Scenery: Very good

Highlights: Isolation through a winding, shallow gorge

Fishing: Smallmouth bass, walleye, northern pike, muskellunge; creek is affected by acid mine drainage.

Camping: Many potential primitive sites, but likely to be on private land

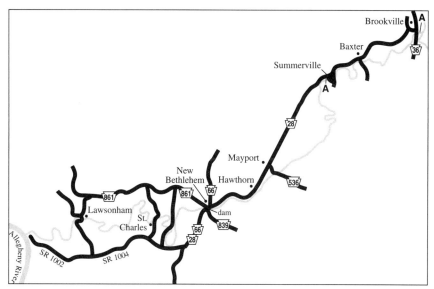

147. Red Bank Creek, Brookville to Allegheny River

Lying in the shadow of the popular Clarion River, Red Bank Creek is one of western Pennsylvania's best-kept paddling secrets. This river-sized creek features miles of fine scenery and relatively little development through an increasingly deepening gorge.

Sand Lick Creek and North Fork join in Brookville to form Red Bank Creek. As you leave Brookville you enter a beautiful shallow wooded gorge that is 200 feet deep with little development; hemlock and rhododendron adorn the banks. Roads usually stay away from the creek, but the railroad makes use of the Red Bank, crossing it several times. This wilderness setting continues down to Baxter, where there is a bridge and a few homes. There are no rapids, but several easy riffles over gravel bars and cobblestones. There is a PFBC access at Summerville where the setting becomes pastoral with fields and farms.

Below Summerville the Red Bank meanders up against steep wooded bluffs and soon resumes its lonely ways as it returns to another shallow, forested gorge down to Mayport. The section between Summerville and Mayport is particularly scenic and isolated. From Mayport to New Bethlehem there is more development as the creek enters a broad valley. Most of the development is on the right, while the left is wooded. There is a dam above the PA 28 bridge in New Bethlehem that you must portage.

New Bethlehem to Allegheny River

Length: 24 miles

Water level: USGS St. Charles Gauge should be 3.6 feet.

Difficulty: Easy

Hazards: None

Scenery: Very good

Highlights: Isolation through a meandering gorge

Fishing: Smallmouth bass, walleye, northern pike, muskellunge; creek is affected by acid mine drainage.

Camping: Many potential primitive sites, but likely to be on private land

This section may be Red Bank Creek at its best. Hemlocks adorn the left bank as the creek meanders through a deepening gorge. This gorge is surprisingly precipitous and reaches a depth of almost 500 feet. Development is scant and limited to cottages near the few bridges that cross the creek; the isolation grows as you proceed downstream. Easy riffles are more common along this section, as are sandstone boulders. As you near the mouth, the current becomes slower as the creek is backed up by a lock and dam on the Allegheny River. Take out on the left at SR 1002.

148. Mahoning Creek

Section: Mahoning Creek Dam to Allegheny River

Length: 25 miles

Water level: Dependent on releases from Mahoning Creek Dam (contact USACE). A release of 600 cfs should be sufficient.

Difficulty: Easy

Hazards: None

Scenery: Good to very good

Highlights: Meandering gorge

Fishing: Smallmouth bass, trout, muskellunge

Camping: Potential primitive campsites exist, but likely to be on private land

Like its sister stream to the north, Red Bank Creek, the Mahoning Creek is a fine float trip through the rolling hills and narrow valleys of western Pennsylvania. Flow is dependent on releases from Mahoning Creek Dam, so call before you put in.

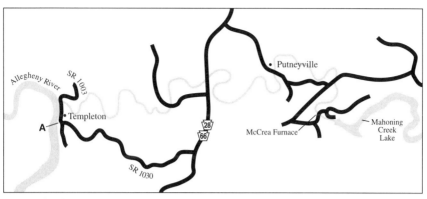

148. Mahoning Creek

You can put in below the lowdam that is just downstream of the Mahoning Creek Dam. However, most paddlers begin at a bridge about a mile farther downstream. The scenery is similar to Red Bank Creek. Paddle down the meandering shallow gorge that is 200–400 feet deep. At Eddysville, Pine Run joins from the left, as does a railroad. There is occasional development with cottages and cabins, particularly around Putneyville. Reenter a shallow gorge that opens up into a valley as you near the PA 28/66 bridge crossing. Below the SR 1007 bridge the creek flows through a deepening gorge that is more isolated and scenic than the previous section. This 400-foot-deep gorge is steep and winding as the creek flows up against wooded bluffs. As you near the Allegheny River, there will be backwater from Lock and Dam No. 8. Proceed onto the Allegheny River for a mile and take out at a PFBC access in Templeton on the left, or the SR 1003 bridge at the mouth of the creek.

149. Crooked Creek

Section: Crooked Creek Dam to Allegheny River

Length: 8 miles

Water level: Dependent on releases from Crooked Creek Dam, contact USACE

Difficulty: Easy

Hazards: None

Scenery: Good

Highlights: Gorge

Fishing: Smallmouth bass, trout, muskellunge

Camping: Very limited; most land along the creek is privately owned.

Crooked Creek drains a vast swath of countryside in Indiana and Armstrong counties. The creek is dammed at Tunnelville and there is a USACE access

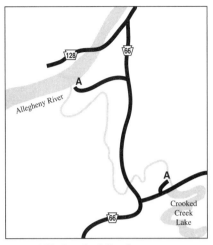

149. Crooked Creek

below the dam at the outflow area. Flows are dependent on releases from the dam, so make sure to call before putting on the creek.

This is a pleasant paddling trip as the creek winds between steep 200–300-foot wooded bluffs over easy riffles and pools. Keep an eye out for any strainers, particularly where the creek bends. There are more cottages and development below where Campbell Run joins the creek. Crooked Creek enters the backwater of the Allegheny River and docks appear along the shore. Paddle up the Allegheny River a short distance to the PFBC access at Rosston.

150. Kiskiminetas, Conemaugh, and Stoneycreek Rivers

Greenhouse Park to Conemaugh River Lake

Length: 46 miles	
Water level: USGS Seward gauge should be 3.0 feet.	
Difficulty: Easy to moderate	
Hazards: Rapids, dam below Seward	
Scenery: Poor to very good	
Highlights: Conemaugh River Gorge, gorge through Chestnut Hill	
Fishing: None. Some trout are possible in the side streams where they enter the river.	
Camping: Primitive camping is possible along the river, but most land is privately owned.	

These three rivers are names of different sections of the same river system; as a result, they are described together. The Stonycreek River joins the Little Conemaugh River in Johnstown to form the Conemaugh River. The Conemaugh River joins the Loyalhanna Creek at Saltsburg to form the Kiskiminetas River, which ends at the Allegheny River.

As you can tell by the orange-tinted water, the Stonycreek is affected by acid mine drainage. While this river system has been abused by industry and coal mining, it is also a river that is the subject of intense cleanup efforts and renewal. Bike trails and parks line sections of the river, which is a major regional asset that has begun to attract the attention of paddlers.

The first available access is at Greenhouse Park along the Stonycreek River. The Stonycreek is one of my favorite rivers; several miles upstream there are exciting Class III–IV whitewater rapids in a beautiful gorge. There is even a whitewater park at Greenhouse.

The first 9 miles of this section are less than desirable. Upon leaving Greenhouse Park, the river flows over riffles as it bends into an increasingly urban setting with steep forested bluffs on the right that rise 400 feet. Thereafter, the river enters Johnstown in a flood control channel that is completely concreted. To make matters worse, this concrete canal is colored orange from the acid mine drainage. The Little Conemaugh joins in downtown Johnstown to add its own orange-colored water. The setting is urban and at times industrial.

The Conemaugh eventually breaks free of the city to enter one of its highlights, and the one reason you would want to paddle this section—the impressive Conemaugh River Gorge. Here, the river cuts a 1,600-foot gorge through Laurel Ridge with towering forested bluffs and rock outcrops. Although referred to as a gorge, it is probably more accurate to call it a water gap since the river slices through a ridge, not a plateau. This is one of the deepest gorges in the eastern United States.

As the river leaves the gap, there are Class II rapids below Findley Run, which you can either run or portage to the right. There is access at Seward, and a dam less than a mile downstream that you must portage to the left. For the next 11

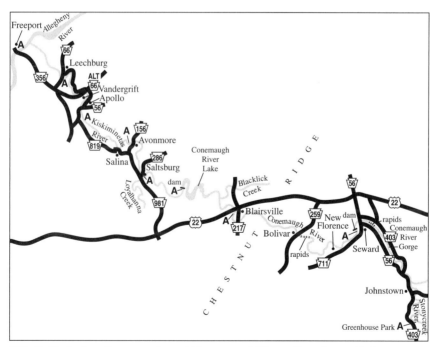

150. Kiskiminetas, Conemaugh, and Stoneycreek Rivers, Greenhouse Park to Allegheny River

miles the river flows through a scenic pastoral setting with steep wooded hill-sides, fields, and small towns. Just above Bolivar is another Class II rapid that you can run or portage to the right. Bolivar provides an access area on the left, about 300 feet upstream from Tubmill Creek.

For the five miles below Bolivar, the Conemaugh flows through another high-light—a 1,000-foot-deep gorge through Chestnut Hill. This gorge has a railroad but no roads and offers great scenery with its steep forested slopes.

Most paddlers will want to take out at the access in Blairsville on the right. Below Blairsville, Blacklick Creek joins from the right and the river enters the narrow, winding backwaters of Conemaugh River Lake. With its twisting forested hillsides and four impressive stone arch bridges that are now a part of the West Penn Trail, this lake is worth paddling (see page 248). However, the Conemaugh River Lake has no developed access areas, and no portage is avail-able around its dam, so you must take out. The only possible access on the lake is a walk-in access along Aultmans Run.

Conemaugh Dam to Allegheny River

Length: 40 miles

Water level: USGS Vandergrift gauge should be 3.5 feet.

Difficulty: Easy

Hazards: Possible strainers

Scenery: Good to very good

Highlights: Pastoral scenery, shallow wooded gorges, Roaring Run Park

Fishing: Below Apollo, there are smallmouth bass, yellow perch, and panfish. Trout at the outlets of side streams. This is a recovering river, so please throw back all fish caught.

Camping: Primitive camping is possible along the river, but most land is privately owned.

The 7-mile section between the dam and Saltsburg is popular with paddlers, as it should be, since it is fairly isolated as the river flows through a gorge-like set-ting with steep wooded hillsides that rise 300–400 feet. There is access on the right at Riverside Park in Saltsburg. The Loyalhanna Creek joins from the left, combining with the Conemaugh River to form the Kiskiminetas River, the final incarnation.

The Kiskiminetas, more commonly called the "Kiski," meanders through a shallow wooded gorge that is fairly undeveloped all the way down to Apollo. Along the way, you will pass Roaring Run on the right, which is also a park with a beautiful series of waterfalls in a glen. The Kiski and its surroundings become more developed as it flows through Apollo and Vandergrift, and thereafter, Leechburg. Below Leechburg, the river becomes more remote for its final 4 miles before joining the Allegheny River. To take out, paddle down the seemingly vast Allegheny for a mile to a take-out in Freeport, on the right.

Below Saltsburg, this section has access areas at Avonmore, Roaring Run Watershed Association a mile above Apollo on the right, and Leechburg.

151. Loyalhanna Creek

Section: Latrobe to Kiskiminetas River

Length: Approx. 20 miles

Water level: USGS Kingston gauge should be about 3.4 feet.

Difficulty: Easy

Hazards: Possible strainers

Scenery: Very good

Highlights: Wildife, isolation

Fishing: Trout

Camping: Primitive camping is possible along the river, but most land is privately owned.

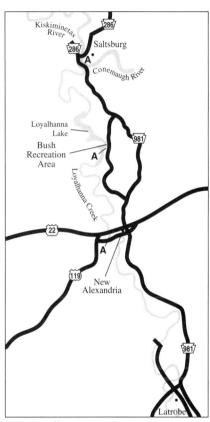

151. Loyalhanna Creek

The Loyalhanna is popular with paddlers of southwestern Pennsylvania. This stream is famous for its trout fishing and offers miles of pastoral scenery below Latrobe. The creek is surprisingly undeveloped and is usually enveloped by woodlands with occasional fields. Hills and ridges rise to about 200 feet above the creek. Expect riffles and easy rapids; strainers are also a possibility, but are not common. Expect to see a variety of waterfowl, ospreys, and even bald eagles on your trip.

There is an access at U.S. 22, which is also a popular put-in for paddlers. Below U.S. 22, the creek becomes even more isolated as it enters the backwaters of attractive Loyalhanna Lake. The inlet features sandbars and provides good opportunities to observe wildlife. Take out at the Bush Recreation Area, halfway down the lake on the eastern shore.

The creek below the dam offers similar scenery as above; however, the flow is controlled by the dam and there is no developed access below the dam. The Loyalhanna flows through a shallow 200-foot-deep gorge. Take out at Saltsburg.

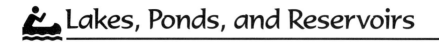 Lakes, Ponds, and Reservoirs

152. Allegheny Reservoir

Size: 12,080 acres (summer pool)

Ownership: USACE

Horsepower restrictions: Unlimited horsepower

Scenery: Very good to excellent

Fishing: Largemouth bass, smallmouth bass, northern pike, catfish, muskellunge, crappie, carp, walleye

Location: Along PA 59, the reservoir is located 7 miles east of Warren and 30 miles west of Smethport. Various access areas are located off PA 321, PA 346, and the Longhouse National Scenic Drive (FR 262). From Warren, follow SR 1013 north to the Webbs Ferry and Roper Hollow launches on the western shore.

The Allegheny Reservoir is in a class by itself. It is one of the premier paddling destinations in Pennsylvania and features superb scenery, excellent water quality, and several fine backcountry campgrounds that offer primitive camping.

This is a large reservoir—it is more than 24 miles long, and in places, more than a mile wide. There are countless coves and bays that invite exploration. Willow, Sugar, and Kinzua bays are the largest. Some of the most scenic coves are on the western shore, particularly the inlets of Cornplanter, Hodge, and Billies runs where the terrain is very steep as the buttresses of the plateaus descend to the reservoir. The shoreline is almost completely undeveloped and features massive boulders. Forested plateaus rise 800 feet above the water.

One of the most scenic places to paddle is behind the Kinzua Dam where the reservoir narrows into a precipitous canyon. Massive boulders adorn the shore and offer great places to eat lunch, sunbathe, or swim. The most famous is Refrigerator Rock, a towering rectangular boulder on the western shore. When the reservoir is high, people jump from the top of the rock into the water below. In summer the water of the reservoir is a deep translucent blue-green. Boulders are also common along the northern half of Kinzua Bay. The only scenic drawback to the reservoir is that when it is low, the shores are exposed with mud and rock. The reservoir is typically drawn down beginning in late September or October.

As you can expect, the reservoir is popular with powerboats. Due to the size of the lake, it rarely feels overrun and there are many coves that offer peaceful paddling. However, larger kayaks are a good idea on the reservoir. Because the water surface is sheltered by the plateaus, wind is not usually a major problem.

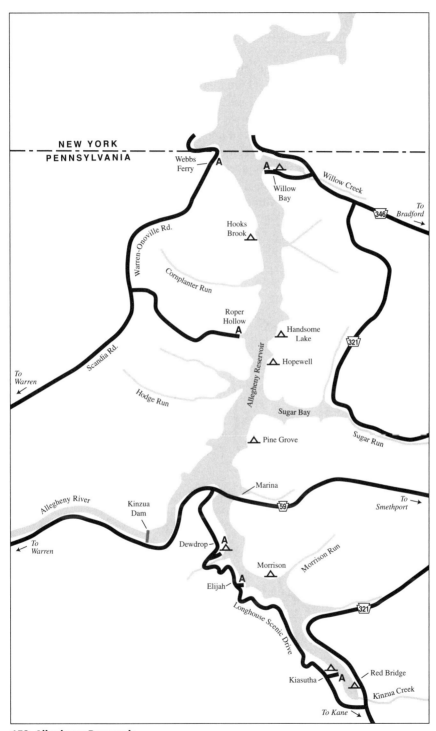

152. Allegheny Reservoir

The Allegheny Reservoir offers the finest primitive camping opportunities of any lake in the state. It is particularly ideal for multinight canoe or kayaking trips. Developed campgrounds with showers and vehicle access are located at Willow Bay, Dewdrop, Kiasutha, and Red Bridge. Primitive campgrounds with pit toilets, water, picnic tables, and fire rings are located at Hooks Brook, Handsome Lake, Hopewell, Pine Grove, and Morrison. These campgrounds can only be reached by boat or hiking. Reservations for the primitive campgrounds are first come, first served and there is an honor system when paying the fee. The primitive campgrounds are located along scenic coves and offer exceptional camping experiences. Morrison is probably the most popular of all the primitive campgrounds. A total of seven boat launches access the lake; only campers are allowed to use the one at Dewdrop. All launches require the payment of a fee.

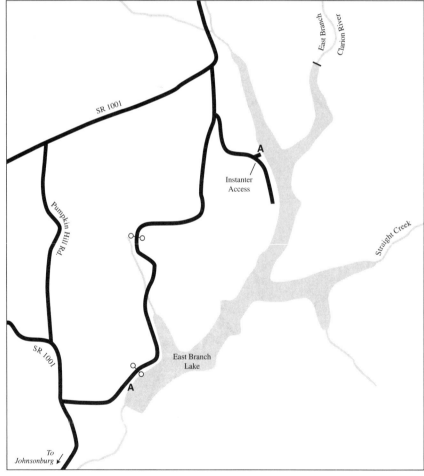

153. East Branch Lake

153. East Branch Lake

Size: 1,160 acres

Ownership: USACE, DCNR, Elk State Park

Horsepower restrictions: Unlimited horsepower

Scenery: Very good

Fishing: Muskellunge, walleye, smallmouth bass, brook, brown, rainbow, and lake trout

Location: The state park is located 9 miles north of Johnsonburg and is reached by following SR 1004 to Glen Hazel and then turning left on SR 1001. Both access areas can be reached from SR 1001.

Much of East Branch Lake is surrounded by Elk State Park, although the dam area is owned and operated by the Army Corps of Engineers. This is a flood control dam and the level of the lake is variable; when the lake is low, the shoreline is exposed.

The lake is located in an isolated area of low plateaus with deep valleys and gorges. Plateaus rise 300 feet above the lake, which is fairly narrow. Hardwood forests cover the surrounding plateaus and offer a fine foliage display in autumn. East Branch Lake feature several inlets that invite exploration, particularly the inlets of Straight Creek, Five Mile Run, and the East Branch Clarion River. Two boat launches provide access; however, paddlers will probably prefer the Instanter Road access since it is closer to the inlets and bays.

154. Beaver Meadows Lake

Size: 37 acres

Ownership: ANF

Horsepower restrictions: Unpowered boats only

Scenery: Very good

Fishing: Bluegill, pumpkinseed, yellow perch, bullhead

Location: From Marienville, follow North Forest Street, which becomes Beaver Meadows Road; follow for a total of 3.8 miles. Turn right on FR 282, a gravel road, and follow .9 mile to a parking area.

Despite being just a few miles north of Marienville, you feel as if you're in the middle of a vast wilderness when paddling Beaver Meadows Lake. This small lake is surrounded by the low rolling plateau and a diverse forest of red and white pine, spruce, hemlocks, and various hardwoods. The water is opaque with tannin from the swamps and wetlands upstream. Since all motors are pro-

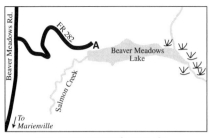

154. Beaver Meadows Lake

hibited and the lake isn't very popular with anglers, expect a lot of solitude while paddling. A highlight of Beaver Meadows is its wildlife; expect to see herons, ducks, geese, and yes, even beavers. Small coves and bays line the shore, but the most interesting places to explore are the wetlands and sedges at the eastern end of the lake where Salmon Creek enters. One boat launch near the camping area and dam provides access.

155. Tionesta Lake

Size: 480 acres (summer pool)

Ownership: USACE

Horsepower restrictions: Unlimited horsepower

Scenery: Very good

Fishing: Walleye, muskellunge, northern pike, perch, bluegill, largemouth bass, smallmouth bass, catfish, brown trout, brook trout

Location: From Tionesta, follow PA 36 south for 1.3 miles. Turn left to Tionesta Lake and cross the top of the dam to a traffic circle. Follow signs to the boat launch.

Tionesta Lake meanders for 6 miles between steep wooded hillsides and bluffs that rise several hundred feet above the lake. Tionesta is fairly narrow and averages a quarter-mile wide. The lakeshore is virtually undeveloped and is surrounded by hardwoods and some pine. Because there are no limits on horsepower, Tionesta is popular with motorboats in the summer. The narrow lake offers few coves, and those that do exist are small; one notable cove is the inlet of Johns Run, across the lake from the Dam Site boat launch. The inlet of beautiful Tionesta Creek is also an excellent place to explore and offers great opportunities to view wildlife in an untouched setting.

Tionesta is unique in that it offers extensive primitive campsites along its shores; these campsites have fire rings and site posts and can only be reached by boat. There are a total of forty-eight campsites on both the northern and southern shores of the lake; no reservations are required and the only charge is the boat-launching fee.

Two boat launches access the lake. One launch is at the Dam Site; the other is the Nebraska Access Area at the eastern end of the lake.

155. Tionesta Lake

156. Chapman Lake

Size: 68 acres

Ownership: DCNR, Chapman State Park

Horsepower restrictions: Electric motors

Scenery: Good to very good

Fishing: Largemouth bass, bluegill, sunfish, yellow perch, sucker, brook trout, brown trout

Location: From Warren, proceed 4 miles east on U.S. 6 to Clarendon. At the traffic light, turn right on Railroad Street (SR 2006) and drive 5 miles to the park.

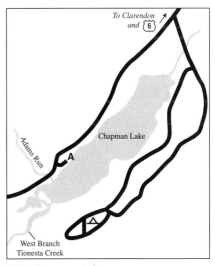

156. Chapman Lake

Bordered by the Allegheny National Forest and State Game Lands 29, the rolling wooded hills that surround Chapman Lake convey a sense of isolation. Hemlocks and pine border the lake, while hardwoods dominate the hillsides. Make sure you paddle up the inlet of West Branch Tionesta Creek as it meanders through a forested valley and passes under a footbridge. One boat launch provides access to the lake.

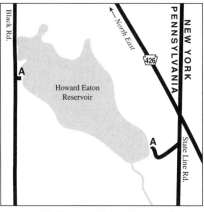

157. Howard Eaton Reservoir

157. Howard Eaton Reservoir

Size: 246 acres

Ownership: PFBC

Horsepower restrictions: Electric motors

Scenery: Very good

Fishing: Largemouth bass, smallmouth bass, northern pike, bluegill

Location: The reservoir is about 6 miles south of North East off PA 426.

Howard Eaton is the perfect place for paddlers in the Erie region who may be too intimidated or inexperienced to go on Lake Erie. This beautiful reservoir is in the northwest corner of the state, perched nearly a thousand feet above Lake Erie, which is about 7 miles to the north. Low, rolling, forested hills surround the lake with a meandering shoreline that offers a small bay along the northern shore. The southeastern half of the lake is the most isolated as it is surrounded by rolling woodlands; the northwestern half is surrounded by fields, woodlots, and a few homes.

The serene countryside makes this lake a memorable place to paddle. While the lake can be popular with anglers, the horsepower restrictions keep heavy boat traffic away; don't be surprised to have this lake all to yourself. Be prepared for strong thunderstorms that can blow off Lake Erie suddenly in the summer.

158. Lake Pleasant

Size: 60 acres

Ownership: PFBC

Horsepower restrictions: Unpowered boats only

Scenery: Good to very good

Fishing: Largemouth bass, bluegill, brook trout, rainbow trout

Location: From I-90, follow PA 8 south for about 3 miles. Turn right onto Mark Road, follow a little over a mile, and turn left onto Lake Pleasant Road. Follow Lake Pleasant Road for about 5 miles and the lake will be on your right.

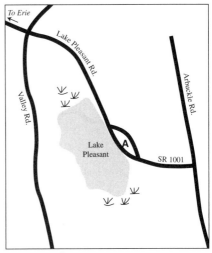

158. Lake Pleasant

This small lake may seem insignificant, but it is unique. Lake Pleasant is a natural glaciated lake, one of the few in the state that is undeveloped and open to the public; it is also the location of the Western Pennsylvania Conservancy's northwest field station, where the rare plants and animals that live here are studied. The lake and its wetlands support eighty different species of plants and three rare species of fish. It is one of the few natural lakes largely free from invasive species. The alkaline springs form fens that in turn harbor nutrient-rich peatlands that are home to three carnivorous plants—pitcher plant, sundew, and bladderworts. These alkaline conditions provide for an incredible biodiversity. Due to its depth and water quality, Lake Pleasant supports a reproducing population of trout.

It is odd to paddle a lake that is a remnant of the ice sheets that once covered this section of Pennsylvania. Today, wetlands and sedges surround the lake as low forested hills rise in the distance. There are a few homes set back from the lake and a few docks, but most of the shore is undeveloped. The meandering southern outlet is an ideal place to paddle, as are the fens and wetlands along the northern shore. You may even be lucky enough to see the ospreys, bald eagles, and loons that have been observed at the lake.

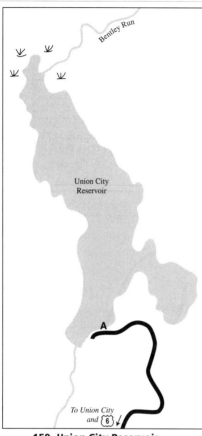

159. Union City Reservoir

159. Union City Reservoir

Size: 32 acres

Ownership: Union City Municipal Authority

Horsepower restrictions: Unpowered boats only

Scenery: Very good

Fishing: Largemouth bass, bluegill, sunfish, yellow perch

Location: The reservoir is located 2 miles east of Union City off U.S. 6; turn left and follow the road .5 mile to the reservoir.

This small lake is one of northwest Pennsylvania's best-kept secrets. Low rolling terrain surrounds this undeveloped lake. The shoreline features a scenic, diverse forest of hardwoods, pine, and hemlock. There is a particularly verdant forest of pine and hemlock along the northwest shore. For the paddler, there are many small coves along the shore; a large bay at the southeast corner is almost enclosed. The highlight may be the northern inlet where Bentley Run feeds the lake. Here you will find meandering channels, wetlands, and sedges that are perfect for birdwatching and diverse plant and animal life. Union City Reservoir may be 2 miles from its namesake town, but when paddling here you feel much farther away. One boat launch, at the southern end near the dam, provides access.

160. Clear Lake

Size: Approx. 140 acres

Ownership: Local government

Horsepower restrictions: Unlimited

Scenery: Good

Fishing: Largemouth bass, bluegill, sunfish, yellow perch

Location: The lake is located in the village of Spartansburg, about 8 miles south of Corry along PA 77.

Aside from a lumber mill and the small town of Spartansburg located at its southern outlet, Clear Lake is undeveloped. The western shore is uniform with few coves. Paddlers will want to explore the northern and eastern shore where there are expansive wetlands and sedges marked with coves, bays, islets, and the winding inlets of the two small streams that feed the lake. Here you will find diverse plant and animal life. The surrounding topography is low and the forest is comprised mostly of hardwoods with hemlocks.

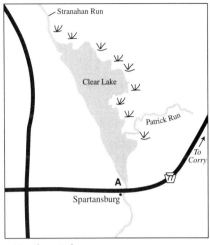

160. Clear Lake

161. Woodcock Creek Lake

Size: 333 acres (summer pool)

Ownership: USACE

Horsepower restrictions: 10 hp

Scenery: Good

Fishing: Smallmouth bass, largemouth bass, muskellunge, catfish, walleye, crappie

Location: The lake is located 4 miles north of Meadville, via PA 86 and PA 198.

This serene lake is surrounded by low, rolling forested hills and fields. Half the lake is managed as Colonel Crawford Park, a county park with camping and a boat access. Due to the horsepower restrictions, Woodcock Creek Lake is a peaceful place to paddle and is popular with sailboats. The eastern half is managed as State Game Lands 435. The lake features many small coves, bays, and stream inlets; it is nearly bisected by a causeway for Huson Road. The best place to paddle is the eastern end of the lake where there is a no-wake zone and the inlet of Woodcock Creek. The lake is shallow at its eastern end. The state game lands offer more isolation with many coves, wetlands and sedges, and excellent opportunities to view wildlife. Watch for powerful summer thunderstorms on hot, humid days that are common in northwest Pennsylvania. The low topography around the lake can also result in windy conditions and waves.

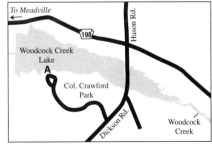

161. Woodcock Creek Lake

162. Conneaut Marsh

Size: Approx. 500 acres

Ownership: PGC

Horsepower restrictions: Unpowered boats

Scenery: Good to very good

Fishing: Largemouth bass, panfish

Location: The marsh is located southeast of Conneaut Lake and various access points can be reached off PA 285.

This large wetland offers a unique paddling experience rarely found in Pennsylvania. The marsh is known by a variety of names, including Geneva Marsh and Conneaut Lake Outlet. The water is fed by an outlet from Conneaut Lake, the largest natural lake in Pennsylvania. The PGC constructed small dams to create these expansive marshlands, which can be accessed from a variety of places, including Brown Hill Road, SR 3021, and off Towpath Road. Do not attempt to run these low dams.

The northern part of the marsh offers the most tranquility and there is an old channel that appears to have been dredged as it intersects with meandering channels. The southern section is not as isolated since I-79, U.S. 19, and a power line cross it. The middle section of the marsh is protected as a propagation area where entry is prohibited.

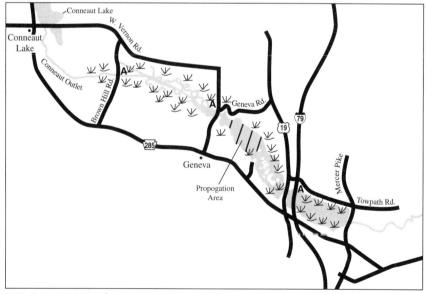

162. Conneaut Marsh

Wildlife and birdlife abound in the marsh, whether it is bald eagles, muskrats, turtles, geese, ducks, herons, or egrets. There is open water and a few sinewy passages that invite exploration. Also expect extensive lily pads, grasses, and other vegetative cover. Thick sedges, wet meadows, and forests surround the marshlands and add a sense of isolation; low rolling hills rise 300–400 feet in the distance. Watch for strong thunderstorms in the summer that can blow in suddenly.

163. Tamarack Lake

Size: 562 acres

Ownership: PFBC

Horsepower restrictions: Electric motors

Scenery: Good to very good

Fishing: Largemouth bass, bluegill, bullhead, catfish, carp, crappie, muskellunge, perch, walleye, pumpkinseed

Location: The lake is located two miles southeast of Meadville.

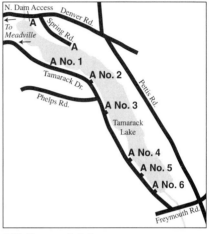

163. Tamarack Lake

Tamarack is a long, shallow, and narrow lake that stretches 3 miles among low forested hills and fields. It is unique in that there are dams at both ends of the lake, with no inlets or tributaries of any size. Tamarack's shore has many small coves and bays and it is a serene place to paddle. The lake is known as a superb bass fishery and is home to many other species of fish. There are a few homes in view of the lake along the western shore— however, most of this shore is wooded and undeveloped. The eastern shore is almost completely wooded and undeveloped.

Watch for powerful summer thunderstorms on the hot, humid spring and summer days that are common in northwest Pennsylvania. The low topography around the lake can also result in windy conditions. Seven launches provide access.

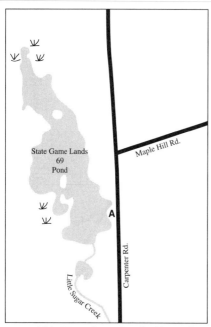

164. State Game Lands 69 Pond

164. State Game Lands 69 Pond

Size: Approx. 130 acres

Ownership: PGC

Horsepower restrictions: Unpowered boats only

Scenery: Very good

Fishing: Largemouth bass, crappie, bluegill, bullhead

Location: From Meadville, follow PA 27 east towards Titusville for 13.5 miles and then turn left onto Carpenter Road towards State Game Lands 69. Drive 2 miles to a parking area on the left.

This relatively unknown lake is a pleasure to paddle with its undeveloped shoreline, many bays and inlets, and pastoral scenery. Fields and meadows are along the eastern shore, while the western shore has scenic woodlands of hardwoods and hemlocks. The lake features two islands, islets, and many coves, particularly on the western shore. The northern end is the inlet of the lake, where there are wetlands, sedges, and tree stumps. There is a parking area and launch at the southeastern corner of the lake near the dam.

The lake is located within State Game Lands 69; to the east are many smaller ponds and lakes that may be worth exploring. However, most will require at least a short hike in from the road.

165. Sugar Lake

Size: 90 acres

Ownership: PFBC

Horsepower restrictions: 6 hp

Scenery: Good

Fishing: Bluegill, yellow perch, black crappie, muskellunge, largemouth bass

Location: The lake is 7 miles northeast of Cochranton and is accessed off PA 173 and PA 27.

Sugar Lake is unique in that it is natural and not man-made like the vast majority of lakes in this guide. Low wooded hills and fields surround the lake. Cottages and homes are on the northeastern and southwestern shores, but the lake is not overdeveloped. Extensive wetlands and sedges located at the inlet and outlet are highlights of this lake, providing opportunities to view plant and wildlife. Paddlers in particular will want to explore the winding outlet of the lake at its southeastern corner. Be aware of strong thunderstorms that can strike suddenly in summer. One launch on the western shore provides access.

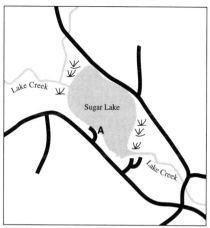

165. Sugar Lake

166. Justus Lake

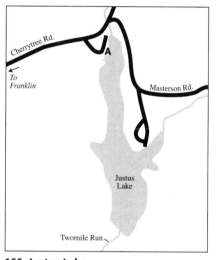

166. Justus Lake

Size: 144 acres

Ownership: Venango County

Horsepower restrictions: Electric motors

Scenery: Very good

Fishing: Largemouth bass, smallmouth bass, trout

Location: The lake is located 8 miles northwest of Franklin via PA 417 and Cherrytree Road.

Justus Lake is surrounded by the steep, forested hills of Two Mile Run County Park. As with many county parks, you will find a beach, picnic areas, and playgrounds. The lake features a few small coves and bays and inlets of two creeks. Rolling forested hills rise 200–300 feet above the lake. However, the real highlight of Justus Lake is its surprisingly deep, clear, and clean water. As a result, it is a fine year-round trout fishery, which is a rare quality among Pennsylvania's lakes. Thanks to the horsepower restrictions, Justus Lake is a serene place to paddle as long as you keep your distance from the beach on hot summer days.

167. Lake Wilhelm

Size: 1,860 acres

Ownership: DCNR, Maurice K. Goddard State Park

Horsepower restrictions: 20 hp; electric motors in the state game lands

Scenery: Very good

Fishing: Smallmouth bass, largemouth bass, muskellunge, perch, walleye, northern pike, crappie, catfish, sunfish, bluegill

Location: The lake is located 13 miles east of Greenville and 13 miles west of Franklin. It is accessed off U.S. 19, I-79, or PA 173.

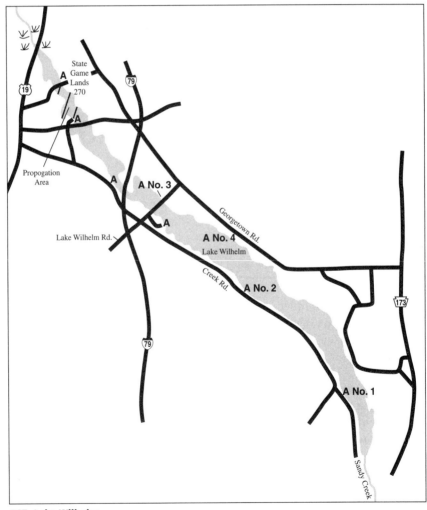

167. Lake Wilhelm

Lake Wilhelm is a long, narrow lake, stretching 9 miles between the low wooded hills of Mercer County. These hills gradually rise to approximately 200 feet above the lake. The meandering shoreline consists of many small bays and coves, but no particularly large ones. Birdlife is a prime attraction of the lake, which hosts eagles, herons, egrets, osprey, and various waterfowl.

Paddlers will be particularly interested in the northwestern end of the lake where horsepower is limited to electric motors. This section is located within State Game Lands 270 and features scenic isolation among its wetlands, quiet coves, meandering shoreline, and sedges. Take time to explore the maze-like inlet of Sandy Creek and its many islets. The middle section of the game lands is a propagation area and entry is prohibited. Seven launches provide access to the lake—four at the state park and three in the state game lands.

Wind can be a problem at Lake Wilhelm. Also be aware that powerful thunderstorms are common in this section of the state, especially on warm, humid days. These storms can form suddenly and move quickly.

168. Kahle Lake

Size: 251 acres

Ownership: PFBC

Horsepower restrictions: Electric motors

Scenery: Good

Fishing: Muskellunge, largemouth bass, bluegill, bullhead, perch, walleye, pumpkinseed

Location: The lake is 6 miles northeast of Emlenton and can be reached off PA 38 or PA 208.

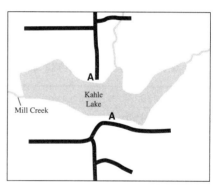

168. Kahle Lake

Kahle Lake straddles the border of Clarion and Venango counties and is surrounded by low forested hills and fields. Kahle is known as a superb largemouth bass fishery and special regulations do apply. Two coves that are also the inlets of the streams that feed the lake are pleasant places to paddle. The lake is accessed by two boat launches.

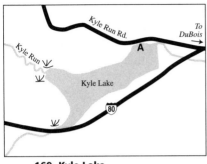

169. Kyle Lake

Size: 165 acres

Ownership: PFBC

Horsepower restrictions: Electric motors

Scenery: Good

Fishing: Largemouth bass, bluegill, catfish, walleye

Location: The lake is 5 miles northwest of DuBois off PA 830.

169. Kyle Lake

Kyle Lake is set in the rolling woodlands of Jefferson County. The serenity and scenery of the lake is somewhat marred by I-80, which traverses close to the southern shore and crosses the southern inlet. You can expect plenty of noise coming from the traffic on the busy interstate as you paddle. Kyle Run, a small stream, feeds the lake at the northern inlet. One boat launch provides access.

170. Mahoning Creek Lake

Size: 280 acres (summer pool)

Ownership: USACE

Horsepower restrictions: 10 hp

Scenery: Very good

Fishing: Walleye, muskellunge, northern pike, perch, bluegill, largemouth bass, smallmouth bass, catfish, crappie

Location: From Dayton, the access areas are reached via PA 839 or SR 1023 to Boat Launch Road.

Mahoning Creek Lake is a hidden gem for paddlers. Thanks to horsepower restrictions, it is a serene setting as the narrow lake meanders for 5 miles between high wooded bluffs and hillsides that rise more than 400 feet. On average, Mahoning Creek Lake is only 1/8 mile wide. With virtually no development, the lake conveys a sense of wilderness. There are few coves in the canyonlike setting of the lake, the only notable one the inlet of Glade Run. There are two boat launches: Sportsman's Area Boat Ramp is operated by the Pennsylvania Fish and Boat Commission and the Milton Loop Boat Launch is operated by Armstrong County. If lake levels are low, it is best to launch from the Sportsman's Area. As a flood-control project, the level of the lake is variable and the shores can be exposed with rock, mud, and boulders.

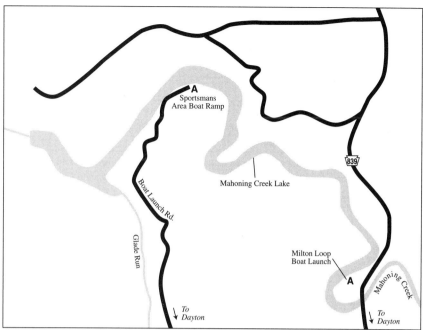

170. Mahoning Creek Lake

171. Hemlock Lake

Size: 60 acres

Ownership: PFBC (leased to Indiana County Parks)

Horsepower restrictions: Electric motors

Scenery: Good to very good

Fishing: Largemouth bass, walleye, saugeye

Location: The lake is 7 miles southeast of Punxsutawney. The lake's eastern access road is located south of Johnsonburg via SR 1033 (Hemlock Lake Road). The park's western access road is located off SDA Church Camp Road.

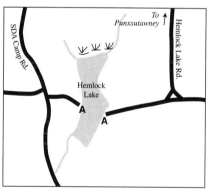

171. Hemlock Lake

With its undeveloped shoreline and forested hills that gradually rise to heights of 200 feet, Hemlock Lake is a peaceful, pleasant place to paddle. The lake is leased by the PFBC to Indiana County to form Hemlock Lake County Park. Make sure to explore the northern end of the lake where there are two inlets with wetlands and sedges. Two launches provide access on opposite shores of the lake where there are also picnic facilities; also be aware that the roads to the lake are not plowed in winter.

172. Keystone Lake

Size: 850 acres

Ownership: Reliant Energy

Horsepower restrictions: 10 hp

Scenery: Very good

Fishing: Largemouth bass, smallmouth bass, walleye, crappie, muskellunge, perch, bluegill, sunfish, pumpkinseed, trout

Location: The lake is 11 miles northwest of Indiana. Access areas are reached via PA 210 for the Atwood access, and PA 85 at Meredith via White Oak Road to the northern shore access.

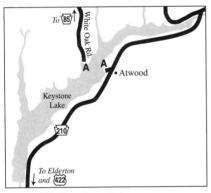

172. Keystone Lake

Keystone Lake is another of western Pennsylvania's best-kept secrets. This beautiful lake stretches 5¹/₂ miles between wooded hillsides that gradually rise 200 feet above the shore. While Keystone is popular with anglers, the horsepower restrictions ensure the lake is a peaceful place to paddle among Armstrong County's rolling countryside.

The lake is owned by Reliant Energy, which uses it as a cooling water supply for the Keystone Power Plant. Fortunately, in cooperation with the PFBC, Reliant Energy permits public use; the PFBC maintains launches on the northern and southern shores.

Keystone Lake features several coves and bays on the northern shore and a particularly long inlet at its eastern end that is ideal for viewing wildlife. Keystone offers fine fishing and is designated as a trophy bass lake.

173. Crooked Creek Lake

Size: 350 acres (summer pool)

Ownership: USACE

Horsepower restrictions: Unlimited horsepower

Scenery: Good

Fishing: Walleye, muskellunge, northern pike, perch, bluegill, largemouth bass, smallmouth bass, catfish

Location: Crooked Creek is 4 miles south of Ford City off PA 66.

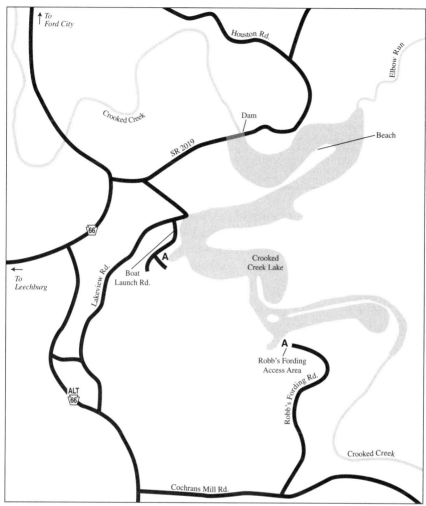

173. Crooked Creek Lake

This narrow lake twists and turns for 5 miles between steep wooded hillsides and bluffs. With no restrictions on horsepower, Crooked Creek is popular with motorboats in the summer. However, there are no-wake zones behind the dam and in several small coves where the creeks enter the lake. One of the best places to explore is the inlet of Crooked Creek, where sediments deposited by the creek have created long peninsulas. The level of the lake will determine how far you can go up the creek. Two boat launches access the lake.

174. Yellow Creek Lake

Size: 720 acres

Ownership: DCNR, Yellow Creek State Park

Horsepower restrictions: 20 hp

Scenery: Very good

Fishing: Walleye, muskellunge, northern pike, perch, bluegill, largemouth bass, smallmouth bass, catfish, brown trout, brook trout

Location: The lake is 8 miles southeast of Indiana and can be reached via U.S. 422, PA 954, and PA 259.

Yellow Creek Lake provides some of the best paddling in west-central Pennsylvania. Forested hills rise 500 feet over the lake. Paddlers will want to explore the narrow gorge behind the dam and the inlets of Yellow Creek and Little Yellow Creek; other coves on the north and south shores invite exploration. A total of five boat launches provide access to the lake.

174. Yellow Creek Lake

175. Loyalhanna Lake

Size: 400 acres (summer pool)

Ownership: USACE

Horsepower restrictions: Unlimited horsepower

Scenery: Very good

Fishing: Walleye, bluegill, largemouth bass, crappie, bullhead

Location: From Saltsburg, follow PA 981 south towards Latrobe for 3 miles. Turn right onto Bush Road and follow for 1.5 miles. Turn right into the Bush Recreation Area.

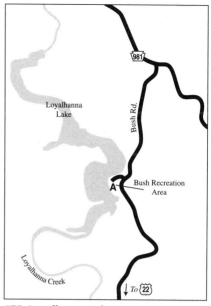

175. Loyalhanna Lake

Loyalhanna is a narrow, curving lake that stretches 4 miles between the wooded hills and bluffs of western Pennsylvania. On average, the lake is 1/4 mile wide. Although Loyalhanna has no limits on horsepower, there are two no-wake zones: one behind the dam, and the other in the middle of the lake near the Bush Recreation Area. Several small coves and the inlet of Loyalhanna Creek invite exploration, where sediments have created a curving peninsula. There is one access at the Bush Recreation Area. This is a flood-control project, so the level of the lake is variable. In higher water, the Loyalhanna Creek offers a fine float trip down to the lake from a variety of upstream access points.

A highlight for paddlers is the Black Willow Water Trail, a self-guided trail with designated stations that point out the natural and manmade features of the lake. A trail brochure is available at the Bush Recreation Area ranger station.

176. Keystone Lake

Size: 78 acres

Ownership: DCNR, Keystone State Park

Horsepower restrictions: Electric motors

Scenery: Good

Fishing: Bluegill, largemouth bass, smallmouth bass, northern pike, catfish, muskellunge, perch, crappie, carp

Location: From New Alexandria, follow SR 1018 (Keystone Park Road) 3 miles to the park.

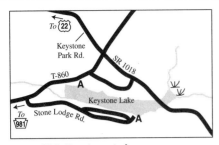

176. Keystone Lake

Keystone Lake is a pleasant place for paddlers who live nearby. Forested hills rise 250 feet above this small lake, which features a few coves and inlets. Two boat launches provide access to the lake: one near the dam and the other off of Stone Lodge Road. Woods, fields, and a beach comprise the shore.

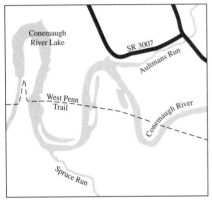

177. Conemaugh River Lake

177. Conemaugh River Lake

Size: 800 acres (normal pool)

Ownership: USACE

Horsepower restrictions: Unlimited horsepower

Scenery: Very good

Fishing: Bluegill, largemouth bass, northern pike, muskellunge

Location: The lake is located between Blairsville and Saltsburg. To reach the carry-in launch at Aultmans Run, follow SR 3009 to SR 3007 from Blairsville.

Conemaugh Lake is a unique place to paddle. First, it is very narrow and winds its way between steep forested hills and ridges. The lake averages 1/8 mile across, and in many places, it is narrower. Even though there is unlimited horsepower, you will likely have the lake to yourself since there are no boat launches for powerboats. Boat access is essentially limited to canoes, kayaks, and small watercraft. There is only a carry-in access at Aultmans Run. Conemaugh River Lake is shallow and averages only 7 feet deep. The Conemaugh River has deposited mud, sand, and gravel bars along the lake.

The most notable cove is the inlet of Aultmans Run. The true highlights are the four scenic stone arch bridges that cross the lake; these bridges once supported a railroad and are now part of the West Penn Trail.

178. Donegal Lake

Size: 90 acres

Ownership: PFBC

Horsepower restrictions: Electric motors

Scenery: Good

Fishing: Catfish, muskellunge, trout, large-mouth bass

Location: The lake is just off PA 711, 2 miles north of Donegal and 11 miles south of Ligonier.

Donegal Lake is nestled among the forested foothills of the Laurel Highlands; Chestnut Ridge gradually rises to the west. This narrow lake is a little over a mile long and features a few small bays and coves. Fields and meadows adjoin the west shore, while the east is primarily wooded. The serenity of Donegal makes it a fine place for local paddlers. Two launches provide access.

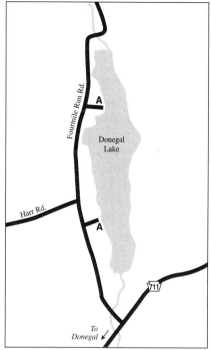

178. Donegal Lake

179. Duman Lake

Size: 19 acres

Ownership: PFBC

Horsepower restrictions: Electric motors

Scenery: Good

Fishing: Trout, smallmouth bass

Location: The lake is along PA 271 between Nicktown and Belsano.

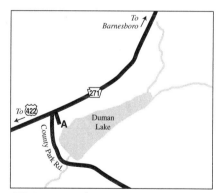

179. Duman Lake

This small lake is owned by the PFBC, but it is also the site of Duman Lake County Park, operated by Cambria County. The park features a campground, picnic facilities, and other recreational amenities. This a quiet place for local paddlers who will enjoy the serene woodlands.

180. Colver Reservoir

Size: 73 acres

Ownership: Cambria Township Water Authority

Horsepower restrictions: Electric motors

Scenery: Good

Fishing: Walleye, saugeye, largemouth bass, bluegill, crappie, perch, bullhead

Location: The reservoir is 2 miles north of Colver.

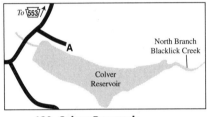

180. Colver Reservoir

This attractive reservoir is set among the rolling fields and forests of northern Cambria County; it is set away from busy roads or highways. The surroundings are pastoral and serene; small coves and bays lie along the shore. The reservoir serves as an industrial water supply and lake levels can be variable. When the level is higher, make sure to explore the winding inlet of North Branch Blacklick Creek.

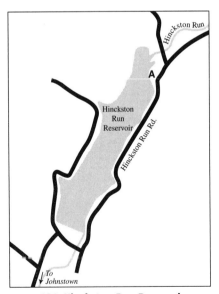

181. Hinckston Run Reservoir

181. Hinckston Run Reservoir

Size: 104 acres

Ownership: Cambria Somerset Authority

Horsepower restrictions: Electric motors

Scenery: Good

Fishing: Largemouth bass, smallmouth bass, crappie, perch, bluegill, bullheads, carp

Location: The reservoir is a mile off PA 271 at Westley Chapel.

The Hinckston Run, Quemahoning, and Wilmore reservoirs are owned and operated by the Cambria Somerset Authority, which purchased them in 2000. This is a blessing for paddlers since these reservoirs weren't previously open to the public. Each reservoir is managed to provide water for commercial and industrial purposes and also for outdoor recreation.

Hinckston Run is located 5 miles north of Johnstown; Laurel Hill rises to the west and steep wooded hillsides surround the reservoir. Hinckston Run, however, is not as undeveloped as Quemahoning and Wilmore. Roads follow the shoreline closely and there are houses near the dam. The reservoir reaches 64 feet in depth and provides habitat for a variety of fish species. A new boat launch at the northern end provides access.

182. Wilmore Reservoir

Size: Approx. 150 acres

Ownership: Cambria Somerset Authority

Horsepower restrictions: Electric motors

Scenery: Very good

Fishing: Largemouth bass, perch, bluegill, bullhead, catfish, pumpkinseed

Location: From Wilmore along PA 53, follow PA 160 north for .9 mile and turn right onto Willow Beech Road. Follow for .4 mile and turn right onto a dirt road and follow for 1.1 miles to the dam and boat launch.

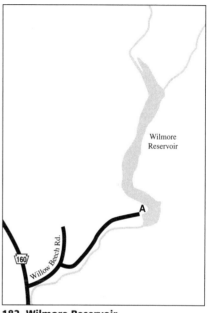

182. Wilmore Reservoir

Wilmore Reservoir, owned and operated by the Cambria Somerset Authority and recently opened to the public, is a hidden gem. It is a long, narrow lake with a winding shoreline. Steep wooded hillsides surround the lake and give it a gorge-like setting that is surprisingly undisturbed and isolated. Explore the inlets of trout streams that feed the lake at its northern end. One launch near the dam provides access.

183. Beaverdam Run Reservoir

Size: 360 acres

Ownership: Highland Sewer and Water Authority

Horsepower restrictions: Electric motors

Scenery: Very good

Fishing: Brown bullhead, yellow perch, bluegill, black crappie, rock bass

Location: From U.S. 219 north of Johnstown, follow PA 869 east for 8.6 miles to a parking and launch area on the left.

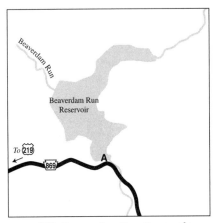

183. Beaverdam Run Reservoir

Nestled high on the Allegheny Plateau, just west of the Allegheny Front, Beaverdam Run Reservoir features miles of undeveloped shoreline. The reservoir is privately owned and provides water for local communities. Thanks to the efforts of the PFBC and other agencies, it is now open to the public.

Low wooded hillsides surround the lake, which is basically comprised of two arms— one to the north and another to the south where small streams enter. The southern arm offers more inlets and coves along its meandering shoreline. Due to its elevation and low surrounding topography, expect windy conditions and cooler temperatures. At almost 2,400 feet in elevation, this reservoir is one of the highest in the state. Thanks to its elevation and western exposure, sunsets are memorable. Two areas are off-limits to boats and are marked by buoys; one area is behind the dam and the other is a small cove on the southern shore. Only boats under 17 feet in length are permitted on the reservoir. One boat launch on the southern shore provides access.

184. Quemahoning Reservoir

Size: 900 acres

Ownership: Cambria Somerset Authority

Horsepower restrictions: Electric motors

Scenery: Very good to excellent

Fishing: Muskellunge, smallmouth bass, largemouth bass, crappie, walleye

Location: From Holsopple, follow PA 601 south for a little over a mile, turn left onto Plank Road, and then make an immediate right onto Quemahoning Dam Road and follow to the reservoir.

Any lake located in the foothills of the Laurel Highlands is bound to be beautiful and Quemahoning Reservoir is no exception. This is one of western Pennsylvania's premier lake paddling destinations, offering miles of undeveloped shoreline and fine mountain scenery. The reservoir, recently opened to the public, is poised to become a major regional asset for outdoor recreation and tourism. Besides paddling, there will be miles of hiking and mountain bike trails, camping, and whitewater releases to the beautiful Stonycreek River (see page 222).

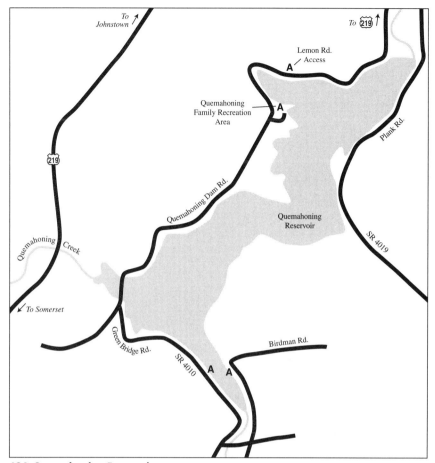

184. Quemahoning Reservoir

The reservoir is nearly 5 miles long and has 14 miles of shoreline. The mountain scenery is particularly impressive along the southeastern shore where a peninsula nearly divides the lake. Forested hills and ridges also surround this pristine lake. There are many quiet coves and bays along the meandering shoreline that invite exploration. Geese, swans, ducks, and herons frequent the reservoir.

The reservoir was completed in 1913 to provide water to the Cambria Steel Company in Johnstown. A subsidiary of the Bethlehem Steel Company ultimately acquired the lake and in 2000 sold it to the Cambria Somerset Authority, which manages it for outdoor recreation and as a water source for industry. It is a blessing to have a lake this beautiful available for the public's enjoyment.

Due to the horsepower restrictions, the reservoir is serene and rarely overcrowded. The authority has its own fees for vehicles and launching boats. Four launches provide access; three are free, while launching from the Quemahoning Family Recreation Area requires a fee.

Monongahela River Watershed

The Monongahela River was excluded from this guide because of its many locks and dams, but its watershed has many fine paddling destinations. The beautiful Youghiogheny is a classic Appalachian river with deep gorges and boulders. The lesser-known Casselman River winds through forested gorges and offers superb flatwater paddling along the section from Salisbury to Rockwood. The Laurel Highlands define the rugged terrain in this corner of the state and harbor several scenic ponds and lakes.

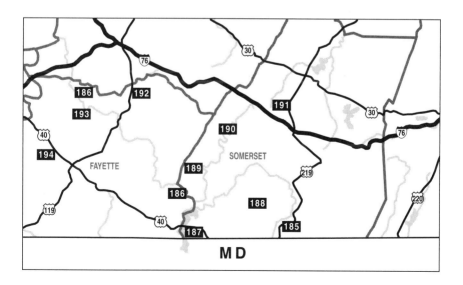

 # Rivers and Creeks

185. Casselman River

Section: Salisbury to Rockwood	
Length: 20 miles	
Water level: USGS Markleton gauge should be 2.7 feet.	
Difficulty: Moderate	
Hazards: Class I–II rapids, particularly between Garrett and Rockwood	
Scenery: Good to very good	
Highlights: Isolated gorge between Garrett and Rockwood, Great Allegheny Passage rail trail	
Fishing: Trout, smallmouth bass	
Camping: None available. Most land along the river is privately owned.	

As I was rushing to finish the manuscript for this book, my buddy Bob Holliday from Tennessee gave me a call. He, I, and our friend Bryan Mulvihill have kayaked and rafted many rivers together. Bob is originally from Somerset, Pennsylvania, and when I told him I was trying to finish this book, he immediately asked if the Casselman was included. No, I replied. He then began to prattle all about the river, the Great Allegheny Passage, the scenery, and how he wanted to take his wife kayaking on the Casselman. I placated Bob with a couple "yeahs," without seriously considering that I would include this river.

And then I thought it over. The Casselman, oddly enough, was one of the first rivers I ever kayaked. It is a beautiful river with winding canyons, boulders, and fun rapids. So, the Casselman may have been the last destination to be included in this book, but it should not be last on your list.

This guide covers the section from Salisbury to Rockwood, which has riffles and some Class I–II rapids between Garrett and Rockwood. This book does not cover the Class II–III section between Rockwood and Harnedsville.

Between Salisbury and Garrett, the Casselman flows through a pastoral setting with farms, fields, homes, and roads along its route. Forests occasionally abut the river, usually along steep slopes and hillsides. A few miles below Boynton is an oxbow loop where the river curves along a 300-foot-high bluff. The water quality along this river is improving and you may have luck fishing for trout and smallmouth bass.

Just before Meyersdale, U.S. 219 crosses the river and follows it down to Garrett. Just after Meyersdale, the Great Allegheny Passage rail trail crosses the

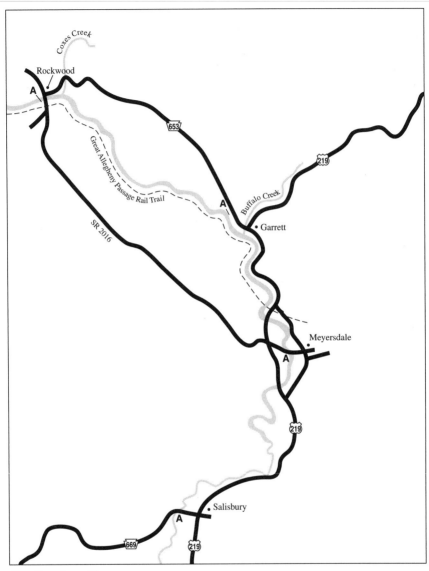

185. Casselman River

river over a high trestle. This trail will eventually connect Pittsburgh to Washington D.C. For the remainder of this section down to Rockwood, this trail will be off to your left.

The real highlight of this section is between Garrett and Rockwood where the Cassleman meanders through a beautiful, steep, wooded canyon that is more than 600 feet deep. No roads enter this beautiful setting, only a railroad on the right and the rail trail on the left. The Casselman has few islands, and that includes this section through the canyon.

You must be aware there are Class I–II rapids through the canyon, most of them in the first 2 miles. At normal levels, they are easy, fun, and straightforward, but some paddling experience is recommended, as is a sprayskirt if you are paddling a kayak. The fun begins immediately as there is a bouncy rapid alongside boulders that flows between old bridge abutments. A mile and a half farther is an island, and soon thereafter, the river enters the deepest parts of the canyon. The fine scenery continues right until the end. Take out at Rockwood, after the bridge, on the left.

186. Youghiogheny River
Ramcat Access to Ohiopyle

Length: 11 miles

Water level: USGS Confluence gauge should be 1.8 feet.

Hazards: Class I–II rapids, rapids and Ohiopyle Falls below take-out

Difficulty: Moderate

Scenery: Excellent

Highlights: Yougiogheny River Gorge, boulders, Ohiopyle State Park, deep pools, good fishing

Fishing: Trout, smallmouth bass

Camping: None available

The Youghiogheny, usually referred to as the "Yough," is a classic Appalachian river featuring incredible scenery, spectacular rapids and waterfalls, huge boulders, and deep pools. It is one of the most famous, and popular, rivers in the eastern United States.

This guide describes the river from the Ramcat put-in to Ohiopyle, and below Connellsville. The section between Ohiopyle and Connellsville contains Class III–IV rapids and is isolated with limited access, so it is not suitable for canoes or flatwater kayaks.

This section is often referred to as the Middle Yough; the Upper Yough in Maryland has Class V rapids, while the Lower Yough has Class III–IV rapids. Needless to say, the Middle Yough is the most placid of these three sections with several easy Class I–II rapids, deep pools, and boulders. Even though the rapids are easy and fairly straightforward, it is advisable that you have some paddling experience before

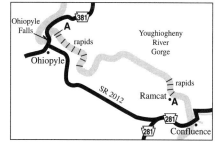

186. Youghiogheny River, Ramcat Access to Ohiopyle

undertaking this section because the eddies, waves, and crosscurrents can still flip a boat and the swift currents and isolation can make rescue difficult. A sprayskirt is advisable for kayaks. You should only attempt this section in lower water flow conditions.

From the put-in, you will encounter several easy rapids and a few small islands. Unlike other rivers, the rapids and riffles here are usually formed by ledges and boulders, not cobbles and gravel bars. The Yough is a deep river with pools that separate the rapids. As the river enters the deepening 1,600-foot gorge, it widens for 4 miles and a headwind can make paddling more arduous. A railroad is on the right, while the Youghiogheny River Trail, a superb and popular rail trail, is on the left.

The gorge begins to close in on the river and rapids and boulders are more common for the last 3 miles of the trip. Take out at the state park boating access on the left before Ohiopyle and the PA 381 bridge. It is essential that you take out here because the rapids grow more difficult below the PA 381 bridge and Ohiopyle Falls is below the rail-trail bridge.

Connellsville to West Newton

Length: 26 miles

Water level: USGS Connellsville gauge should be 2.1 feet. The river is usually runnable all year.

Difficulty: Easy

Hazards: None

Scenery: Good to very good

Highlights: Remote gorge between Dawson and Layton, good fishing

Fishing: Trout, smallmouth bass

Camping: Limited. Most land along the shore is privately owned. Commercial campgrounds are along the river. Primitive camping is available 5 miles below Dawson.

This section is the remainder of the Youghiogheny River before it joins the Monongahela at McKeesport. The section from Ohiopyle to Connellsville is not included due to its Class III–IV rapids and limited access. You should definitely experience that incredible stretch of river, just not in a flatwater canoe or kayak.

The 6-mile section from Connellsville to Dawson is fairly remote with limited development. Pass a commercial campground at Adelaide, where there are also the remains of beehive coke ovens in the hillsides. The 7.5-mile stretch from Dawson and Layton is the gem of the lower Youghiogheny—the river winds through a gorge more than 500 feet deep and large boulders dot the shoreline. The setting is almost completely remote and untouched. There is primitive camping 5 miles below Dawson on the left. Layton offers a commercial campground and paddlers have camped on the islands downstream from the bridge.

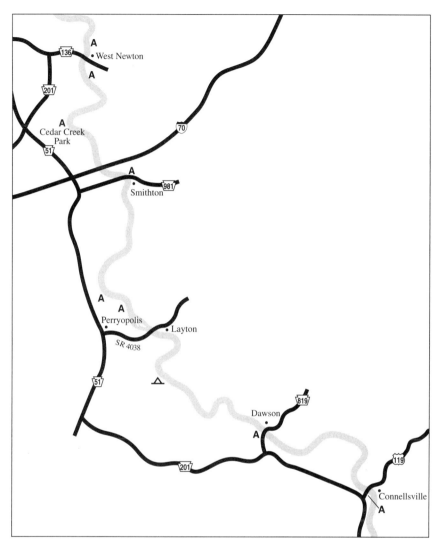

186. Youghiogheny River, Connellsville to West Newton

The river is mostly wooded with steep bluffs and occasional islands and homes down to Smithton, where there is an access. Below Smithton the river gradually becomes more pastoral with wooded hills and fields. Three miles below Smithton, on the left, is Cedar Creek Park, with waterfalls and other natural features. The pastoral setting continues to West Newton. Downstream from here the river becomes more developed with cottages and homes. Upon reaching McKeesport, the Youghiogheny enters an urban setting with more development and industry.

Access points are at Connellsville, Dawson, Perry Township, Whitsett, Smithton, West Newton, and Cedar Creek Park.

🛶 Lakes, Ponds, and Reservoirs

187. Youghiogheny River Lake

Size: 2,840 acres (summer pool)

Ownership: USACE

Horsepower restrictions: Unlimited horsepower

Scenery: Very good

Fishing: Smallmouth bass, walleye, muskellunge

Location: The lake is located just south of Confluence and can be accessed by roads off PA 281 and U.S. 40.

This 16-mile-long lake straddles the border of Pennsylvania and Maryland, occupying a narrow valley between broad, forested mountains. As a flood-control project, the lake level is variable and during dry seasons mud and rock can be exposed along the shoreline. Powerboat traffic can be heavy on summer weekends. There are also occasional homes and cottages along the shore, particularly the midsection of the lake. However, most of the shoreline is undeveloped.

This winding lake has many coves and inlets. The inlets of Hall, Tub, Braddocks, and Reason runs are no-wake zones that are ideal for paddlers. Five launches on the Pennsylvania side provide access. The Somerfield North and South, Tub Run, and Jockey Hollow launches provide the best access to the middle section of the lake, where most of the coves and inlets are located.

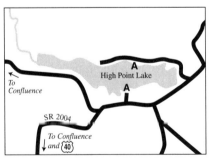

188. High Point Lake

188. High Point Lake

Size: 338 acres

Ownership: PFBC

Horsepower restrictions: Electric motors

Scenery: Very good

Fishing: Northern pike, smallmouth bass, crappie, largemouth bass, bluegill, bullhead, perch, walleye

Location: The lake is 7.5 miles east of Listonburg via SR 2004.

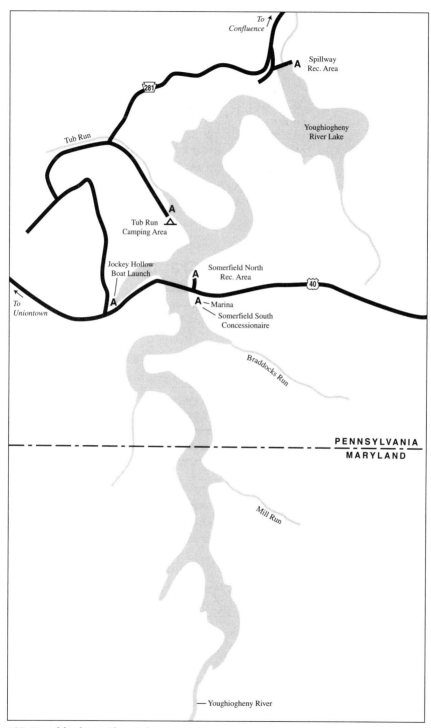

To
Confluence

A Spillway
Rec. Area

281

Tub Run

Youghiogheny
River Lake

A
Tub Run
Camping Area

Jockey Hollow
Boat Launch

Somerfield North
A Rec. Area

40

A
A — Marina
To   Somerfield South
Uniontown   Concessionaire

Braddocks Run

PENNSYLVANIA
MARYLAND

Mill Run

— Youghiogheny River

187. Youghiogheny River Lake

High Point Lake is another of Pennsylvania's best-kept paddling secrets. This is a beautiful lake featuring impressive mountain scenery; after all, the lake sits in the shadow of Mt. Davis, Pennsylvania's highest point. The forested ridge of Glade Mountain rises to the north and Winding Ridge to the south. Mt. Davis is to the east. With an elevation of 2,480 feet, High Point is also the state's highest lake open to the public.

The lake is 2 miles long and narrows behind the dam between forested shores; there are few coves or bays of any size. Meadows and fields are along the north shore; a few cottages are also in view of the lake. There are two small coves and a small stream inlet at the eastern end of the lake. However, it is High Point's isolation, serenity, and mountain scenery that make it such a fine paddling destination. Two launches provide access.

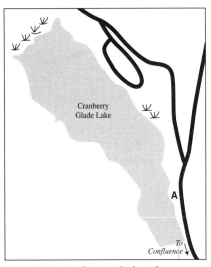

189. Cranberry Glade Lake

189. Cranberry Glade Lake

Size: 112 acres

Ownership: PFBC

Horsepower restrictions: Electric motors

Scenery: Very good to excellent

Fishing: Largemouth bass, bluegill, crappie, perch, northern pike

Location: The lake is located 7 miles north of Confluence in SGL 111.

This scenic lake is nestled in the Laurel Highlands at an elevation of more than 2,200 feet. The isolation and mountain scenery make Cranberry Glade an ideal paddling destination. The ridge to the west rises 700 feet above the lake. The lake is very shallow and almost resembles a swamp in summer with lily pads. Cranberry Glade is also a good largemouth bass fishery. The northern end of the lake has wetlands and small-stream inlets. There are some cottages on the eastern shore, but they are obscured by trees. One launch provides access.

190. Laurel Hill Lake

Size: 63 acres

Ownership: DCNR, Laurel Hill State Park

Horsepower restrictions: Electric motors

Scenery: Very good

Fishing: Largemouth bass, perch, trout, bluegill, crappie, sunfish

Location: From Somerset, follow PA 31 for 8 miles, turn left onto Trent Road and follow the signs to the park.

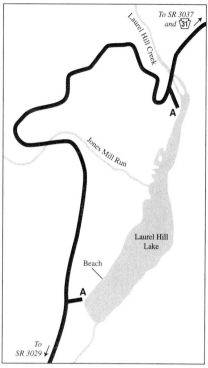

190. Laurel Hill Lake

This beautiful lake is set at an elevation of 2,000 feet in the Laurel Highlands, which rise to the west. Laurel Hill Lake is mostly undeveloped and is surrounded by forested hills. Paddlers will be most interested in the wooded eastern shore, and the many coves, inlets, and islets along the northern half of the lake where Laurel Hill Creek enters. There is a beach along the southwestern shore of the lake, near the dam. Two launches provide access; one near the dam and beach, and the other at the northern end near the inlet of Laurel Hill Creek. Use the northern access as it provides access to the more scenic areas of the lake.

191. Lake Somerset

Size: 253 acres

Ownership: PFBC

Horsepower restrictions: Electric motors

Scenery: Good

Fishing: Walleye, largemouth bass, bluegill, muskellunge, bullhead, sunfish, crappie, catfish

Location: The lake is 1 mile north of Somerset and can be accessed off PA 601.

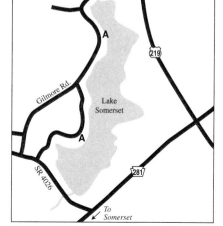

191. Lake Somerset

This lake is a pleasant place to paddle with a meandering shoreline set among forested hills and fields. Small streams feed the lake and there is one bay on the eastern shore. Somerset Lake is between the Pennsylvania Turnpike and U.S. 219, and although the highways are largely out of sight, you may hear the traffic. One boat launch provides access.

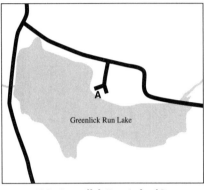

192. Greenlick Run Lake (Green Lick Reservoir)

192. Greenlick Run Lake (Green Lick Reservoir)

Size: 101 acres

Ownership: PFBC

Horsepower restrictions: Electric motors

Scenery: Good to very good

Fishing: Largemouth bass, walleye, catfish

Location: The lake is located 4 miles south of Mount Pleasant, off PA 982.

Greenlick Run Lake offers peaceful coves among the hilly farms and woodlands of northern Fayette County. The northern shore is mostly fields, while the southern has more woodlands. To the east are views of Chestnut Ridge. The lake is managed as a county park and one launch provides access.

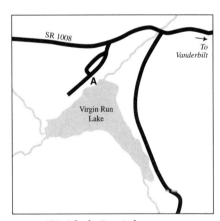

193. Virgin Run Lake

193. Virgin Run Lake

Size: 33 acres

Ownership: PFBC

Horsepower restrictions: Electric motors

Scenery: Good

Fishing: Bluegill, crappie, catfish, largemouth bass

Location: The lake is 4.5 miles west of Vanderbilt off SR 1008.

This small lake is A-shaped with two inlets that meet at the dam. Forested hills border the lake with a few houses near the dam. One launch provides access.

194. Dunlap Creek Lake

Size: 44 acres

Ownership: PFBC

Horsepower restrictions: Electric motors

Scenery: Good

Fishing: Largemouth bass, saugeye, rainbow trout

Location: From Uniontown, follow U.S. 40 towards Brownsville for 3.5 miles and turn left onto Haddenville Road/T537 and follow for 1.3 miles. Turn right, and then left, following T612 to the lake.

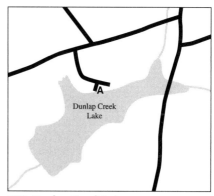

194. Dunlap Creek Lake

Dunlap Creek Lake is surrounded mostly by fields with a few woodlots; homes can be seen from the lake. The surrounding terrain is low and rolling. The lake features small coves and stream inlets. The lake is managed as a county park and there is one launch and a parking area on the northern shore.

Ohio River Watershed

The Ohio River itself may hold little interest for paddlers, but the rivers, creeks, and lakes in its watershed offer great paddling opportunities, including some of the best wildlife viewing in the state. Some of the largest lakes in Pennsylvania are found here, as are two worthwhile rivers, the Shenango and Raccoon Creek.

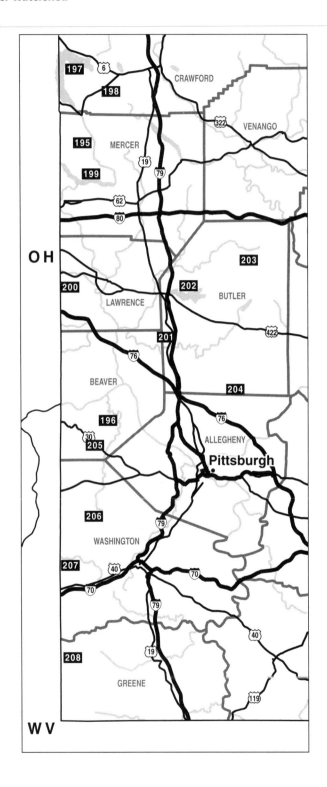

 Rivers and Creeks

195. Shenango River

Section: Pymatuning State Park to Shenango River Lake (Big Bend Access Area)

Length: Approx. 20 miles

Water level: Flows dependent on releases from Pymatuning Dam. USGS Transfer gauge should be at least 2.5 feet.

Difficulty: Easy

Hazards: Numerous strainers

Scenery: Good to very good

Highlights: Isolation, wildlife, Kidd's Mill Covered Bridge

Fishing: Smallmouth bass, trout, catfish

Camping: The creek flows mostly through private property; primitive camping may be possible with permission.

Western Pennsylvania is laced with many beautiful rivers, and the Shenango is one of the most unique. It is a river with tremendous recreational potential and thanks to the Shenango River Watchers, a nonprofit group that protects and promotes this river, it is poised to become a superb paddling destination. This group is working to make this section of the river a part of Pennsylvania's Water Trail System.

Put in below the dam at Pymatuning State Park and you will soon encounter the one thing you must know about this river—there are many strainers. Because the river tends to have a lazy current during normal flows, they are not deathtraps, but they will make your trip slow going. There is an effort to clear the river of the strainers, so the condition of the river should improve in the future.

As you near Jamestown, there are houses on the left, with some development as you pass through town. Below the town, the river enters a thick riparian forest as it twists

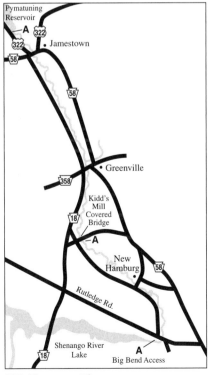

195. Shenango River

and turns. Even though the river is fairly close to a road (off to your right), there is a surprising sense of isolation and superb opportunities to observe myriad birdlife. Bald eagles and ospreys are often seen along the river. Before you reach Greenville and Crooked Creek, there is a park and access on the left. The river passes through Greenville—where there is a large mill on the left—rather quickly. Down to Kidd's Mill Road, the setting is more pastoral with occasional homes and fields, as well as a buffer of forest. The lower section of the river below Greenville has fewer strainer problems compared to the upper section.

The scenic Kidd's Mill Covered Bridge is a highlight of this river and is also an access point. The section down to Big Bend is an excellent trip with isolation in a jungle-like riparian forest. The river continues to meander heavily with some islands and braids. Off to the left is the Shenango Trail, a hiking trail. Take out on the right at the Big Bend access area, before the river enters the lake.

Below the Shenango River Lake, the river flows through urbanized Sharon with steel mills and a few dams. The section from West Middlesex to New Castle is worth paddling as the river returns to its meandering ways through a thick riparian forest with surprising isolation and little development.

196. Raccoon Creek

Section: Witherspoon Road to Rocky Bottom	
Length: 28 miles	
Water level: The USGS gauge at Moffet Mill should read at least 2.2 feet.	
Difficulty: Easy	
Hazards: Strainers	
Scenery: Good	
Highlights: Pastoral scenery	
Fishing: Limited due to acid mine drainage	
Camping: The creek flows almost exclusively through private property; primitive camping may be possible with permission.	

Raccoon Creek offers an enjoyable float through the countryside of western Pennsylvania. The creek does suffer from acid mine drainage, although water quality is improving. With a watershed of less than 200 square miles, Raccoon Creek is a fairly small creek when compared to others in this guide.

You can begin as far as Witherspoon Road; however, the creek is small there, so many paddlers begin at Raccoon Creek State Park along U.S. 30 or Independence Marsh along PA 151.

The first 17 miles of the creek from Witherspoon Road feature pastoral scenery of wooded hills, extensive fields and farmlands along the creek, and occasional houses. The creek is often bordered by trees. A nice place to stop and explore is the wildflower preserve at Raccoon Creek State Park.

The setting becomes urbanized briefly near the juncture of Green Garden Road and Route 60. However, after passing under Route 60 a second time, Raccoon Creek enters a scenic gorge-like setting that is forested and somewhat isolated. Take out at Rocky Bottom on the left.

Raccoon Creek is easy to paddle, with riffles over gravel bars and pools. There are surprisingly few braids or islands for a creek this small, but strainers are always a possibility, particularly at sharp bends and along islands.

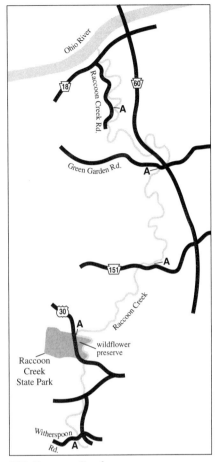

196. Raccoon Creek

🛶 Lakes, Ponds, and Reservoirs

197. Pymatuning Reservoir

Size: 17,088 acres

Ownership: DCNR, Pymatuning State Park

Horsepower restrictions: 10 hp

Scenery: Very good

Fishing: Smallmouth bass, largemouth bass, muskellunge, perch, walleye, northern pike, crappie, catfish, sunfish, bluegill, carp

Location: Pymatuning is 15 miles west of Meadville and is accessed by U.S. 6, PA 285, or U.S. 322.

Pymatuning is in a class by itself. It is one of the largest lakes in the state and one of the largest and most popular state parks. The reservoir is a renowned fishing destination, particularly for walleye. And of course, a lake this big is perfect for paddling. The shoreline contains many coves and small inlets; a causeway carrying PA 285 across the lake and into Ohio essentially divides the lake in half.

Paddlers will be most interested in the northern section of the lake with its islands, numerous coves and inlets, plentiful access, and two state park natural areas. A total of four launches provide access to this part of the lake; Wilson, Alcatraz, and Linesville Marina launches provide the closest access to the more scenic areas of the reservoir. Three developed campgrounds border the lake, but there are no primitive, boat-in camping areas as found at the Allegheny Reservoir, Tionesta Lake, or Raystown Lake.

Black Jack Swamp Natural Area is at the northern end of the lake and protects extensive wetlands and sedges harboring many species of birds and plantlife. The 161-acre Clark Island Natural Area is only accessible by boat and is home to a mature hardwood and white pine forest. Harris, Whaley, and Glenn islands also invite exploration. This section of the reservoir is arguably the most scenic.

The southern half of the lake is worth paddling, although more homes are in view from the lake. There are a few islands as the lake narrows behind the dam, as well as several small coves and bays on the western shore.

Pymatuning is particularly famous for its waterfowl and wildlife; you may also see herons, countless ducks, egrets, bald eagles, various hawks, and ospreys. Pymatuning provides some of the best opportunities to observe wildlife in Pennsylvania.

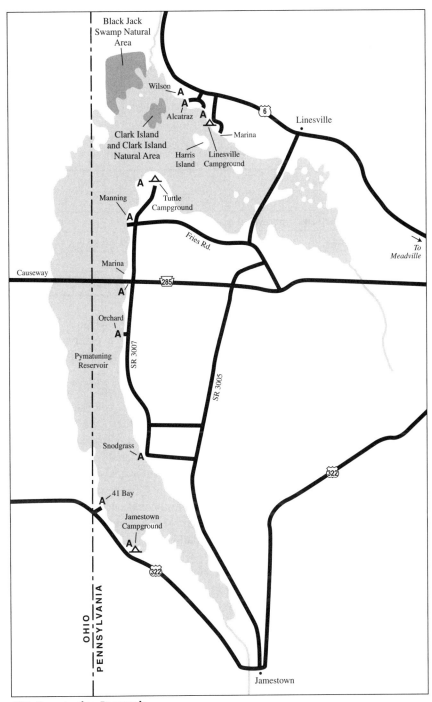

197. Pymatuning Reservoir

The Pymatuning Reservoir is popular and can receive heavy boat traffic in the summer. Fortunately, the lake is so large it can accommodate a lot of boats and there is always a quiet place to paddle. The wind is often a problem and can create large waves, and powerful thunderstorms often occur in hot and humid weather.

198. Hartstown Swamp

Size: Approx. 1,000 acres

Ownership: PGC

Horsepower restrictions: Unpowered boats only

Scenery: Very good

Fishing: Largemouth bass, bullhead, crappie, bluegill, carp

Location: Hartstown is 5 miles west of Conneaut Lake along U.S. 322.

Hartstown Swamp may very well be the Serengeti of Pennsylvania paddling. The swamp is famous for its phenomenal birdlife and diverse plant and animal life. Towering grasses rise along the shore while lily pads blanket the surface. There are extensive wetlands, islets, and sedges.

This is not a single swamp. Rather, four low earthen dams, or dikes, have created a series of shallow lakes along what was Crooked Creek. This was done to provide habitat for waterfowl. These lakes also have their own names, such as Randolph Run Lake, Crystal Lake, Mud Lake, Crooked Creek Lake, and Hartstown Dike, but collectively they are also known as the Hartstown Swamp.

Randolph Run Lake is the most southern and features fields and woodlands. The northern inlet contains extensive wetlands. Just to the north are Crystal and Mud lakes, which feature several islands and coves. North of U.S. 322 is Crooked Creek Lake with more islands. The most northern is Hartstown Dike with islands, tree stumps, and extensive wetlands.

The surrounding terrain is low and rolling with gradual hills rising to the east and west. For the most part, forests and a few fields surround the swamp, which is mostly undeveloped. There are a few homes along U.S. 322. The swamp contains numerous coves, inlets, channels, islands, and islets. A total of four launches provide access. You can easily spend several days exploring this complex of shallow lakes and wetlands.

To the east of the swamp are remnants of the old Erie Extension Canal. Just to the north is the Pymatuning Swamp, the source of the Shenango River, which in turn flows into the Pymatuning Reservoir. This region is famous for its wetlands and superb birdwatching, with more than 100 documented breeding species.

To
Conneaut Lake

Hartstown Dike

A

322

Mud
Lake

A   A

Hartstown •

322

Lower
Lake

Pine Rd.

A

18

A

Adamsville •

Crooked Creek

198. Hartstown Swamp

199. Shenango River Lake

Size: 3,560 acres (summer pool)

Ownership: USACE

Horsepower restrictions: Unlimited horsepower; western end of the lake is limited to 10 hp.

Scenery: Good to very good

Fishing: Smallmouth bass, largemouth bass, muskellunge, perch, walleye, crappie, suckers, sunfish, bluegill, carp, trout

Location: The lake is located just north of Sharon and is accessed by PA 846, PA 18, and PA 258.

Shenango River Lake stretches 11 miles through low, rolling countryside. The lake is surrounded by extensive fields, but a buffer of trees and forests usually lines the shore. The irregular, meandering shoreline contains extensive coves, inlets, and bays that invite exploration. Furthermore, the eastern and western thirds of the lake offer many islets and islands. Although there is unlimited horsepower and the lake is popular with motorboats in the summer, there are many places to find seclusion. The western end of the lake, at the inlet of Pymatuning Creek, is limited to 10 horsepower. There are also no-wake zones behind the dam; at the eastern end of the lake where the Shenango River enters; and in the bays and coves on the northern shore between PA 846 and PA 18. Overall, the best place to paddle is west of the PA 846 bridge since this section has a combination of forested shores, relative isolation, countless coves, bays, and inlets, and numerous islands. Make sure to explore the maze-like

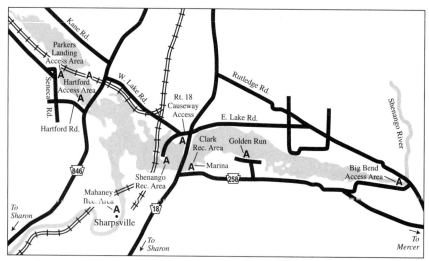

199. Shenango River Lake

inlet of Pymatuning Creek with its thick forests and superb opportunities to observe wildlife.

Shenango is well-known for its birdlife, particularly waterfowl, egrets, herons, hawks, ospreys, and bald eagles. The Shenango River enters the lake at its eastern end and makes for an excellent float trip (see page 271).

Wind can be a problem due to the low topography that surrounds the lake. Also be prepared for strong thunderstorms in the summer.

Six launches provide access to the lake. Use the following launches to reach the corresponding areas of the lake: Parkers Landing Access Area to reach the 10 horsepower zone at the western end of the lake; Golden Run to reach the no-wake zone at the eastern end of the lake; and the Shenango Recreation Area or Route 846 access to reach the bays along the northern shore.

200. Bessemer Lake

Size: 28 acres

Ownership: PFBC

Horsepower restrictions: Electric motors

Scenery: Good to very good

Fishing: Sauger, rainbow trout, brown trout

Location: The lake is a half-mile west of Bessemer along PA 317.

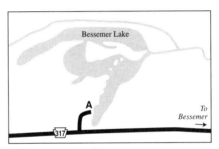

200. Bessemer Lake

This small lake is unique, featuring winding channels, coves, and islets that make it a joy to explore. Deciduous woodlands surround Bessemer, which is undeveloped. The surrounding topography is low and rolling. There is one launch at the southern end of the lake that provides access.

201. Lower Hereford Manor Lake

Size: 45 acres

Ownership: PFBC

Horsepower restrictions: Electric motors

Scenery: Good

Fishing: Largemouth bass, channel catfish, saugeye, rainbow trout

Location: The lake is 2 miles north of Zelienople, off PA 288.

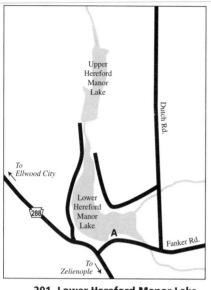

201. Lower Hereford Manor Lake

This L-shaped lake is surrounded by forested hills and features small coves. Roads follow much of the shore and the lake can be accessed from different parking areas, but the lake is otherwise undeveloped. There is a launch on the southern shore near the dam.

The upper lake is located just north of the lower lake; it covers 23 acres and is open to fishing. Its water level has been lowered to reduce pressure on its dam. Together, these two lakes are sometimes referred to as Hereford Manor Lakes.

202. Lake Arthur

Size: 3,225 acres

Ownership: DCNR, Moraine State Park

Horsepower restrictions: 20 hp

Scenery: Good to very good

Fishing: Northern pike, largemouth bass, catfish, crappie, bluegill, muskellunge, walleye, catfish

Location: Moraine State Park is 10 miles west of Butler and 10 miles east of New Castle. It is accessed by U.S. 422 and PA 528.

Lake Arthur is one of western Pennsylvania's premier paddling destinations. The lake has more than 40 miles of meandering shoreline, creating an incredible number of bays and coves. The largest and most isolated coves are along the southern and eastern parts of the lake, including Porter's Cove, Big Run, Shannon Run, Swamp Run, and Muddy Creek. Be aware that the eastern end of Swamp Run is a propagation area and entry is not permitted. The winding bays and inlets just north of the dam are fine places to paddle as they meander through woodlands.

Wildlife viewing is very good and includes egrets, herons, ospreys, bald eagles, and waterfowl. In summer, many of the coves are covered with lily pads and lined with high grass and sedges.

Lake Arthur is surrounded by low forested hills that rise 200–300 feet and conditions can get windy; wind surfing is popular on the lake. Moraine State Park has ten launches to access the lake. The following launches provide the

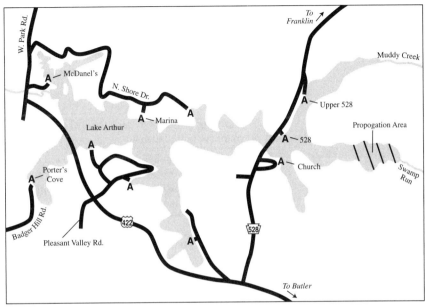

202. Lake Arthur

best access to some of the more isolated coves and bays: Porter's Cove, McDanel's, Old Route 422, Upper 528, 528, and Church.

203. Glade Dam Lake

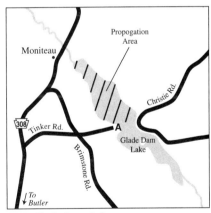

Size: 170 acres; up to 400 acres

Ownership: PGC

Horsepower restrictions: Unpowered boats only

Scenery: Good to very good

Fishing: Largemouth bass, catfish, crappie, bluegill

Location: The lake is near the village of Moniteau, which is located 13 miles north of Butler along PA 308.

203. Glade Dam Lake

This lake is set among low, rolling hills with fields and forests. A large section of the lake behind the dam is a propagation area and is restricted; there are signs. The southeastern third of the lake contains inlets, wetlands, and islets. This is a fine place to explore and observe wildlife. Glade Dam is famous for its birdlife, with more than 200 species, including bald eagles. Be aware the level of the lake is changeable and the surface area can grow as large as 400 acres.

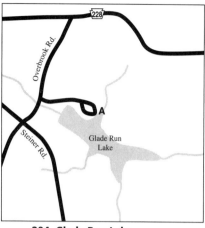

204. Glade Run Lake

204. Glade Run Lake

Size: 52 acres

Ownership: PFBC

Horsepower restrictions: Electric motors

Scenery: Good

Fishing: Largemouth bass, channel catfish, rainbow trout, bluegill

Location: From Bakerstown, follow PA 8 north for 3.6 miles towards Butler. Turn right onto Overbrook Road and follow for 2.2 miles. Turn right to the lake access.

Located just north of the Pittsburgh metropolitan area in south Butler County, Glade Run offers several small coves along its northern, southern, and eastern shores. The lake is also known as Glade Lake or Glade Mill Lake. Two small creeks enter the lake at its eastern and southern ends. Low forested hills gradually rise above the meandering shoreline of the lake. One launch provides access.

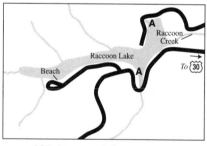

205. Raccoon Lake

205. Raccoon Lake

Size: 101 acres

Ownership: DCNR, Raccoon Creek State Park

Horsepower restrictions: Electric motors

Scenery: Very good

Fishing: Bluegill, sunfish, bullhead catfish, crappie, yellow perch, smallmouth and largemouth bass

Location: From Imperial, follow U.S. 30 west 9.6 miles to the state park. Turn left onto the park road to reach Raccoon Lake.

This narrow lake is located in a wooded valley with steep hillsides that rise 200 feet. Interesting places to explore are Traverse Creek inlet and the inlet near the boat launch. With the exception of the swimming area, the lake is undeveloped with a diverse forest of hardwoods, hemlock, and pine along its shore.

206. Cross Creek Lake

Size: 258 acres

Ownership: Washington County

Horsepower restrictions: 10 hp

Scenery: Very good

Fishing: Largemouth bass, catfish, bluegill, walleye, muskellunge

Location: From Washington, follow PA 18 north for 8.5 miles and then turn left onto PA 50. Go 4 miles and turn left onto County Park Road and follow into the park.

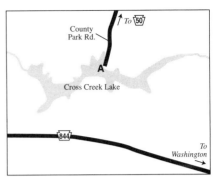

206. Cross Creek Lake

This attractive lake is surrounded by Cross Creek County Park's 3,400 acres of rolling forested hills and fields. Most of the shoreline is wooded. Cross Creek stretches more than 2 miles and is narrow, featuring many coves and small bays on both the northern and southern shores that will interest paddlers. Another place to visit on the lake is the inlet of Cross Creek, where there is a covered bridge. This lake probably offers the best lake paddling in this corner of the state. Cross Creek is also known for its good fishing, particularly largemouth bass.

A permit and fee are required to boat on the lake. For more information, contact the Washington County Department of Parks and Recreation at (724) 228-6867.

207. Dutch Fork Lake

Size: 91 acres

Ownership: PFBC

Horsepower restrictions: Electric motors

Scenery: Good

Fishing: Crappie, largemouth bass, catfish

Location: From Claysville, follow U.S. 40 west for 3.7 miles. Turn right and go 1 mile to the lake.

207. Dutch Fork Lake

This narrow, winding lake is about 2 miles long and is set among the rolling farmlands and wooded hills of western Pennsylvania. Interesting places to paddle are the coves and small bays near the dam, as well as the inlet at its southern end. Two launches provide access.

At the time of this writing, the lake was drawn down pending repairs to its dam.

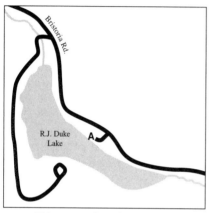

208. R. J. Duke Lake

208. R. J. Duke Lake

Size: 52 acres

Ownership: DCNR, Ryerson Station State Park

Horsepower restrictions: Electric motors

Scenery: Good

Fishing: Largemouth bass, smallmouth bass, brown trout, bluegill, sunfish, crappie

Location: From Wind River, follow PA 21 for 2 miles and turn left onto Bristoria Road/SR 3022 and follow it for a mile into the park.

This small lake is surrounded by relatively steep forested hills that rise more than 400 feet, creating surprisingly rugged terrain. Thanks to horsepower restrictions, R. J. Duke Lake is a serene place to paddle. Paddlers will want to explore the winding inlet of the North Fork. One boat launch provides access.

At the time of this writing, the lake was drawn down due to the condition of the dam.

Lake Erie Watershed

No other lake in Pennsylvania is like Lake Erie, a vast freshwater expanse that is among the largest in the world. Immensely popular Presque Isle is a bird lover's—and paddler's—paradise. Like many other smaller streams in this watershed, Elk Creek has cut impressive shale cliffs as it has carved its way down through the gentle plains above Lake Erie, providing scenery unique to Pennsylvania creeks.

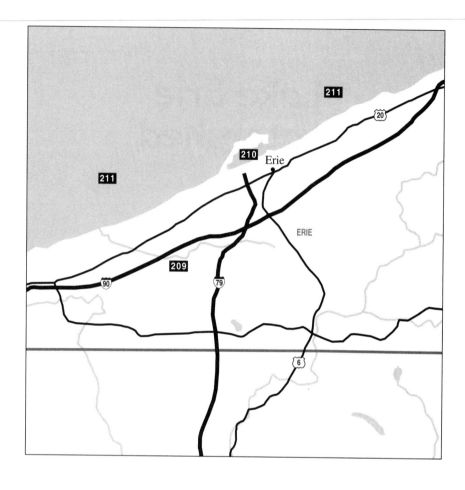

Rivers and Creeks

209. Elk Creek

Section: PA 98 to Lake Erie

Length: 13 miles

Water level: As an approximate correlation, USGS Walnut Creek gauge should be 4.65 feet.

Difficulty: Moderate

Hazards: Strainers, Class I–II rapids

Scenery: Very good to excellent

Highlights: Impressive shale cliffs, sidestream waterfalls

Fishing: Steelhead

Camping: None. Almost all land is privately owned.

Elk Creek is the smallest of all the rivers and creeks described in this guide, but it is included because it is so unique. The creek flows through the gentle plains above Lake Erie, but along the way it has cut beautiful shale cliffs that rise 100 feet above the creek, often forming curving amphitheaters on the outside bends. In places, small side streams and tributaries cascade down beautiful waterfalls.

Paddling experience is recommended before attempting this creek. Paddlers often put in at Follys End Campground along PA 98. The creek is not difficult to paddle, but you can expect many riffles, easy rapids, strong currents with eddy lines, and pools. There are also many gravel bars and rapids formed by low, sloping ledges and gravel bends. Watch Razorblade Rapids about 2 miles below the put-in. These Class II rapids are not difficult but feature a wave and hole that whitewater kayakers enjoy surfing. Recreational paddlers can paddle through the wave as long as you stay straight with some forward momentum, or you can portage to the left. Wave trains may also be encountered that can swamp an open kayak, so a sprayskirt is advisable.

The creek then meanders along the beautiful bends of shale cliffs and passes under a covered bridge at Gudgeonville Road. A very nice spot is just downstream where Little Elk Creek joins on the left from its own shale gorge. Most of these impressive shale cliffs are from PA 98 down to the I-90 bridge.

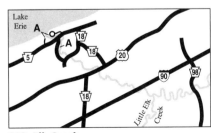
209. Elk Creek

Most of the creek is undeveloped and seemingly isolated. There are homes in view where U.S. 20 crosses at Girard; however, the creek soon returns to a more natural state. Paddle under a high railroad trestle as the creek continues to meander down a shale gorge. A mile farther, the Elk flows through a tunnel under a railroad; you can paddle through this tunnel, but a flashlight is a good idea to help look for strainers. There is an access on the left before the tunnel. Strainers may also collect where PA 5 crosses the creek, just farther downstream. Take out on the left before Elk Creek enters Lake Erie; it is worth paddling to the lake just for a shocking change of perspective and to explore the creek's winding outlet and sandy beachheads.

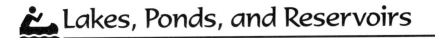# Lakes, Ponds, and Reservoirs

210. Presque Isle Bay

Size: 3,718 acres

Ownership: Commonwealth of Pennsylvania, DCNR, Presque Isle State Park

Horsepower restrictions: Internal combustion engines are not permitted in the interior lagoons.

Scenery: Good to very good

Fishing: Walleye, smallmouth bass, perch

Location: From I-90, take Exit 18 and follow PA 832 north; it leads directly to the state park. The Lagoon Launch is an ideal place for paddlers to put in on the bay. The entrance to Presque Isle is located just west of Erie.

Although a part of Lake Erie, Presque Isle Bay is described separately since it is a very popular paddling destination. Presque Isle is in a class by itself—the state park attracts more than four million people a year, and there are beautiful beaches, world-class birdwatching, diverse ecosystems, and plentiful wildlife. Presque Isle is one of the most biodiverse places in the state. Further, if it were enclosed, Presque Isle Bay would be by far the largest natural body of water completely within Pennsylvania. The bay is 4.6 miles long and 1.8 miles wide.

The city of Erie is on the southern shore and paddlers must anticipate that there can be heavy boat traffic, including large commercial vessels. It is advisable that you stay closer to the northern shore along the state park. Paddlers are permitted into the interior ponds and lagoons of Long Pond, Big Pond, and Grave Yard Pond. These maze-like interconnecting bodies of water offer exceptional opportunities for birdwatching and wildlife that should not be missed. More than 320 species of birds have been documented at Presque Isle. The interior ponds feature wetlands, sedges, and deciduous forests. Misery Bay features the famous Perry Monument, commemorating American victory in the 1813 Battle of Lake Erie. The best boat launch to use is the Lagoons launch on Misery Bay, near the Perry Monument.

Thompson Bay and Gull Point are also worth exploring, though you will have to leave the protection of the bay and go into the lake. Gull Point is a specially protected natural area where access is forbidden from April 1 to November 30 so migrating birds can rest and nest. It is another excellent place for birdwatching. The remainder of the lakeshore is protected by breakwaters, so you will want to stay a safe distance from the shore if you want to paddle farther. Exercise caution around the breakwaters and the waves and surf along the shore.

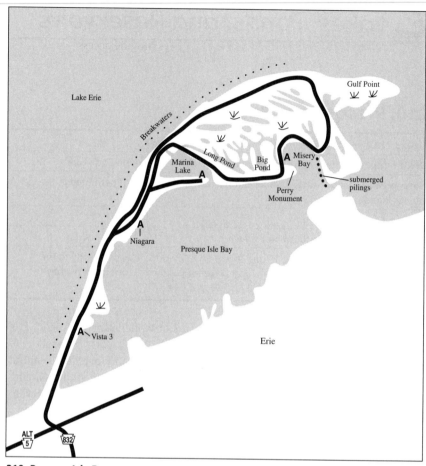

210. Presque Isle Bay

211. Lake Erie

Size: 9,950 square miles; Pennsylvania's section is 749 square miles.

Ownership: Commonwealth of Pennsylvania

Horsepower restrictions: Unlimited

Scenery: Good to very good

Fishing: Walleye, steelhead, bass, coho, chinook salmon, trout, perch

Location: A variety of access areas are located off PA 5.

Lake Erie is Pennsylvania's only Great Lake, and it provides a paddling environment unlike anywhere else in the state. Paddling here is like paddling a freshwater ocean—an incredible expanse of water. Pennsylvania has 51 miles of lakeshore. With the exception of Presque Isle and the outlet of Elk Creek, this shoreline is largely uniform with few significant features like bays or harbors. Outside of Presque Isle, eight public boat launches provide access.

Paddlers who want to explore the lake will likely prefer the western shoreline, where there is less development, particularly west of Elk Creek. Here, bluffs rise 90 feet above the lake and small streams cut through mini-gorges. These bluffs harbor 3,000 bank swallows and the undeveloped Erie Bluffs State Park is home to more than eighty species of birds. Ideal places to put in or take out are the PFBC access at Elk Creek and a local government access at Raccoon Creek.

Only experienced paddlers should attempt an extended sojourn along the shore. Thunderstorms and high winds can occur suddenly and there are few harbors or bays to provide protection. The beaches are often narrow, rocky, and offer little protection; they are fully exposed to waves, surf, and high winds. The most significant bay along the western shoreline is the outlet of Elk Creek. You will also want to keep some distance from shore to avoid being tossed by the surf and waves as they reach the shore. You must be fully prepared for inclement weather.

With great scenery, ample wildlife, phenomenal sunsets, and isolation, paddling this vast lake can be an unforgettable experience.

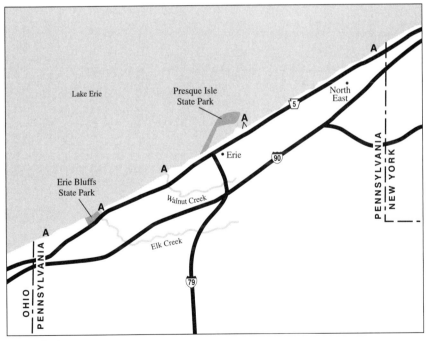

211. Lake Erie

Index